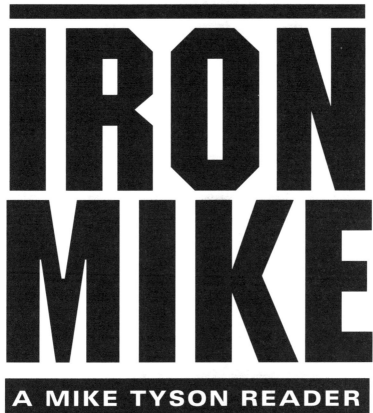

IRON MIKE

A MIKE TYSON READER

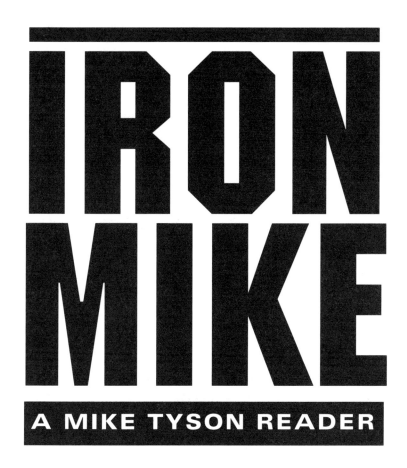

IRON MIKE

A MIKE TYSON READER

EDITED BY DANIEL O'CONNOR

FOREWORD BY
GEORGE PLIMPTON

THUNDER'S MOUTH PRESS

IRON MIKE: A MIKE TYSON READER

This compilation and Introduction © 2002 by Daniel O'Connor
Foreword © 2002 by George Plimpton

Published by
Thunder's Mouth Press
An Imprint of Avalon Publishing Group Incorporated
161 William St., 16th Floor
New York, NY 10038

Library of Congress Cataloging-in-Publication Data is on file with the publisher.

ISBN 1-56025-356-8

9 8 7 6 5 4 3 2 1

Frontis-piece "Portrait" reprinted by permission of the *Wall Street Journal,* © 2002 Dow Jones & Company, Inc. All rights reserved worldwide.

Designed by Paul Paddock
Printed in the United States of America
Distributed by Publishers Group West

WILDERMUTH

This book is dedicated to
K.O. Craig
and
Darryl Pierre

ACKNOWLEDGMENTS

I am grateful to George Plimpton and to all of the contributors who allowed their work to be reprinted, with special thanks to Katherine Dunn, Gerald Early, Rudy Gonzalez and Martin Feigenbaum, Michael Katz, Robert Lipsyte, Steve Lott, Joyce Carol Oates, and Jay Allen Sanford. Thanks to all my colleagues especially Kevin Votel, Ghadah Alrawi, Matthew Lore, Sam Erman, Paul Paddock, Tracy Armstead, Mike Walters, Will Balliett, Catheline Jean-Francois, Nate Knaebel, Erik Kahn, Carl Bromley, Dave Riedy, Steve Toole and Shawneric Hachey for your help in making this a book; Thanks also to Neil Ortenberg who allowed me to start this and then forced me to finish it.

Daniel O'Connor

CONTENTS

"For some reason, people don't want fighters just to be fighters."

—Garry Wills

FOREWORD

by

George Plimpton

I met him once, just for a moment, shaking his hand at some function, remembering the two gold teeth, the surprisingly high, almost whispery voice, that he was shorter than expected, only 5'11—women in the room were taller than he was—and then the awe that I had been in the presence, if only for a few seconds, of the youngest heavyweight champion ever (only twenty when he knocked out Trevor Berwick in the second round). In those days they referred to him as Kid Dynamite.

If I were starting my sports-writing career over again, callow, energetic, full of beans, I would have begged, had the opportunity come up, to do a feature on Mike Tyson. Whatever one's opinion, most of it thoroughly negative, he has surely been the most interesting fighter around—yet another in that long line of controversial yet colorful characters going back through Muhammad Ali, Archie Moore, Sugar Ray Robinson, to Jack Johnson, just to mention a few. That assignment had never happened.

So here is this book as compensation, whose pieces fill out a fascinating portrait of this disturbed and disturbing young fighter—one side of his character (the Bad Tyson) described by Joyce Carol Oates as:

"a prehistoric creature rising from a fearful crevice in our collective subconscious."

There are kinder views. The Good Tyson is splendidly evoked in an essay by Pete Hamill who describes his visit to the Indiana Youth Center to see the fighter, then in the second year of a six year sentence (it was commuted after three) on a most dubious conviction for raping an eighteen-year-old beauty-pageant contestant. It turns out that an old con had suggested to Tyson, "Go to the library. Read books. Work your mind. Start with the Constitution"—advice which got Tyson going on a considerable program of self-education (often by his own volition reading in a solitary confinement cell where he could concentrate) . . . Machievelli, Voltaire, Dumas, F. Scott Fitzgerald, many biographies, Genghis Khan, Oliver Cromwell, Mao Tse Dung. (Tyson has a tattooed likeness of Mao on one upper arm, Arthur Ashe on the other. Jeanne Ashe, the tennis star's widow, said of the latter, 'If I could sue a body part, I would.')

Perhaps to illuminate a darker side of his nature, Tyson read voluminously about the criminal world, mobsters, Dutch Schultz, Lucky Luciano, Murder Inc., assuring Hamill that he didn't believe gangsters were heroes but one had to understand them. It is a very sympathetic portrait. At its conclusion Hamill suggests, "In prison Mike Tyson is discovering the many roads back to sanity."

Alas, that did not come to pass. The history is a sorry one from the start. It's all here, from the earliest days as an inmate of the Tryon Juvenile detention center (thirteen years old); released into boxing by Cus D'Amato who saw his potential ("This is the one I have been waiting for all my life"); winning the title in 1986; his brief marriage to Robin Givens; the amazing interview with Barbara Walters with Tyson sitting beside his wife hardly saying a word (he said later he was under such heavy sedation he couldn't concentrate) while she speaks of their marriage ("It's been torture. It's been pure hell. It's been worse than anything I could possibly imagine."); his relationship with Donald and Ivana Trump (he was often a visitor on their yacht Trump Princess); the shift of his allegiance to Don King; the loss to the unknown Buster Douglas in Japan; the incident with Desiree Washington, three years in prison, author of some horrendous remarks, among them that he wanted to drive Francois Botha's nose into his brain, that he was going to turn Razor Ruddock into his girl friend, that he wanted to eat Lennox Lewis's children (he knew Lewis didn't have any children and apparently meant it as a macabre joke); the cannibalization of Evander Holyfield's ear (which wasn't a joke); a second visit to jail in 1999 for an outburst of what a judge ruled as a "potentially lethal road rage" (at one point he imagined he saw Sonny Liston standing in a corner of his cell); cursing the press, then a minute or so later breaking into tears at the thought of Cus D'Amato; a second marriage, this time to a doctor, four children . . . all of this rounded out with myriad sketches of the peripheral characters, many of them odious.

We learn his eating habits, a daily bowl of Captain Crunch, which turns out to be his favorite food. The trappings of his wealth. His various homes, including a six bedroom mansion in Southington, Ohio, with a 100-inch television screen, a 1100 pound chandelier . . his bed with a coverlet made of foxtails, seventy two pairs of size 13 shoes and sneakers in a walk-in closet the size of a foyer. His Nevada mansion with its life-sized statues of the heroes he had read about and revered— Genghis Khan, Alexander the Great, Hannibal; a menagerie of young lions and tigers with whom he wrestles. His five dogs, three of them "royal blood" shar-peis. Several hundred pigeons, which were kept in a huge dovecote at Cus D'Amato's house in the Catskills.

I remember a story about him, that after the memorial service for Cus D'Amato Tyson let the pigeons out and then on top of the dovecote raised his arms aloft, either a final salute to Cus or to indicate that he was now free of influences other than those of his own nature.

The cars, of course, which at various times have included a red Lamborghini Countach, a black Ferrari Testarosa, a Range Rover, two Mercedes, two Porches, a Bentley with a bumper sticker that reads "I ♥ Allah", a rare Lamborghini "jeep" originally built for the king of Saudi Arabia ("with a 200 gallon fuel tank, bullet proof, with room for four passengers and six bodyguards"), and, of course, the obligatory Rolls-Royce.

Tyson doesn't like driving. No wonder. He once drove a car into a tree on his own property, hurting himself so badly that it was thought by some that he was trying to kill himself. But he likes "having the cars around", enough of them, it turns out, to give away to his friends—six Range Rovers and BMWs on the occasion of his thirtieth birthday.

By necessity, there is a chauffeur—a young Puerto Rican named

Rudy Gonzalez. He has provided one of the more compelling documents in the collection—a lengthy entry which provides the sort of
inside information that in celebrity biographies one gets from the
butler.

Perhaps most graphic is his account of how Don King breaks up
Tyson's marriage with Robin Givens—suggesting to the gullible Tyson
aboard the yacht Trump Princess that Donald Trump is having an affair
with his wife. Gonzalez describes driving the shaken Tyson to his mansion in Bernardsville where the fighter goes on a rage, breaking furniture, smashing paintings until Robin comes home from a shopping
trip, calling out innocently to her husband that she's back, only to
become a victim of his continuing fury, which includes being beaten
up and the furniture thrown out of their bedroom window. A divorce
follows. The marriage only lasted eight months.

Don King, according to Gonzalez, is also responsible for the
breakup of Tyson's close relationship with his white co-managers, Bill
Clayton, frail at the time, and Joe Jacobs, handball champion and
boxing archivist (he had a collection of twenty-six thousand boxing
films, many of which Tyson studied). The elimination of the old guard
was engineered by two unsavory characters in King's employ (no laurel
wreaths for them in any of the pieces), named John Horne, a second-
rate comic from the Albany area, and Rory Holloway, an old neighborhood friend who according to Jose Torre's 1989 biography of Tyson
once organized a sex marathon for the fighter involving twenty-four
women in a single night.

Who knows what kind of people will be involved in Mike Tyson's
future. As of this writing he is only thirty-five. There will be fights to come,
many involving his own personal behavior. Whatever, the future cannot
fail but to be of interest. Perhaps that assignment will come my way.

INTRODUCTION

by

Daniel O'Connor

"He is inarticulate in the way we all are when more has happened to us than we know how to express; and inarticulate in a particularly Negro way—he has a long tale to tell which no one wants to hear."

". . .he has no reason, on any level, to trust them, and no reason to believe that they would be capable of hearing what he had to say, even if he could say it."
—James Baldwin, "The Fight: Patterson vs. Liston"

After Mike Tyson appeared to start a brawl at the press conference promoting Lewis vs. Tyson, the last such incident treated in this collection, the writers began the familiar knelling of the end of Tyson's career. Tyson seemed to have exhausted, not for the first time, their reserves of tolerance and forbearance. He has been counted out so many times (not including several self-announced retirements) that his perverse insistence on continuing may alone be enough to account for the tone of weary impatience and disgust evinced in the op-eds that followed. For Ralph Wiley, who writes perceptively and sympathetically of Tyson in his book *Serenity* (1989), the fight was the least of Tyson's problems. Wiley was among the many who seemed to think that Tyson's life was beyond redemption. In his column titled "Too Late to Save Tyson," on *ESPN's Page 2*, Wiley fantasized about rescuing Tyson from the gang of hangers-on that represent the ghetto streets from which Tyson had been rescued once before by Cus D'Amato, in the first and most important chapter of his early mythology. "But more likely, these hangers-on would simply drag Tyson down further into the muck of the netherworld, and they did, and he is stuck there now, seemingly for good." In

Serenity Wiley had seen the attraction of that netherworld for himself, and his tone was less despairing: "Tyson likes the word 'pure.' On the streets, the admiration for what he could do, who he was, was pure. He was a bad motherfucker there. Not a meal ticket, or husband, or criminal element of an underclass. In the street he was pure, the 'baddest man on the planet,' in his words. The streets were his mother's milk. No man wants to give that up, no matter what he grows to be."

What to make, then, of the numberless Tyson supporters who haven't yet been convinced that he needs saving? In a brief discussion of Tyson in *Holler If You Hear Me: Searching for Tupac Shakur*, Michael Eric Dyson writes that Tyson "embodied the authentic street brother," echoing Nelson George's pronouncement in his *Hip Hop America*. Dyson continues:

> In [Don] King, Tyson seemed to find the father figure who could turn whites' demonization of him into more than dollars, while offering him a psychic shield from whites' attacks…. Equally important, Tyson became King's field general in the ghetto rebellion against more sedate, sophisticated style adopted by the black bourgeoisie.

Tyson still commands loyalty in the black neighborhoods. "Just hail any nefarious-looking, corner-hanging dude on the street in Brooklyn. He's probably a Tyson hanger-on," wrote Wiley in his column. In the competition among cities for the right to host Lewis vs. Tyson, Washington D.C. emerged as a favored contender. The *New York Times* quoted a D.C. "boxing elder:" " 'Tyson is very popular in the black community, particularly among the young. . . . Maybe a lot of what we call the bourgeoisie wouldn't want this fight, but it really boils down to a Rock Creek-Southeast political situation,' Mr. Finley said, using geographical shorthand for the city's racial dividing lines." Washington's black mayor, Tony Williams, had campaigned for his city, citing the economic windfall that the fight would mean. The *Financial Times* reported, "Most citizens, rich and poor, black and white, think he's pretty good at what he does . . . But the constant niggling complaint about the mayor—and it irritates him—is that he is not considered black enough for a majority, and far-from-affluent black city. So, when the *Washington Post* reported from street level that most ordinary blacks thought Tyson deserved a chance to fight in the city . . . then it appeared that, for once, Williams had demonstrated populist antennae." But Leadbelly's "Bourgeois Town" and Parliament's "Chocolate City" lost the bid—the Lennox Lewis camp deemed support for Tyson so strong in D.C. that they thought staging the fight there was the equivalent of giving Tyson hometown advantage.

Not everybody in the black neighborhoods is in Mike's corner, however. His rape conviction in 1992 sparked many arguments; Edward Lewis, chairman and CEO of *Essence*, "the preeminent lifestyle magazine for today's African-American women," in his "What It Means to be Black Man" writes that he was "dismayed and offended" by the National Baptist Convention's efforts to secure leniency for Tyson. And when Tyson was released from prison in 1995 and feted with a homecoming in Harlem, chaperoned by Don King and Al Sharpton, the celebration drew protests from the hastily convened African Americans Against Violence, a coalition of neighborhood activists.

Beyond Harlem, Tyson's homecoming was condemned by the National Organization of Women who were, in turn, dismissed by Ishmael Reed as a "white supremacist" group. Many strident articles have appeared, most by impatient or plainly baffled whites, scolding black people for continuing to support Mike Tyson. J. Gregory Garrison, the special prosecutor in Tyson's rape trial, and Randy Roberts, in their *Heavy Justice*, quote Anna Quindlen's questioning approvingly: "The most respected reporters had all but pronounced Tyson guilty. Writing for the *New York Times*, Anna Quindlen wondered what sort of person could consider Tyson a role model after hearing his own witnesses testify: 'Why in the world should Mike Tyson, a man who apparently can't pass a ladies room without grabbing the doorknob, be a role model?'" This sentence, from an article in the *New York Times* reporting on the reaction of Tyson's old neighborhood to the Holyfield biting, is even subtler: "People in Brownsville, indeed anywhere, could choose to believe whether Tyson had actually raped Desiree Washington six years ago, but no one could deny what they saw beamed, at a premium price, into their living rooms on Saturday night." The reporter's gratuitous linking of the biting, which everybody saw, or could have seen, with a rape, which nobody saw, is telling. The "indeed anywhere" doesn't save this from condesension.

IRON MIKE

• • •

All controversial episodes in Tyson's life have provoked pontifications from unlikely correspondents. Ellen Goodman, Keith Botsworth, Maureen Dowd, Christopher Hitchens, Richard Rodriguez, Jonathan Yardley, Anna Quindlen, and Geoff Dyer—distinguished writers all— are among the many writers rarely seen in the sports pages who have been compelled to weigh in on Mike Tyson even if only to say that the rest of them don't know what they're talking about: in an ugly review of Joyce Carol Oates article, "Rape and the Boxing Ring," and her book, *On Boxing*, Yardley says that there's really very little good writing on boxing. "Perhaps the reason for this is that boxing is so alien to the actual experience of literary people, the only way they can approach it is via fantasy."

Their (presumably) more knowledgeable brethren in the sports pages have their own axes to grind. Seventeen years of coverage chronicles the erosion of the relationship between Tyson and the press, a relationship that became particularly fraught when Tyson broke with his white manager Bill Cayton, a figure eulogized by the sportwriters, for Don King. (Ralph Wiley, who is black, is alone among the writers I have read in suggesting, in *Serenity*, that Tyson was justified in severing his contract with Cayton, and to offer an explanation for the press's response: "Yet Tyson was castigated from pillar to post in the media, and, of course, this was racist at its core.") The intercession of King also meant that access to Tyson would be more controlled, sometimes denied altogether. Writing last year in the *New York Post*, Wallace Matthews, Tyson's self-proclaimed nemesis, says "For the last twelve years, the former heavyweight champion has carried on a love-hate relationship with the media. Mostly hate. And mostly, the media has responded in kind." That the media has merely "responded" might be debated. Sportswriters often write as surrogates of the fans, directly addressing the athlete, and though it doesn't deny genuine outrage to say so, much of their confrontational writing must be considered required of them. Mike Katz's birthday greeting to Tyson, reprinted in these pages, cited by other writers, and part of the collective Tyson memory, is a model of this genre. (Maureen Dowd mimics this convention when, in her obligatory column on the Holyfield biting, she says "Mike Tyson, you're no Dick Morris.") Implicit in much of the debate about Tyson's behavior is the question of who has the authority to speak about him. What does it mean that those who champion Tyson are those most likely to have no voice, while the rest of us get our news of him from writers who admit to a "mostly hate" relationship? If most can write of Tyson with the confidence that they speak for their readers, many acknowledge in their margins that while the literate chorus decries Tyson as (in Dave Anderson's words) "a thug who got lucky," a vast inarticulate mass looks on him as their champion.

In an interview with Nick Charles Tyson asks, "How am I fascinating? What in the world is fascinating about me besides I fight and beat people spectacularly? Other than that, what's so fascinating about me?" Why, in other words, is Anna Quindlen fascinated by the rape trial of a prizefighter? The answer can only be that we are fascinated not by Tyson as Tyson, not by "who hit whom how hard," but by a mythological Tyson whom we have created, perhaps to give shape to a disorder we fear cannot be disciplined. Montieth Illingworth, according to Gerald Early, "describes the various fables of Tyson's manhood as 'Cus and the Kid,' 'Iron Mike,' and 'The Public Enemy,' to which one might add 'The Regenerate Muslim.'" Of Tyson's "Public Enemy" incarnation, Early says that it was "cooked up" by Don King, suggesting, rightly, that Public Enemy is, like the others, a role inhabited by a Tyson who is, at least in part, *not* the fable. Joyce Carol Oates describes Tyson as "a prehistoric creature rising from a fearful crevice in our collective subconscious," and Ira Berkow discloses in the *Times* sports pages that "Perhaps one of the greatest fears is to open a closet in our minds and find Tyson hulking there." (Both of these quotations place the responsibility for creating Tyson *outside* of Tyson, and echo Leroi Jones' famous invocation of Sonny Liston as "the big black Negro in every white man's hallway, waiting to do him in, deal him under, for all the hurts white men have been able to inflict on his world.") In Mike Lupica's nasty and dismissive profile of Tyson for *Esquire* (February 1988) Tyson says, "A lot of this for me is like Hollywood, like playing a role. I'm supposed to be the epitome of a man, you know? I'm supposed to be macho. So I'm macho. . . . I'm the heavyweight champion of the world." More recently, he snarled at reporters "You wanted a beast? Now you've got a beast." It is fitting that *Time* magazine's coverage of the most decisive fight in Tyson's career, his defeat by

Buster Douglas, was written by Richard Corliss, *Time*'s movie critic, who compared the outcome to that of a *Rocky* picture: " . . . a story like this only happens in the movies."

All great fighters are compared to their predecessors, but for most of the last century the terms of comparison were those employed by whites who had the power to make and break black fighters. Jack Johnson's defiant bad behavior and antagonizing of whites ruined opportunities for other black heavyweights, notably Harry Wills, from 1915 until Joe Louis was finally allowed to fight for the title in 1937. Louis was explicitly warned against emulating Johnson and his image as a polite black man who didn't run around with white women was carefully monitored by his black handlers. As Jeffrey Sammons told Thomas Hauser ". . . the press gave us a model citizen who was white in every way except his color." For those who write about Tyson, one of his most consistent roles is that of foil to Muhammad Ali, or rather, to Ali's rehabilitated image. Tyson, the sullen, lisping brute, taunted for his ugliness—who thought of himself as ugly— is darkened in contrast with the beautiful, dancing, voluble Ali, whose own word for himself was "pretty." Ali, too, was denied a license to fight in Las Vegas, and though his crime, defiance of the draft, is considered, in retrospect, a noble one of conscience, Ali was reviled with a violence greater than any Tyson has ever occasioned. "I'm a bad nigger now," he said. Some part of the enmity he earned was from those seeking to punish him for his embrace of Elijah Muhammad and Malcolm X. Tyson has also con-verted to Islam—a conversion most writers find unconvincing—but in common their conversions announced a turning away from whites. In his introduction to *The Muhammad Ali Reader*, Gerald Early writes, "Ali was essentially a comic. This explains why, although he was deeply hated by many whites at one point in his career, he was able to come back.... Ali offered the public the contradictory pleasure of having to take him seriously while not having to take him seriously." Tyson "offers" no such pleasure. Echoing Ali's famous "I don't have to be what you want me to be," Tyson obstinately refuses to concur with the judgments of his interlocutors. His insistence that he has been mis-treated, that he is a victim, is what most offends. If Ali is not quite an "honorary" white American, as Leroi Jones wrote of Floyd Patterson, his bad self has been forgiven, or more likely, forgotten. This forgetfulness signals a hope that the troubling conflicts that Ali represented in his bad incarnation have been redressed; Mike Tyson is a reminder that they have not. Many writers note Tyson's attentiveness to ring history, anomalous among fighters, another legacy of Cus D'Amato; nobody is more aware of Ali than Tyson. But Tyson's fascination with Sonny Liston is also recorded. He has visited Liston's gravesite in Las Vegas; and he has spoken of identifying with Liston, the "ugly bear" whom Ali defeated twice.

Joyce Carol Oates, in her generous note permitting her work to be reprinted here, called Mike Tyson's life a "tragedy in progress," a view to which almost all of the assembled contributors subscribe. But Tyson steadfastly refuses to bear the responsibility for that tragedy himself and this is the source of the great anxiety and outrage that he provokes, the fascination that he exerts. Two scant generations after the passage of the besieged Civil Rights Act, when words like "affirmative action," "black reparations," and "underclass" roil the language of an avowedly classless nation, Mike Tyson is not a grotesque anomaly but the avatar of a question whose answer we fear: Whose tragedy is it? Richard Steele, writing of Tyson's appearance before the Nevada State Athletic Commission, quotes commissioner Amy Ayoub's response to Tyson's heard-before pleas: "Mr. Tyson," she concluded, "I know you're a human being, but I deeply feel that you're not a victim anymore." To which Steele, a black man, adds, "I second that." Steele does not quote Tyson's reply, maybe because he's tired of hearing it: "You don't know me, miss. You don't know nothing about me. You only know what you read. You don't know my horror stories. You don't know if I'm a victim or not."

IRON MIKE

MIKE

A MIKE TYSON READER

CUS D'AMATO

People, July 15, 1985

by

William Plummer

The old man stood in the dressing room beneath the Albany Convention Center and watched his kid warm up, watched him wheel around the room in time with the music. *Lovergirl, Square Biz*, the pop-soul sound of Teena Marie was little more than white noise in the old man's head, which was teeming with other themes. At 6 feet and 212 pounds, the kid was an impressive physical specimen. Plus, as the veteran pugs liked to say, he carried a cure for insomnia in either hand. Still, the old man was worried about the fight. He was concerned that the opponent, one Hector Mercedes, was three inches shorter than his kid and that the public would perceive his fighter to be a bully. Above all, the old man was concerned that his kid stay within himself, that he demonstrated in this—his pro debut—how far he'd come toward mastering the mutiny of emotions that warred within him nearly five years ago, when as a virtual feral child he was plucked from the New York streets and deposited upstate in the Tryon School for boys, an anteroom to prison.

In a word, D'Amato was back. The man who outsmarted the boxing monopolists of the '50s to make Floyd Patterson king of the sport, the man Muhammad Ali asked to manage him, the man Norman Mailer called a student of Zen—the storied Cus D'Amato was back and maneuvering on the margin of boxing's Big Time after an absence from the major fight circuit of nearly 20 years. At 77, D'Amato announced that within two years he expected to match Mike Tyson, his 19-year-old ward, for all the marbles—meaning he was out to make his kid the youngest heavyweight champ in history.

For years D'Amato had been holed up, locked in a deep sleep, as far as much of the boxing world was concerned, in Rip Van Winkle country. He had been living in Catskill, N.Y. as guest of Camille Ewald, whose sister had been married to his older brother. He had the run of Camille's 14-room Victorian house, overlooking the Hudson, which, thanks to the largesse of fight-film entrepreneur Jimmy Jacobs, he had turned into a sort of year-round training camp. At any given moment there might be half a dozen fighters in residence, working under D'Amato's tutelage in a gym carved into the loft above the Catskill Police Station. D'Amato trained the local talent as well, but the best kids tended to be the ones sent to him for fine tuning or general over-haul by managers with a direct tap into the urban miasma.

Then, one evening in 1981, Bob Stewart, a former fighter who worked at the Tryon School, brought over a 14-year-old kid for the Master's look-see. "We deal in losers up here," says Stewart. "But Mike Tyson had something. In the back of my mind was the knowledge that Cus took in fighters, and maybe if I brought Mike down six or seven times, he'd take a liking to him. The first night we boxed three rounds. I had to fight my head off because Mike was charging me. Boom! I hit him in the second round and his nose was blown all over the place and Cus' trainer says, 'We better stop it at two.' But Mike says, 'No, I want to go three.' Here I am hoping that maybe after two or three months Cus will say something. But, no, this very first night what does Cus say? 'That's the heavyweight champion of the world. If he wants it, it's his.'"

With Mike, as with former light-heavyweight champ Jose Torres and Patterson before him, Cus was no mere trainer, but a teacher of the thoroughgoing sort that frequented the gymnasia of ancient Greece. Cus spent two hours a day working with him in the gym. He spent much of the waking portion of the remaining 22 teasing out his kid's inner man. Cus learned that Mike had grown up fatherless in the Brownsville section of Brooklyn, robbing cars and stores, sometimes sleeping in abandoned buildings. He discovered that the kid extended unqualified love only to his pigeons, the "street rats" he caught in the park and cooped on the roof of a burned-out tenement. He discovered that the kid was mortified by not being able to read, that this was the source of his truancy. "My feeling is this," he told the boy. "There are no stupid people. There are only uninterested people." Cus got Mike private tutoring and gave him reading that would appeal to him—books about main eventers such as Joe Louis and Jack Dempsey, Napoleon and Alexander the Great. Cus discovered that Mike was not merely suspicious of white people, he was distrustful of everyone. "See," says D'Amato, "people, especially if they come up in a rough area, have to go through a number of experiences in life that are intimidating and embarrassing. These experiences form layer upon layer over their capabilities and talents. So your job as a teacher is to peel off these layers."

Which is to say that early in their conversations the old man started talking to the boy about fear, coming at the topic from different angles. "Fear," he would say, "is like a fire. If you control it, as we do when we heat our houses, it is a friend. When you don't, it consumes you and everything around you." And: "Imagine a deer crossing an open field. He's approaching the forest when his instinct tells him, 'Think! There may be a mountain lion in the tree.' The moment that happens, nature starts the survival process. Normally a deer can jump five or 10 feet. With adrenaline he can jump 15 or 20 feet. Fear, you see, is nature's way of preparing us for struggle. Without it, we'd die." And: "Any fighter who fought Muhammad Ali was intimidated by him. You see, Ali's secret weapon was a tremendous will to win; an ability to take his own fear and project it as an irresistible force, which immediately tended to inhibit the ability of his opponent to execute what he knew."

When Mike first came to Cus and Camille, his promise was obvious only at ringside. Otherwise, says Camille, "He was sloppy, rude, wild." He seldom spoke at the dinner table and spent most of his time in his room. Then, bit by bit, he let Cus and Camille into his life. Recently he bought Cus a Father's Day card. Mike, whose natural mother is dead, also brought home a friend and introduced him to Camille, saying, "I want you to meet my mother." Camille laughs at the memory. "I thought that kid's eyes would pop from his head when he saw my white skin."

CUS D'AMATO

Cus had no choice but to turn Mike into a money fighter. In three years he won every major amateur tournament in America, losing only in the Olympic Box-off to subsequent gold medalist Henry Tillman, who spent much of the fight in thoughtful retreat. All told, Mike had just 25 amateur fights. His talent had outstripped his experience and, perhaps, D'Amato worried, his development as a human being.

Constantine "Cus" D'Amato is that wonder in the fight game, a student of the inner man, a self-created Freudian in a profession overrun with dim behaviorists. The seventh of eight sons of an Italian immigrant who delivered ice in a horse-drawn wagon, he rose to maturity in the tumultuous Frog Hollow section of the Bronx—an area that also gave rise to Dutch Schultz and other leading men whose pictures hung in the post office. Decades later, when a couple of mugs climbed the stairs of his 14th Street gym and tried to steal a fighter from him, D'Amato found himself saying, "You can do anything you want. Cut me up into little pieces. I won't give in!" He realized afterward that he'd heard his father use that precise language 30 years earlier on a pair of toughs who wanted in on his ice business.

It seems strange that D'Amato himself never boxed, but there is a reason. At 12 he had a street fight with a man—"one of those men who push kids around because they know they can't push men around." It left him virtually blind in one eye. There is another reason. In his youth, D'Amato confides, he had "what you might call a religious interest." It had grown out of a preoccupation with death, one that found him observing funeral processions with a longing to trade places with the fellow in the box. D'Amato declines to speculate upon the roots of this preoccupation—whether it issued from the fact that his mother died when he was 4 or that three of his seven brothers had gone the same way by the time he came along. Did he ever think about joining the priesthood? "Yes," he answers, his white brow arching in surprise. "How did you know that?"

It's written all over him. It is there in the precocious acts of self-denial. At 16, D'Amato went four days without eating—this, he says, so no one could ever intimidate him with threats of starvation. Later, drafted into the Army during World War II, he would shave only with cold water, stand at attention for hours on end, sleep on the barracks floor. It's there too in the acts of self-mortification, the monkish proofs that the spirit is superior to the flesh. "I had a habit of coming in late at night," he remembers, "and my father used to try to break me of it." Damiano D'Amato used a bullwhip on his seventh son, crashed it down on the boy's bare shoulders even as he lay shuddering but unrepentant beside his bed. Cus, who reveres his father—"He was like granite"—and who has a way of locating the sweet spot in adversity, says the beatings only did him good. "I didn't have a regard for getting hit the way other people did."

The priestly aspect is there as well in the young D'Amato's rejection of the world of getting and spending. Cus would not work for anybody, especially not for money. Nor would he waste his time in high school, which he quit in his second year when he discovered it was interfering with his education. The latter consisted largely of lying under trees "just thinking about things" and reading. (Mark Twain was an early favorite; Cus later dipped into Clarence Darrow, Bertrand Russell— even Einstein—to see what all the fuss was about.) Otherwise he hung around the gyms where his brothers trained or assisted his friends and neighbors as a sort of folk-lawyer paladin—helping them deal, say, with insurance companies reluctant to make good on claims or with two-bit shysters who'd taken fees but provided no services. D'Amato would accept no cash for these offices. But he would, if the offer were made according to an unspoken protocol, accept expenses or a quid pro quo. It was in this manner that Cus obtained the Gramercy Gym. Learning that a childhood friend wanted to get into the gas station business, Cus had gone down to city hall, where he looked over maps and discovered that Bruckner Boulevard was about to be cut through the Bronx. The friend ended up building five stations along the route, making a fortune in the process. "Not long after that I happened to mention to somebody else that I was looking to open a gym," Cus remembers. "Well, this fellow I'd helped found out about it and asked if he could stake me. It sounds crazy, but that's the way we operated in those days, one fellow helping another."

A third-floor walk-up on 14th Street, above a dime-a-dance hall, the Gramercy was something more than a gym. It was Cus D'Amato's laboratory. All those years that Cus had seemed to be wandering fancy-free through the Bronx, he had actually been developing novel ideas about the Manly Art. He was still experimenting in 1949, when a group of men headed by James D. Norris Jr., a Chicago millionaire, paid Joe Louis $150,000 to retire and simultaneously signed the top four heavyweight contenders to exclusive contracts. The International Boxing Club moved systematically through professional boxing, buying up talent in each division, until it controlled virtually every fighter, every arena and all the TV revenues. It was a seemingly foolproof scheme that erased managers from the fight-game picture. At least that was the idea—only Norris and Co. had failed to take into account an obscure manager-trainer from New York whose sole address was a gym on 14th Street, where he slept alone each night with a ferocious police dog. "I couldn't fight them myself," says D'Amato, who had been spoiling for a showdown with the IBC and had been training for it, in a sense, his entire life. "I had to wait for a fighter to fight them with, a kid who was not only good but loyal. If he was good but not loyal, it wouldn't help me. I couldn't expose myself, because they were going to get to my fighter, pay him off or do something to get him to leave me."

In 1952 Floyd Patterson won the gold medal in the Helsinki Olympics. On his return to the U.S., D'Amato met him at the airport accompanied by a pack of newsmen. He announced to the world that the 17-year-old Patterson, a mere middleweight, was turning professional with the object of becoming heavyweight champion of the world. D'Amato had been working with Patterson since Floyd was 14 and recently out of the Wiltwyck School for Boys, a school for disturbed children in Esopus, N.Y. He had taught Patterson to hold his gloves inordinately high—in a style the IBC would lamely deride as the "peekaboo"—while his elbows guarded his ribs from body blows. Thus armored and slipping and weaving in the manner D'Amato rehearsed in the gym, Patterson could punch largely without fear of being punched, and could therefore take on the appearance of a crowd-pleasing go-for-broke slugger.

But there was more to the making of Floyd Patterson than technique. "The only thing Patterson showed at the beginning," Cus remembers, "was that he was game and determined. I knew he was a good kid. I waited. I watched him, studied him, until I learned his character and personality." Patterson was dominated by an inferiority complex. He was so introverted and sensitive that mere conversation seemed to leave him covered with fingerprints. D'Amato's tactic was not to criticize or lecture or even talk to Floyd directly, but to speak to some third person within Patterson's earshot. He would converse with this person about the uses of fear and intimidation, about the deer approaching the forest. But the performance did not end there. D'Amato would carry himself in a self-assured way, be expansive in company. Normally casual, he became an elegant dresser, donning a homburg hat, a blue serge suit, a pearl gray overcoat. His purpose? To convey to Patterson that he had nothing to be ashamed of, that he was someone of importance, top of the mark. "Floyd would watch me and never let on that he was watching me," Cus remembers. "But I knew."

Meanwhile D'Amato was watching too—for his chance. In 1956 he managed to match his fighter with Hurricane Jackson, the IBC's No. 1 contender. When Patterson won a decision over Jackson, the IBC had no choice but to match Cus' kid with the venerable Archie Moore, whom Floyd subdued with a leaping left hook in the fifth round. With that victory D'Amato drove the IBC to its knees. He went on to bury it by never letting his kid fight for an IBC-controlled promoter—this despite threatening phone calls in the middle of the night, despite regular abuse in the dailies from sportswriters on the IBC pad. Eventually the IBC was declared a monopoly and dismantled by the government.

Back in Albany, Mike Tyson's fight with Hector Mercedes was all over by 1:47 of the first round.

"The term is quick, not easy," D'Amato told a ringside reporter. "This fellow Mercedes came to fight."

"Mike is an irresistible force," said Jimmy Jacobs, who co-manages Tyson. "He's the most aggressive talent to come along since Joe Frazier."

Privately Jacobs and D'Amato were less sanguine. The fight, short as it was, told little about Mike that Cus did not already know. With the bell it was as if Mike had been released from a cage. He went after Mercedes with a fury that had everyone at ringside gasping, backing him up from the outset, battering him with either hand, finally forcing Mercedes to call it a night with a left hook to the body that cut his legs out from under him.

"We're going to have this problem with Mike, getting him opponents," Jacobs said to D'Amato.

"Yes, I know that," said Cus.

CUS D'AMATO

On the way back to the dressing room, D'Amato was waylaid by a reporter who asked the inevitable question: How did it feel being back after nearly 20 years? D'Amato objected. He hadn't been away. The reporter tried again. What difference had Mike Tyson made in his life? "He's meant everything," said the old man. "If it weren't for him, I probably wouldn't be living today. See, I believe nature's a lot smarter than anybody thinks. During the course of a man's life he develops a lot of pleasures and people he cares about. Then nature takes them away one by one. It's her way of preparing you for death. See, I didn't have the pleasures any longer. My friends were gone, I didn't hear things, I didn't see things clearly, except in memory. The last time I had an erection was 15 years ago. So I said I must be getting ready to die. Then Mike came along. The fact that he is here and is doing what he is doing gives me the motivation to stay alive. Because I believe a person dies when he no longer wants to live. He finds a convenient disease, just like a fighter, when he no longer wants to fight, finds a convenient corner to lie down in. It's like boxing. It's all psychological."

DR. K. O.

Village Voice, December 10, 1985

by

Jack Newfield

All fighters come from mean streets and lower depths. Champions such as Sonny Liston, Archie Moore, Jake LaMotta, Dwight Braxton, and Macho Camacho have survived prison detours. Mike Tyson, who could be the next great fighter, comes from the mean streets of Bed-Stuy and is a survivor of a penal institution for incorrigible boys. When Tyson was 13 years old he moved directly from an upstate reformatory—where he'd spent two years—into the communal home of Cus D'Amato—boxing's supreme teacher, psychologist, moralist, saver of souls, and father-substitute. D'Amato died last month at 77, and Mike Tyson, at 19, is his unfinished masterpiece.

At this point, only boxing buffs know Mike Tyson's name. He's had only 13 professional fights—all awesome knockout demolitions, nine in the first round—but he hasn't appeared yet on network television. On March 23, 1985, he started his professional career fighting for $500. Since then he has fought in Albany, Houston, and Atlantic City. He does not have the kind of six-figure, multifight television contract that the 1984 Olympic champions received at the birth of their pro careers. He has been booked, and then bumped, from four cable-TV fights. This Friday night he makes his 10-round debut on his native ground at the Felt Forum, against Sam Scaff for $5000.

Tyson started in boxing's outside lane because he did not have the marketing advantage of an Olympic gold medal. He did not have the headstart glitz of past Olympic boxing champions like Muhammad Ali, Sugar Ray Leonard, Joe Frazier, Michael and Leon Spinks, Floyd Patterson, or George Foreman—or even of Tyrell Biggs and Henry Tillman, the Olympic super-heavyweight and heavyweight gold medalists of the 1984 games in Los Angeles. All Tyson has is the power, speed, and character that might constitute ring genius.

The politics of amateur boxing cheated Tyson out of his rightful place on America's 1984 Olympic boxing team. Cus D'Amato was advised in a friendly way, not to even enter Tyson in the super heavyweight trials because that berth was reserved for Tyrell Biggs, and Tyson was robbed of two decisions in elimination fights with Tillman for the right to be the heavyweight on the Olympic squad. In one of those three-round fights Tyson scored a clean knockdown, and in the other he nearly chased Tillman out of the ring. But he lost split decisions each time. Afterward, Tyson smashed the second-place trophy against the wall of his dressing room.

Tyson was not even a New York City Golden Gloves champion like current pro contenders Carl "The Truth" Williams, Eddie Gregg, and Mitch Green. Tyson had only 25 amateur fights. He never entered the Gloves during the years he was a secret being sculpted by Cus D'Amato in a gym above the police station in rural Catskill, New York, 100 miles from the deprivations and temptations of Bed-Stuy.

During those decisive years, when Tyson was between 13 and 19, Cus D'Amato taught him everything he knew about boxing, for which Tyson had an instinctive aptitude, and about life—which is so much harder to learn, and for which Tyson had only the primitive preparation of the streets and jail.

Inside the ring, Tyson quickly mastered the signature D'Amato moves of elusive aggression that made Floyd Patterson and José Torres (both former pupils of D'Amato) champions bending at the knees to maintain balance and position; holding your gloves high, next to the cheekbones; keeping your chin down; getting under and inside the opponent's jab; punching straight, short, and fast from the shoulder;

and stepping to the side and throwing a left hook to the liver. ("The punch nobody can take," Tyson says.)

During the long country walks, communal meals, and quiet evenings of watching grainy black and white films of the boxing masters of the past, D'Amato imparted to Tyson his special blend of psychology and philosophy. The key to it is what D'Amato called "cultivation of character." To Cus, "character" was a mystical combination of will, courage, self-denial, self-respect, and intensity. Cus told all his fighters, "The hero and the coward both feel exactly the same fear, only the hero confronts his fear and converts it into fire."

Cus also said that fighters of good skill and great character will often beat an opponent of superior skill but less character.

Cus also conveyed to Tyson his idea of the goal of the trainer-fighter relationship: for the fighter to eventually become completely independent of the trainer, and for the trainer to make himself obsolete. This was one reason why D'Amato himself never worked in Tyson's corner; he wanted to nurture in Tyson the confidence of self-sufficiency during a fight, so he would not feel dependent on an external adviser.

Five years ago my friend José Torres told me that D'Amato had found a troubled 14-year-old "kid from Brooklyn who is going to become the heavyweight champion of the world." D'Amato had discovered José in the squalor of Ponce, Puerto Rico, in 1957 when José was still an amateur, and guided him not just to a world championship but to a successful second act as a writer and state commissioner after his boxing career was over. Along the way Cus never had a written contract with José, Cus never took a dime from all the money José earned during his career, because Cus felt he was making enough money to live on from Floyd Patterson's purses. When José was broke and on the way up, Cus paid for his wedding. When Cus died, he left no material assets or estate; he hadn't had a bank account for 15 years. Jim Jacobs, Cus's best friend, paid all of his expenses.

So one morning in 1980, José and I went to the gym above the police station in Catskill, and we saw the future. Tyson was then 14 years old, 200 pounds, and about five-six. Outside the ring he seemed withdrawn and sullen. Inside the ring he was a manchild prodigy puncher. Toward Cus he displayed the beginnings of trust and affection.

On the day Cus died last month, Tyson cried and was inconsolable.

DR. K.O.

The next day José Torres drove back to the train that would take him back to Catskill and spoke to Tyson fighter-to-fighter, brother-to-brother, since Cus had been a father to both of them.

"Who is going to teach me now?" Tyson asked. "I was learning every day with Cus."

Torres answered: "Cus had enough time. You know everything already. You now know everything Cus could teach you. Cus gave you inspiration. All you need now is experience, confidence, and desire."

That same night I happened to read my daughter the end of E. B. White's *Charlotte's Web*; the chapter where the brave old spider dies, consoled by the knowledge that her eggs are rescued and about to be hatched.

The history of boxing is the history of immigrant succession in America. Fighters don't come from prep schools or seminaries. The best way to understand this dangerous, corrupt, and disorganized sport is through the eyes of Charles Darwin.

When the Irish were the urban underclass after the famine of 1848, the great champions were John L. Sullivan, James J. Corbett, Philadelphia Jack O'Brien, and Terry McGovern. The generation of Jewish immigrants fleeing the pogroms of Russia and Europe produced, during the '20s and '30s, Benjamin Leiner, known as Benny Leonard, and Beryl David Rosofsky, known as Barney Ross.

In the '30s and '40s, blacks found boxing as an exit from the slum, and started to dominate the sport. Out of the jobless Detroit ghetto, at the bottom of the Depression, stormed Joe Louis and Sugar Ray Robinson. From Los Angeles came the first triple champion, Henry Armstrong.

In the '60s and '70s, great fighters emerged out of Latin America's third world poverty: Roberto Duran from Panama, Wilfredo Gomez from Puerto Rico, Carlos Monzon from Argentina, Alexis Arguello from Nicaragua, Jose Napoles from Cuba, Ruben Olivares and Salvador Sanchez from Mexico.

And so Mike Tyson was born in Brooklyn's Bedford-Stuyvesant in July 1966 into an environment of riots, heroin, crime, disintegrating family structure, and collapsing public schools. He was born on Franklin Avenue, between De-Kalb and Willoughby, not far from where another fighter of the future, Mark Breland—the 1984 Olympic welterweight gold medal winner—was growing up. When Tyson was about nine, he moved to Brownsville, which is even more impoverished than Bed-Stuy.

It is probably a miracle that Mike Tyson did not die in a shootout with police, or end up doing 25 years in Attica. By the time he was 10 or 11 years old he was a remorseless predator, disconnected from society, doing muggings, stick-ups, and holding the gun during armed robberies, "because I was a juvenile." Once he was knifed in the face by someone he had beaten in a fair fight.

Tyson attended the same public school I did—P.S. 54, at the corner of Nostrand Avenue and Hart Street. He was a good student at the beginning, but by fifth grade he had become a chronic truant. "I knew who my father was, but he never lived with us," Tyson says. Abnormally strong for his age, he was able to knock kids five years older unconscious in street fights. They would jab and jive like Ali, and Tyson would rush in and land his punch of natural power.

"I started hanging out with a bad crowd," he recalls now, "After I was about 10, I lived on the street. We robbed stores, gas stations, everything. I got arrested lots of times. I can't count how many. They put me in a lot of different places that I escaped from. I just walked out in the middle of the night because they had no fences. I was in Spofford House in the Bronx for about eight months. Then I got convicted of assault and they sentenced me to 18 months in Tryon, a school for bad boys. But they held me overtime. I did two years because I knocked out a few guards and some residents. I was hyper in Tryon, and I couldn't escape. I felt cooped up and frustrated with all my energy, so I had a lot of fights. But please, don't think I was a murderer or anything like that I wasn't that bad."

The confidentiality provisions of the state's social services law prohibited the administration and counselors at the Tryon School in Johnstown, New York, from talking for quotation about Tyson. But off-the-record they are all proud of the kid they remember as originally the most difficult of 35 residents who lived in medium security Elmwood Cottage. In April 1984, the state's youth services commissioner, Leonard Dunston, presented Tyson with a plaque for accomplishment after being a resident in a state juvenile facility.

DR. K.O.

When Tyson first arrived at Tryon he was "violent, depressed, and mute," according to one of his counselors. After a couple months he discovered boxing with gloves instead of fists. One of the guards at Tryon was Bobby Stewart, a former pro boxer who knew about D'Amato's boxing club in nearby Catskill. Stewart arranged a meeting during which he sparred with Tyson in front of Cus. Eventually, Tyson was paroled into Cus D'Amato's custody. He moved in with Cus; Cus's companion of 45 years, Camille Ewald; Kevin Rooney, Cus's loyal fighter from Staten Island, who would become Tyson's friend and trainer; and the other young boxers who were part of the extended D'Amato family.

Things did not go smoothly at first. Cus enrolled Tyson in the local public school, but Tyson knocked out a few classmates, and Cus had to arrange for a private tutor to visit the house.

For the next six years D'Amato and Tyson worked and talked together every day. Tyson not only learned how to box from Cus, he learned the rules of civilized society. He also learned Cus's code of honor: loyalty, perfectionism, courage. And no contact with—and no compromise with—the corrupters and connivers of boxing.

By being such a gifted pupil, Tyson, in return gave Cus the treasure of looking forward to the future. He made Cus feel young again. Cus felt like it was 1962 again, and José Torres was undefeated, and Paul Pender, the middleweight champion, was ducking his fighter. With Tyson's father absent and his mother (now deceased) living in Brooklyn, Cus became Tyson's legal guardian.

Some fighters can be obnoxious bullies outside the ring. But every fighter Cus ever trained was a considerate gentleman. And under Cus's tutelage, Tyson, too, began to feel free to display playfulness and even tenderness. He returned to an old hobby he'd had in Brooklyn—collecting pigeons. Tyson now spends hours training and playing with his collection of 100 pigeons. The birds give him peace, and are his second favorite form of recreation.

His favorite relaxation—also a solitary pursuit—is studying old boxing movies on a big screen in his bedroom. His co-managers, Jim Jacobs and Bill Cayton, own the world's largest collection of boxing films and tapes—about 26,000. Their company, Big Fights Inc., is a $20 million corporation that sells the rights to show these films. So Tyson has access to his own vast film archive of past champions. He has become an authentic historian and scholar of the sweet science.

When I asked Tyson about the champions of the past he most admired and identified with, I got answers that were surprising and revealing. I had anticipated his identification with pure punchers like Liston and Foreman, but he dismissed them as "just ponderous guys without too much brains."

His favorite fighter, he said, was Rocky Marciano. "He broke their will," Tyson said with reverence. "He was constantly coming in. But he swayed low, so the punches hit him on the shoulder. He didn't get hit as much as people think he did. And we have in common fighting guys with longer reach."

The second champion Tyson mentioned was Tony Canzoneri, the clever-aggressive, five-four, two-time lightweight champion during the 1930s.

"Canzoneri had incredible guts and desire," Tyson said. "And he was so smart."

"And I love Henry Armstrong," Tyson volunteered. "You know, Cus thought he was the best boxer who ever lived."

Six days after Tyson was a pallbearer at Cus D'Amato's funeral, he was scheduled to fight Eddie Richardson in Houston, Texas, for $2500. Jim Jacobs, Tyson's co-manager with Bill Cayton, contemplated calling the fight off when he saw how "traumatized" Tyson had been by the death of D'Amato. But Tyson wanted to go through with the fight; whatever grief and loss he felt, he would not let it interfere with Cus's radical plan of fighting every 10 days to acquire experience and confidence. When boxing writers in Houston asked him if he was emotionally prepared to fight so soon after Cus's burial, Tyson told them: "I have certain objectives, and I'm going to fulfill them." Jim Jacobs never saw him so "resolute and determined."

Cus had been telling the boxing community for years that Tyson was going to be "the youngest heavyweight champion in history," and Tyson wants to make Cus a prophet. Under Cus's direction, Floyd Patterson became champion at 21 years and nine months, and Tyson, not yet 20, has set his mind to break that record, even though it places him under the pressure of an artificial timetable.

At this infant stage of Tyson's career, there are naturally unanswered

DR. K.O.

Cus D'Amato

questions about what hidden weaknesses might lurk beneath his growing aura of invincibility. Other fighters have looked like unbeatable monsters, only to have tiny flaws exposed and broken open under pressure from great rivals in big fights. Muhammad Ali unmasked George Foreman's lack of stamina and mechanistic inability to adjust his tactics and style. Larry Holmes revealed Gerry Cooney's lack of confidence in his own endurance, and his demoralization when someone took his best shot and was still standing. Sugar Ray Leonard found weakness in Thomas Hearns's chin, and ignorance of how to clinch when dazed.

So in Texas, the herd of boxing writers seized upon Tyson's height and reach as the potential flaw in this jewel. Tyson, at five-eleven and a half, is short when compared to Foreman, Ali, or Holmes. Since Jack Johnson won the heavyweight title in 1908, only two heavyweight champions have been under six feet—Rocky Marciano and Joe Frazier. And Tyson's reach is not nearly as long as future rivals like Pinklon Thomas, Tyrell Biggs, Tim Witherspoon, Greg Page, Carl Williams, Gerry Cooney, or Michael Spinks. And his opponent in Houston was Eddie Richardson, who is six feet six inches tall, with a reach advantage of about nine inches.

"Are you too short to be a heavyweight?" the skeptical writers kept asking Tyson before the fight.

"None of my past opponents say that," was Tyson's standard reply.

Richardson was an adequate journeyman fighter—he had 12 wins and two losses going into the bout, with eight knockouts. Tyson had won all his 11 fights by knockouts.

The fight in Houston lasted 77 seconds. The first punch Tyson threw—a freight-train overhand right—knocked Richardson down. He got up, but Tyson, advancing in crouch, hit him with a left hook so fast that Richardson never saw it coming. Richardson seemed to be lifted off the canvas by the force of the blow, and fell backwards like a sawed-down tree. He was counted out.

In the dressing room before the local writers could formulate their questions, a pumped-up Tyson asked: "Do you still think I'm too short?" When an interviewer asked Tyson what lessons he had learned from D'Amato, he answered: "To face your problems."

Several viewings of the tape of this fight, and the tape of Tyson's one-round knockout in September of the six foot four Donnie Long, suggest the simple essence of Tyson's distinction. *He punches harder than any body else*. It was this raw natural power that Cus D'Amato saw when Tyson was 13 years old and still in a prison for adolescents. D'Amato merely concentrated and refined this power by teaching Tyson to punch in a shorter arc, improve his timing and hand speed, and develop a left hook that is just as powerful as his right. D'Amato discovered Tyson, but he didn't invent him.

Tyson's victims all say afterward that they have never been hit so hard. Donnie Long, who had never been knocked out before, said Tyson's punch "felt like a blackjack." Sterling Benjamin, who succumbed in 54 seconds, said it felt "like a sledgehammer hit me." He was put down by a left hook to the liver—Tyson's punch "nobody can take."

John Condon is the head of Madison Square Garden's boxing department. He has been around fighters for 30 years. He told me: "I have never seen anybody punch like Tyson. Not Marciano, not Liston. Nobody. He would knock out Gerry Cooney today in one round. His trouble will be no one is going to want to fight him."

Nobody can give a professional fighter this magnitude of punching authority. It comes from nature's chemistry of leverage, upper-body strength, timing, and quickness of hand that prevents the opponent from preparing his nervous system for the impact. Professionals get knocked out by the punch they don't see coming.

One-punch destroyers have come in all shapes and physiques. A surprising number of legendary hitters have been tall and thin: Ray Robinson, Sandy Saddler, Bob Foster, Thomas Hearns, Carlos Zarate, and Alexis Arguello. An equal number have been compact, strong, and stocky: Stanley Ketchel, Joe Frazier, Archie Moore, Sonny Liston, Wilfredo Gomez, and Rocky Marciano.

Whatever the secret formula is, Tyson was born with it. But a punch by itself is no guarantee of success or greatness. It must exist in combination with other qualities—"character," defense, and intelligence. And there must not be that small vulnerability that some future foe will find and exploit in a contest the whole world is watching.

Perhaps the most common unseen vulnerability in young prospects is the inability to take a punch. This quality cannot be taught, and it cannot be known until it is tested in an actual fight. Cus thought the ability to take a punch was a reflection of character and will. Other trainers believe the ability to relax in the ring and the thickness of the neck as a shock absorber are also factors in avoiding being knocked out. This capacity to survive the other man's best blow was one of the dimensions that made Ray Robinson, Muhammed Ali, Rocky Marciano, Harry Greb, Henry Armstrong, Carmen Basilio, Sandy Saddler, and Sugar Ray Leonard boxing immortals. Tyson told me: "I know I can take a great punch, but I don't want to have to prove it."

Tyson's extraordinary 19-and-a-half-inch neck is a good indication he can probably take a great punch. But he was once tested in this regard, in his toughest amateur fight.

This involuntary experiment occurred in the heavyweight finals of the Empire State Games in April of 1984, just before the Olympic trials. Tyson, then not yet 18, was fighting Winston Bent, the reigning New York City Golden Gloves champion.

During an exchange in the second round, Bent jolted Tyson with a right hand to the temple. Tyson punched back with fury. He did not go down. He did not retreat. And in the next round he knocked Bent out. It was an example of what Cus D'Amato meant when he talked about "character" in a fighter.

On November 22—nine days after his knockout in Texas—Tyson was in the ring again. The location was Albany, and his opponent was Conroy Nelson, six foot five inches, and with a professional record of 19 wins and five losses. He had a 10-inch reach advantage.

The venue was a music tent, sold out—with 3000 people plus 400 standees—on a cold, rainy night. They'd all come to see Tyson, who has become a hero in the Albany-Troy-Schnectady area. (The television networks are now considering showing Tyson for the first time in February, and staging the fight in the Albany area so there will be an enthusiastic live crowd rather than the usual indifferent gamblers and tourists who attend the fights staged in the Atlantic City and Nevada casino hotels.)

The second Tyson departed his trailer dressing room—wearing no socks and no robe, as is his tradition—the crowd started screaming. And Tyson, who learned from Cus there is an entertainment and personality aspect to boxing, smiled and interacted with his fans.

At the opening bell Tyson sprang to the attack immediately

imposing his will and energy level on his opponent. Nelson retreated and covered his head with his gloves. Tyson stepped to the side and went to the body with supersonic hooks to the liver and kidney.

George Foreman at 26 did not have enough poise, flexibility, or intelligence to do this with Muhammad Ali in Zaire. Foreman kept trying to punch through Ali's parrying gloves, and hit him in his bobbing and twisting head, instead of his stationary body. Foreman kept missing, got frustrated and exhausted, and Ali knocked him out. But Tyson, at 19, had the wisdom and patience to feast on Nelson's exposed ribs until his hands came down, his breath came in gasps, and his legs lost their spring.

Twenty seconds into the second round Tyson hit Nelson with one short, perfectly timed left hook that smashed the bridge of Nelson's nose into pieces. Nelson went down, managed to get to one knee at the count of nine, and then with his fearful eyes and tentative body language, signaled the referee that he didn't wish to continue.

As soon as the bout was over a 10-year-old kid named Tony, who trained with Cus, jumped into the ring, and held up a homemade sign that said: GOODEN IS DR. K—BUT TYSON IS DR. KO.

Afterward, in the trailer, with a trace of irritation, Tyson answered unusually silly questions from some of the local press. One scribe asked about a local politician who wanted to shut down Cus's Catskill gym because it was "dirty." Tyson and Kevin Rooney said they never heard of the crazy idea.

Another reporter asked Tyson if he expected to win all his fights by knockouts. "That's not possible," Tyson the Historian replied. "Joe Louis didn't knock out every opponent. Schmeling didn't either. Nobody can."

After the local press left, I followed José Torres behind a curtain, where he embraced Tyson. Tyson whispered, "Cus would have been proud."

The following morning, Tyson told Camille: "It was just like Cus was there. Everything he taught me came back to me."

Boxing, is now in a phase of transition. The Age of Muhammad Ali is over. Marvin Hagler is so magnificent he has run out of relevent competition. Boxing is at such a low ebb that Gerry Cooney, who has never beaten a legitimate contender under 35 years old, is being considered for a heavyweight title fight when his only credential is his white skin.

But about to dance on stage is the next generation of Mark Breland, Pernell Whitaker, and Mike Tyson. If boxing is going to be cleansed of its monopolistic manipulations and counterfeit crowns, it will occur when these three rising stars with honest managers become free and independent champions, liberated from phony rating organizations and option contracts to promoters.

So watch Mike Tyson, Cus's kid from Brooklyn, this Friday night at the Felt Forum. He has overcome every adversity to redeem a wayward life and become a role model to a lost generation of the ghetto.

But while watching him, remember he is just 19. Inside his man's body are teenage emotions and inexperience. He has been a professional boxer less than nine months. He has never gone more than four rounds outside the gym. He has never gone 10 rounds, much less the championship 15.

There will be more tests to find hidden flaws in Tyson. We haven't seen what will happen the first time some freak just shrugs off his punch. We don't know how Tyson will handle the money and celebrity that are about to crash into his orderly, ritualized life.

The Tyson we will see Friday night is not yet Muhammed Ali, or Joe Frazier, or Rocky Marciano. But at 19 he is more advanced than they were at 19. And 12 or 15 months from now Mike Tyson could become the youngest heavyweight champion in history. Just as Cus D'Amato and his extended family knew years ago.

FROM FIRE AND FEAR

1989

by

José Torres

J im Jacobs had broken the news of Cus's imminent death to Tyson as gently as possible. "It didn't help," he said. "Mike was devastated."

"I was in Cayton's office," Tyson recalled, "and Jimmy said, 'Mike, I have bad news. They don't think Cus is going to make it through the night and I have to arrange the whole thing for the funeral.' I couldn't take it. I ran outside. I didn't want no one to see me cry. I just went crazy and took a subway to Brooklyn. I knew he was going to die, but one can never tell, you know, miracles happen."

The next day a friend of Tyson's heard about D'Amato's death on the radio. "They saw me in the street," Mike said, "and said, 'I have bad news; they say Cus is dead.' I said, 'I know.' "

A few days later, Mike was asking himself, "What am I going to do? I should take care of Camille . . . make sure she is all right. They don't have no money. So much responsibility. I felt real bad, but Cus told me that if anything happened to him I should depend on Jimmy [Jacobs]."

Jacobs was concerned that Mike might be too upset for his fight with Eddie Richardson, which was scheduled for November 13, nine days after D'Amato's death. "We can call it off and reschedule it as easy as drinking a soda," Jacobs told Mike.

"Do you think Cus would want it that way?" Mike asked.

"I don't think so. He wouldn't want anything to interfere with your career, not even his death."

"I feel the same way."

"It's up to you."

When the press interviewed him, Tyson was prepared. "The only way I could make Cus proud of me is by becoming champion of the world," he told the writers. "Nothing should interfere with that. I'm going to fight in a week and am going to fight better."

A few days later, Cus was buried in Catskill not far from the house he loved so much. I delivered the eulogy to a multitude of Cus's friends, speaking through my tears about how much Cus had helped young fighters and how the only thing he really wanted in return was saving young lives. The three most successful fighters he developed— Floyd Patterson, Mike Tyson, and myself—and Rooney, Jacobs, Bright, and Tom Patti, a light-heavyweight in Cus's stable, were the pallbearers.

Tyson, now nineteen, was truly desolate. "You know," he said to me in tears, "I really feel like taking my own life. If I really had any real guts, I would just kill myself. That's the way I feel. But I have no fucking heart."

"You know deep down that you have to realize what Cus set out for you to do," I tried to console him. "You have to work hard, and I promise you in two to three years Cus will come to you again. He wants to see Mike the champion."

He leaned on my shoulders and cried. "Did you ever see Cus cry?" I asked.

Mike nodded his head.

"When?" I asked.

"When Joe Louis died," he said, wiping his eyes with his shirtsleeves, "and last week when he felt he was not going to make it and might not be able to marry Camille as he planned."

After the funeral Mike went home to rest. He had to travel to Texas in a day or two. On November 13, 1985, he stopped Eddie Richardson in the first round. The first time the six-foot-six Richardson did not move his jaw fast enough from one of Mike's lethal left hooks, he was hit and his body went down—hard. When he got up eight seconds later, another left hook was patiently waiting for him and finished the job, one minute and seventeen seconds into the first round.

A memorial for D'Amato was held in the old Gramercy Gym in Manhattan six days later. "We should celebrate Cus," Jacobs suggested. "It should be a memorial to make people happy . . . about what Cus was able to accomplish . . . all his generous achievements in behalf of the young. All that should be celebrated, and now is the time."

Floyd Patterson, whom Cus helped put into the record books, was conspicuously absent. A previous engagement, he said, "prevents me from attending." But Pete Hamill, Gay Talese, Norman Mailer, and Budd Schulberg were there, and so were Dick Young, Bob Lypsite, Georgie Colon, Simon Ramos, Joe Shaw, Nelson Cuevas, and dozens of others, famous and not so famous, who were touched by Cus. We ate and drank and cried and laughed, bonded together by our love for an old man.

That day Mike sat quietly next to Camille and Jay Bright until he spotted a tall, slender girl—a friend and neighbor of my older brother's family, who lived in Brooklyn. She thought Mike was "cute." And he wasted no time setting up a date with her. She was a teenager who believed in serious relationships and was genuinely impressed with the undefeated boxer's growing fame. She began seeing Mike between fights and eventually sex became a part of their relationship. She was taciturn about her friendship, except with my wife, to whom she confided that Mike would show up unannounced at her home in Brooklyn, say he was hungry, and soon her mother would whip up a colossal Spanish meal that he would wolf down as if he had just ended a two-week hunger strike.

It was hard for Tyson to spend much time with her. He was fighting every two weeks or so and had little time for a normal social life. But somehow he found time for this pretty Puerto Rican girl from Brooklyn. With Cus and his counsel gone, no one could predict what Mike would do with fame, fortune, and women. For the time being, though, the priority was boxing.

Mike's training was now being carefully supervised by Kevin Rooney and Matt Baransky, who found themselves trying to measure the effect of Cus's death on their charge. Nine days after the Richardson fight, at the Colonie Coliseum in Latham, New York, Tyson disposed of Conroy Nelson in about three-and-a-half minutes. If you asked his opponents, Tyson was unstoppable. But a few boxing writers, whose expertise often seemed to be based on an obligation to be clever, were still skeptical.

From December 6, 1985, through February 16, 1986, Tyson traveled from New York City to Latham to Albany to Atlantic City to Troy, New York, for a scheduled 144 minutes of boxing, one eight-round and four ten-round fights. But the fans only saw Tyson for about thirty-nine minutes, barely thirteen rounds of action.

The fight on February 16, 1986, against Jesse Ferguson established Tyson as a true drawing power. No other boxer, with the exception of champions like Marvin Hagler, Sugar Ray Leonard, and "Macho" Camacho could spark the same enthusiasm. The 12,000-seat R.P.I. Houston Field House in Troy was filled to capacity. It was Mike's first exposure on national television. And the crowd behaved just like the wild fight fans of yesteryear. No one could hear the announcer call out Ferguson's name. It was drowned out by deafening boos. And it was almost as hard to hear Tyson's name because of the cheers.

In the first round, Tyson rushed Ferguson and was greeted by a cool pro who knew what he was doing. Tyson missed with a jab and a right cross and got hit with a jab in return. Mike walked in again. Ferguson just waited for him. There were a few inside exchanges. Both fighters felt comfortable in close. Mike was forced to think because Ferguson was countering every time Tyson missed a punch. Suddenly, Mike threw a right-hook-to-the-ribs-right-uppercut-to-the-chin combination. Ferguson went down and remained there for the obligatory eight count. From that point on the fight was not the same. His confidence buoyed by the knockdown, Mike chased Jesse around the ring. Every time they came close, Ferguson would hold Tyson with all his might, making it difficult for referee Luis Rivera to separate them. Rivera warned Ferguson several times. After struggling to untangle Jesse's hands from Tyson's arms in the sixth round, he turned toward the judges and crisscrossed his hands vigorously, signaling Ferguson's disqualification. The audience roared in approval, and Tyson loved it.

In the postfight press conference Tyson was asked about the vicious uppercut that floored Ferguson in the first round. "Well," Mike said, "I was trying to push his nose bone up to his brains."

By then, Jacobs, Cayton, and Rooney knew that the teenager from Brooklyn had reached boxing adulthood. Tyson's busy boxing schedule had escalated the level of his competition. Now, he had to fight legitimate contenders, and if he really had the right stuff, the time had come to prove it. He was on the road of no return—make-or-break time.

The scarcity of good heavyweights and the resulting probability of a mismatch whenever Tyson was in the ring scared most boxing commissioners to no end, myself included. As commissioner, I'd asked Peter Della, NYSAC's supervisor of officials, to assign only the best referees to Tyson's matches. I also told Dr. Frank Folk, our chief physician, to watch Tyson's rivals closely and not to hesitate to stop any match when in doubt. I've always thought it preferable to stop a bout too soon rather than too late.

Several days before his death, Cus and I discussed what would be a major problem for Tyson during the early part of his career. Basically, the teenager was much too powerful, smart, and sharp for heavyweights who matched his limited experience, but he could be very vulnerable to guys with know-how and seasoning. Before he stepped in the ring with this higher class of opponent, he would have to be exposed to a wide variety of boxing styles, but in a manner that allowed him to correct his weaknesses without incurring risk. The problem, therefore, was finding "ideal opponents" who were limited enough to represent a probable "W" in Mike's win column, but skilled enough to expand Mike's repertoire—opponents who wouldn't be defeated so convincingly that Mike would be catapulted to the next level. Finding and securing these ideal opponents often boiled down to politics—back-room game playing.

As it turned out, Jacobs and Cayton had been able to hold off the procession of "ideal opponents" for one more fight that promised a respectable payday and not much work. Mike's nemesis would be a fighter named Steve Zouski, and the bout would be part of a pay-television doubleheader that featured the Marvelous Marvin Hagler—John "the Beast" Mugabi world middleweight title bout. Although the Hagler-Mugabi fight was being staged in Las Vegas, Nevada, and the Tyson-Zouski bout at the Nassau Coliseum in Uniondale, Long Island, the television audience, supposedly tuning in to watch the championship fight, would be enhanced significantly in New York, where Tyson had become boxing's biggest attraction.

Tyson had trouble sleeping the night before this bout, and at five o'clock in the morning he asked his assistant, Steve Lott, if he could go to the gym and do some training. Steve in turn asked Rooney, who thought it was a great idea.

"So we went to the gym at six," Steve recalled, "on the morning of the fight, and Mike loosened up a bit, went on the bike for about twenty minutes, did some calisthenics, shadow-boxed for a while, and then jumped rope."

That night, as was his habit, Tyson jumped at his opponent, forcing him to use his hands and legs as defensive tools rather than weapons. The first and second rounds followed the same pattern: Tyson chasing, Zouski backing up and then grabbing until the referee separated them. Now and then, Zouski would throw desperate punches and one or two would graze Mike's face, delighting the few Zouski fans at the Coliseum. Then, during the third round, as Zouski tried to formulate an effective attack, Tyson threw a few soft right hooks to Zouski's hanging left ribs and with the same hand, launched two powerful uppercuts, following through with a vicious left hook. Zouski's large frame collapsed over his inanimate feet. As Mike walked to a neutral corner—his white trunks with red stripes spotted with his opponent's blood—Arthur Mercante, one of the sport's best referees, completed his ten-second count. Zouski had expired with eleven seconds remaining in the third round.

This was to be the last time Tyson would fight someone at this level. Jacobs and Cayton knew that the degree of competition would have to go up several notches, but not so much, of course, as to constitute a grave danger to their fighter.

Tyson had fought nineteen times in the past twelve months, many times twice a month and sometimes more frequently, knocking out most of his adversaries in the first round. Now he would face the first of his "ideal opponents," James "Quick" Tillis, who would also become Tyson's first formidable rival.

In this fight, both boxers were looking to advance their ratings, although Tyson was the main attraction, the hot item. His reputation was overwhelming and that meant good business. So the fight had been scheduled to take place in Tyson's backyard—the Civic Center, in Glens Falls, New York.

People came by the busload and Glens Falls transformed itself into a huge carnival. The theme was the Tyson fight, and every one of the mostly white faces was rooting for their favorite son. Quick Tillis became public enemy No. 1. This was Tysonland. And when the two fighters entered the ring to settle things, the electrified atmosphere at the arena brought memories of the old noisy, brawling club fights in New York City in the 1940s, 1950s, and 1960s, a time when fans were divided into neighborhood or ethnic factions and extra cops were always needed.

Quick Tillis was definitely not from this neighborhood, and the fans, their faces beet-red, booed him with real venom. Some of them appeared to want to jump into the ring to take on Tyson's opponent themselves. At 215 ½ pounds, Tyson—dressed in black shoes, black trunks, no socks, and no robe—looked fit. But he was aware that Tillis had a reputation for being wily in the ring, and consequently, he was on guard.

At the sound of the first bell there was a solemn silence. The fans were very much aware that Tyson had a habit of dispatching his adversaries in a matter of seconds, and they expected him to score a knockout in the first round.

After the first two minutes of the fight, with Tillis evading Mike's punches skillfully and throwing some leather of his own, punches that at times made contact with Tyson's face and body, the fans began chanting, "First round! Come on, Mike. One! One! One!" And then the bell sounded to end the first round and the crowd sighed in disappointment.

I couldn't hear what Tyson said to Rooney, but his eyes and expression showed concern. Mike had connected with some of his best shots, and Tillis had taken them without batting an eye. Obviously, Mike would have to work harder—much harder. And most important, he couldn't allow his emotions to get the best of him. This was probably the first time in his short career that he'd have to appeal to the various psychological switches Cus had installed in his head.

As the fight continued, Quick Tillis maintained a consistency in moves, punches, and attitude, and at times, he even outpunched Mike in the in-fighting. For the first time in twenty bouts, Tyson had lost more than one round. But at the sound of the last bell, though some were displeased by Tyson's performance, everyone knew that the teenager had prevailed. A few boxing writers, notably Mike Katz and Wally Matthews, still groused that Tyson was a myth invented by Cus, Jacobs, and Cayton, but they didn't find much support.

Seventeen days later, Don King Productions and Madison Square Garden were copromoting Tyson against Mitchell Green, a six-foot-five-inch hulk who was managed by Don King's son, Carl. It was the first fight in which Tyson would make a substantial amount of money. Home Box Office (HBO) was bankrolling this match and two more Tyson bouts to the tune of half a million each. As a matter of fact, HBO was paying Tyson directly, the first television-to-fighter transaction in boxing history. The only stipulation was that Mike had to fight one of the three or four contenders from any of the bonafide international organizations.

I'd seen Mitch Green in action some years back. If there was a heavyweight in 1980-82 with real potential to challenge for the top, it was this giant of a man. I hadn't watched him fight recently but had heard about his troubles with the law and wondered if perhaps he was one of those prospects too wild to be tamed. In any case, Green was a fighter who scared me. Cus had been dead for six months, but I was trying to connect with him in my thoughts and learn what would he think of a Mitch Green—Mike Tyson fight. Then I remembered the day Cus conceded to me he wasn't perfect and was liable to make mistakes.

"I think," he had said, "that I know of another person who would probably make less mistakes than me in boxing at this stage of my life . . . Jimmy Jacobs."

"If I was not absolutely convinced that Mike is going to take care of Green with ease," Jacobs told me seriously, "I wouldn't have made the match." For my part, I thought Mike was ready to fight the best in his division, even those with higher ratings than Green. But still, something about Green's size and tenacity worried me.

The morning of May 20, 1986, was hot and humid, and the Tyson-

Green weigh-in was being held in the ring of Madison Square Garden rather than at the usual small room at the New York State Athletic Commission. The venue gave promise of high drama—or at least more drama than usual—and consequently, a large contingent of press was on hand.

As NYSAC chairman, I purposely kept myself a safe distance from both fighters. I was a friend of Tyson's and an acquaintance of Green's. Since Tyson was big news and whatever he did was good copy, there were some sportswriters who weren't above making something of my closeness to him if the opportunity presented itself. That's one reason why, whenever Tyson fought in New York, I always prayed for a knockout. A close fight going Tyson's way might have provided a field day for the press.

It looked as if the press would have its field day anyway when, just before stepping onto the scale, Green, in the company of his mother, claimed to have just discovered that he was only getting $50,000 for that evening's bout while Tyson was guaranteed half a million. He argued that the disparity was unfair. And the fact that Green's manager, Carl King, was the adoptive son of the promoter and seemed to have no clear explanation for the disparity added to the controversy.

I was forced to join the melee when Green began shouting insults and threats against the two Kings and said he wasn't going to show up for the fight.

I told Green that he would have to honor his contract. The agreement had been signed some time ago, I pointed out, and Mitch had known the numbers long before the weigh-in. It took another heated argument between Carl King and Green to resolve the matter, but by now it was no secret in the boxing world that the Kings were rooting against their own man, maybe even hoping he'd get knocked out.

That night Madison Square Garden was not filled to capacity, but the crowd was excited and noisy. With Muhammad Ali out of the limelight and Larry Holmes lacking the charisma and aura of a superchampion, boxing fans were hoping to witness the birth of a new era. They'd missed those special moments that could only be produced by the likes of Jack Johnson, Jack Dempsey, Joe Louis, Rocky Marciano, and Muhammad Ali.

Holmes, a formidable champion, failed to achieve legendary status because he'd followed Ali to the throne. Holmes suffered from "the Ezzard Charles syndrome." (Charles, one of the greatest boxers of his time, followed Joe Louis and his overpowering popularity. Consequently, he never achieved the recognition he deserved.) Another problem Holmes faced in his time was the resurgence of the various international boxing organizations. The organizations' refusal to consolidate their rankings resulted in at least three different "champions" in each weight class, devaluing the worth of any one title.

The night of the Tyson-Green encounter, my older brother, Andresito, was more nervous than usual. He had gone to the Gramercy gym, where Mike had trained the past week, and had noticed that Mike was "unnaturally scared."

"I would be too," I said.

Andresito, whose opinion Tyson respected, told me that Mike had asked him whether he'd looked okay in sparring. "Did I make any big mistakes?" Mike asked him.

"You're not busy enough inside," my brother told him. "You've become too lazy in the in-fighting." Mike nodded thanks. The next day Tyson tried to fight inside more and was much more active. Again he solicited opinions on his gym work.

The night of the fight I visited both dressing rooms. Mike was quietly sitting in a chair. He was tense and I didn't want him or anybody else to think that the commission would give him special treatment. So I told him, "No one can guarantee you just and fair treatment better than I can. But if you want to win, no one but you must do it." Then I lowered my head and whispered in his ear, "But I'm sure you can and will. Good luck." I shook his hand and he winked at me.

In the other dressing room I told Green that there was only one way he would carry some weight in this business. "And that is by winning fights," I said. "You beat Tyson and you'll get lots of attention . . . and money." I also wished him luck and shook his hand. He had a nonchalant attitude and seemed unafraid. To be honest, I hoped my impression was wrong. A fearless person had no chance against Tyson. No one could take gratuitous chances with him and survive. Against Tyson a boxer needed the protection of fear.

When referee Luis Rivera called the fighters to the center of the ring, Mike appeared to be angry. His upper lip was contracted and his mouthpiece was covered with saliva foam. He was breathing hard through his nose. Across from Tyson, Green was not timid either. He was moving around and moving his lips, trying to unnerve Tyson with insults.

The first punch was thrown by Mike, who, like most D'Amato fighters, would try to catch his opponent cold, unprepared for a quick, hard blow. Cus had taught that most heavyweights draw confidence from their size rather than talent: at heart they're just big bullies. Tyson was hoping Green fit that profile.

But Mitch was moving smartly, and remembering how able and efficient he'd been in the past, I worried that Mike could find himself in a very tough fight. Eventually it became clear that Tyson had decided to throw bombs until one of them hit the bull's-eye. But at the end of ten rounds Mitch was still there, and Mike had failed to knock out his second rival in a row.

Tyson detractors were quick to tsk-tsk over the fact that Mike had permitted Green, and before that Tillis, to finish on his feet. They were so exultant at seeing their low opinion of Tyson confirmed that they failed to notice that Mike's vast superiority had prevented either fight from being close.

Mike badly needed to relax so that before—and during—his fights he could achieve that state of mind Ernest Hemingway called "grace under pressure." The obvious solution was a confidence-building fight that would restore his belief in himself, and for that reason I encouraged Jim Jacobs to "get Marvis Frazier." I told him: "He has an incredible name, but he's also made to order for our style." By "our style" I meant the so-called peekaboo appearance Cus's fighters projected by carrying both hands high with the gloves resting over the cheekbones and moving, blocking, and punching from that position. "He wouldn't go over two to three rounds with Mike" was my belief.

Though Frazier wouldn't be slotted in immediately, perhaps that conversation was what convinced Jim to match Mike against three "fair" but unknown fighters. He needed to build up Mike's confidence and he chose the summer months of 1986 to do it. Of the three boxers scheduled to fight Mike—Reggie Gross, William Hosea, and Lorenzo Boyd—I was most concerned with Gross. I had seen him in a vicious battle in Pennsylvania against a boxer named Jimmy Clark just a few months before D'Amato's death and was so impressed with both fighters that I urged the old man to keep an eye on them and put them on his list of possible opponents for Mike.

The first of this not-too-dangerous series of bouts would pit Tyson against Gross on June 13, 1986, at Madison Square Garden. When I told Jim about my chat with Cus regarding Gross, he smiled.

"As a matter of fact, every single fight we've selected for Mike is from a list given to us by Cus; he thought that by now Gross would be just right for Mike."

Mike entered the ring to thunderous applause that in itself had to revitalize his confidence. Some sportswriters had begun reporting that Tyson's unconventional boxing gear—no socks, no robe, black shoes, black trunks—was some sort of ghetto superstition. After Rooney put his arms around Mike's immense shoulders and whispered final instructions in his ear, he planted a big Irish kiss on his fighter's mouth. Was this something new in the mystical world of prizefighters?

Tyson walked menacingly toward Gross and opened up with a barrage of swift and powerful punches that forced his opponent into a defensive shell. Some of the punches found the intended target, mainly the ones to the body, but there was no indication that Gross was ready to sign off. Mike persisted with his cannonball shots until Gross returned one of his own—a piercing right uppercut that landed flush under Mike's jaw. The crowd let go a collective murmur as if they'd shared the pain. It did not diminish Mike's relentlessness. He kept up his attack, and as Gross connected with another uppercut, Mike let go a left hook to the jaw. Gross's legs folded under him. Referee Johnny LoBianco started to count and Gross looked up with sad eyes as if to announce that he'd had enough. But his pride got him to his feet. Tyson did not wait; another left hook was already on its way toward Gross, who did not see it coming. The punch exploded on his right temple, sending him back to the dusty canvas, his coordination gone for the night. A look at the fighter's eyes prevented LoBianco from starting the count, and he signaled instead the end of the fight. Tyson was the victor by a technical knockout (TKO). The match was only two minutes and thirty-six seconds old.

Two weeks later, William Hosea, a rough-looking boxer from somewhere out west, came to Troy's R.P.I. Houston Field House to challenge Tyson. Two minutes into the first round, Hosea was on the soft floor, holding on to his right side, screaming with pain. He tried to say something, but nothing came out of his mouth. Referee Harry Papacharalambous made clear motions with his hands that the fight was over.

Fifteen minutes later, Hosea, his pain somewhat subdued, said a few words to the media. His breathing still heavy, he said, "I was hit with a sledgehammer." He held his right side, his face full of sweat. "The bastard hits like a sledgehammer."

Two weeks later on July 11, 1986, Tyson was back in a boxing ring. The venue was the Stevensville Country Club, Swan Lake, New York, and the fight was billed—privately, of course—as "a preparation match" for Tyson. His rival was Lorenzo Boyd, a youngster—just like Tyson—with a decent record but with no experience. Boyd's manager didn't deserve a medal for accepting this bout.

It had been labeled a "preparation match" by Jacobs and Cayton because an important fight had just been negotiated for Mike. On July 26, 1986, his opponent was going to be a youngster from a tough boxing town named Philadelphia with a legendary last name: Frazier . . . Marvis Frazier.

"So you wouldn't bother us anymore with Marvis, we made the match," Jacobs told me jokingly. "If anything happens to Mike, nobody but you is to be blamed."

Stevensville, because of its limited capacity, was the perfect spot for a tune-up fight. Also, since it was located in Tysonland, the crowd was highly partisan. For those who preferred lengthy bouts it was fortunate Mike was not up for this fight. He was probably fighting Boyd with his fists and Frazier in the back of his mind. The battle actually lasted four minutes and forty-three seconds. It was the second-longest time Sid Rubenstein had had to work in the seven Tyson fights he'd refereed.

To say that I would be a disinterested observer of the upcoming Tyson-Frazier fight because of my position as chief of boxing in New York would be a falsehood. Tyson had slept in my house and was loved by my family as if he were a relative. We always wanted him to win. Everyone in the boxing business was aware of our friendship. However, as far as I knew, no member of the boxing community had ever doubted my honesty and integrity regarding Tyson's matches. Thus, when Papa Joe Frazier made public remarks criticizing my friendship with Mike, I called him to the side. "The one who should be concerned about my relationship with Mike is Mike himself," I told him. "My officials are human beings and just by nature they would bend over backwards to be objective. That may affect Mike much more than his opponents. So, don't worry."

The former heavyweight champion of the world smiled and walked away. A few days later, however, he repeated his concern publicly. This time when the press approached me with the question, I was a little angry.

"Mike Tyson," I said, "needs help from no one. And much less against Marvis Frazier."

This fight would be in the heart of Tysonland: the Civic Center in Glens Falls where Mike had lost his perfect knockout record after nineteen straight KOs about twelve weeks before. The referee would be Joe Cortez, one of the top referees I'd asked Peter Della to designate for Tyson's fights. Meanwhile, because of Joe Frazier's comments about my closeness to Mike, I decided to stay away from the boxers as much as possible. Still, just before the match, I visited both dressing rooms and wished each fighter good luck. I must admit that I reminded Mike about his need to keep cool. "Don't you get excited," I said. "Keep your mind clear at all times and the rest will come automatically."

Mike nodded and gave me the thumbs-up sign. He was concentrating fully, a sure sign he'd matured. "Oh, God," I reassured him, "are you looking good." I went out and told Jacobs I had not seen his fighter in a better boxing disposition. For this fight, Steve Lott, an assistant trainer, had gotten hold of two patches displaying the colors of the American flag—one with the letters "Go America," the other "USA"— and sewed them on the front of Tyson's trunks.

As we waited for the opening bell, I thought of all the misfortunes good fighters had been subjected to by one punch; the sure winners whose one foolish mistake had gotten them knocked out. I hoped Mike was not having these same thoughts. I stared at him from my first-row seat, studying his eyes, and concluded he couldn't be readier. As Cortez repeated what the boxers already knew in the middle of the ring, Mike's legs moved in anticipation. His belly, just like Marvis's, was trembling involuntarily. Marvis had his father next to him, staring insults at Tyson while massaging his fighter's back. And then the fighters walked back to their corners and we heard the first stroke of the bell.

By the time Joe Frazier ushered himself into a position where he could shout instructions at his son, Tyson had backed Marvis into a corner and was throwing nasty bombs from every angle. The crowd, anticipating the inevitable, rose to their feet. As Marvis looked for refuge in his own corner, close to Pops, Tyson dispatched a murderous right uppercut that landed perfectly on his opponent's jaw. Marvis's superb condition kept him on his feet, but though his limbs and body maintained a semblance of consciousness, his eyes indicated a lack of brain function. Tyson, sharp as a laser beam, threw a five-punch combination. Three caught the falling body of his rival, and Cortez rushed in to prevent Frazier from being unnecessarily injured. The fans went crazy, their demand for a first-rounder fulfilled. Marvis Frazier had been pounded so soundly that the referee did not have to give the ten count. Instead, Cortez called the fight doctor into the ring as Marvis struggled to regain consciousness. While still in the ring just after the knockout, Cortez told me he'd never seen a greater puncher than Tyson in all his years in boxing.

Immediately after the postfight press conference, Tyson called his sister, Denise. "He was very happy," she recalled. "The first thing he said was, 'Did you see how fast I got rid of this guy? It was funny how his father, Joe, stood next to him during the instructions, looking at me like he wanted to hit me. I thought he was going to take a swing at me.' Then we laughed." Denise said Mike told her he would probably be fighting for the championship soon. "He said it made him scared to think about fighting for a world's title."

Three weeks later, Mike was at Trump Plaza Hotel in Atlantic City, preparing to take another step toward the heaviest of all crowns in the sports world. His opponent was José "Niño" Ribalta, not a great threat, but good enough to expose flaws in any fighter. Niño, not the easiest man to hit cleanly, was the type of awkward boxer that could make any boxer look awful. And in fact, there were a few rounds in the fight that Tyson's detractors loved. Mike missed punches like an amateur, some of the sportswriters claimed. But when he connected, he connected solidly—no less so in the tenth round, when Niño put his jaw in the

Defeating Trevor Berbick to become the youngest heavyweight champion in history, November 22, 1986

way of one of Tyson's right-uppercut-left-hook combinations and dropped to the canvas. He went down twice more, forcing the third man in the ring, referee Rudy Battle, to stop the match and declare Tyson the winner by TKO—at one minute and thirty-seven seconds of the last round.

The third bout in the deal HBO had struck with Tyson would be in Las Vegas against Alfonso Ratliff, a six-foot-five-inch giant. This time Don King was involved in the promotion but not on the most favorable terms. He would get a fixed fee, instead of a percentage. While Tyson and his crew had been busy in the East, Don King, ever searching for huge profits, had formed a partnership with pal Butch Lewis, which he'd dubbed "The Dynamic Duo," and in conjunction with the Las Vegas Hilton Hotel and Home Box Office he was promoting something called "The Heavyweight Unification Tournament." In effect, Don would get all the international boxing organizations together and induce their respective heavyweight champions to be part of an elimination contest; the one left standing would become the "Undisputed Heavyweight Champion of the World." This was the appropriate answer to the grim confusion the general public had about the multitude of champions. It made lots of sense, although I'd been truly distressed to see that for some mysterious reason Tyson had not been included.

But to the surprise of many boxing fans, King agreed to embrace the Tyson-Ratliff match as part of the "Unification Tournament." Since he was classified as the No. 1 challenger by the WBA, Tyson was a rightful and deserving contestant. But Tyson's sudden good fortune was not due to King's good heart. The promoter already had an elimination match set for the Las Vegas Hilton between WBA heavyweight champion Michael Spinks and Norwegian Steffen Tangstad, the European heavyweight champ. The trouble was that the advance sale for that fight amounted to only a few thousand dollars—a situation that augured financial catastrophe. Tyson was the best ticket in *any* town. One can only imagine Seth Abraham of HBO and the two Johns— Giovenco and Fitzgerald—of the Las Vegas Hilton, putting pressure on Don to change things around.

Once Tyson's name was added to the program, sales went through the roof, making King and everyone involved in the promotion cheerful. King also realized that without Mike Tyson, the death of the "Unification Tournament" was almost guaranteed, so he needed little prodding to get Tyson involved.

It was Tyson's first professional appearance in Las Vegas, and King and Lewis had said in private that Mike's next fight, "if he beats Ratliff," would be against Trevor Berbick for the WBC crown. I knew right then that this kid so close to my heart was going to be the youngest heavyweight champion in boxing history. Mike called me at the Hilton to say that in just weeks he was going to fight for the title. I didn't want Mike to have added pressure on him. And yet as the professional he was becoming, he should be concerned not just with defeating Ratliff but with looking sensational and exciting in the process. I felt that to do that he couldn't afford to fight two bouts at once in his mind—against Ratliff *and* Berbick.

"Just think about Alfonso Ratliff and forget about any other fight," I told him. "Take this guy out first, then we talk about the next one."

Increasingly attentive and watchful as the fight drew near, Tyson rehearsed moves and punches with me in flawless fashion. How in hell he was able to be so calm was beyond me. "Man," I told him a couple of days before the Ratliff fight, "you are a much better liar than I ever was. You can hide that anxiety and fear much better than I could ever do." Mike would give me only a very deceptive smile.

As I was to learn later, on the very first day Mike trained at the Johnny Tocco's Ringside Gym in Las Vegas, the boy seemed surly and uncomfortable, the pressure of being in a different environment getting to him. No one had noticed that the new pugilistic sensation was there with his crew, so the place was deserted. As it turned out, it was for the best since there were no outsiders to witness the anguish that overtook Mike during that first day of sparring. At the close of the session, Rooney and Tyson, as they always did, walked together into the dressing room and suddenly Mile spoke.

"I wanna go home," he declared. "I don't like this place here. We are packing today." Kevin was shocked. Unable to say a word he went to Steve Lott and gave him the bad news.

"I started to walk into the dressing room," said Lott, "and I'm thinking, 'My God, what would Jim or Bill say to Mike in a position like this?' I gotta do whatever they would do, shit!" As he walked into Mike's dressing room, Tyson was just getting out of the shower. Steve spoke first.

"Mike, how you doing?" Tyson didn't say a word. This was followed by a second gambit. "How ya feeling?"

"I don't like it here," Tyson said. "I wanna go home."

"Why?" Lott asked.

"I just don't like it in here." Tyson stood up. "Let's go home."

"Mike, this is normal. Sit down for a second. You think that coming to Las Vegas is like going to prison, but that's not true. It's a reward. Don't you think that everything Cus told you has come true—that you'd become an exciting fighter, that you'd become a great fighter?"

"Yes."

"Well, now you are bearing the fruit of all that. You've been rewarded with the luxury of coming to Las Vegas and fighting before this large audience. How do you think Spinks feels knowing that he had an advance ticket sale of only eighty dollars and when they added your name on the marquee outside the hotel they sold nine thousand dollars' worth of tickets in two days? Isn't that a credit to what you and Cus have done?"

"Yes."

"This is a reward. Fighters go their whole life praying and hoping to be invited to Las Vegas to fight before a world audience and exhibit their skills, but they are never asked. And here you are, twenty years old . . . the entire world is saying, 'We love to see you. We want you.' And because everything you've got is so exciting, they want to see it.

"Besides," Lott continued, "you fought in the most famous boxing arena in the world: Madison Square Garden; and you went to Atlantic City and to Houston, Texas, and you had nothing but tremendous success in those places. You've already faced the pressure and the turmoil and you overcame. Did you do that before?"

"Yes."

"You just have to do it again. Particularly with this guy. You know that as soon as you hit him he's gonna go."

"Yeah, I know," Mike said. "That's not the problem. It's the place, the moment . . . the circumstances."

"Let's see how you feel in a couple of days," Lott said. "Can you give it a chance?"

"Yeah," Tyson answered, "I can do that."

"Great," Steve said, his insides ready to burst.

In the early evening of September 6, 1986, in the privacy of his dressing room, minutes before fight time, Mike Tyson, as usual, soaked his entire body in Aboline, a heavy moisturizing cream—and started to put on his jock strap and protective cup. It was then that Lott noticed the boy was having some difficulty pinning a dime-size, metal Jewish charm to the tongue of his left boxing shoe. "What are you trying to do?" Steve asked.

"Just trying to put this thing in here," Tyson replied. Lott took the charm and pinned it to Mike's shoe. It was a lucky emblem that became part of the all-black, no-socks, no-robe boxing uniform Mike would wear for every fight.

A few minutes later, the floodlights above the boxing ring at the Las Vegas Hilton shone on referee David Pearl, Alfonso Ratliff, Mike Tyson, and the boxers' cornermen. Pearl repeated some of the rules that most boxers hear wherever they fight. Then the bell sounded and Tyson marched forward. His intimidating steps were followed by even more intimidating punches that established his bad intentions. Ratliff quickly decided that the possibility of victory was too remote to take stupid chances and that the best route to take was the practical one. Let's survive, Ratliff figured. Tyson, for his part, did not want to put on a boring performance and give the media more ammunition to use against him. At the same time, he wasn't willing to risk the opportunity of his life.

Mike put extra pressure on the tall man. Instead of chasing him as most boxers do with a moving opponent, Tyson cut the ring short by moving in the same direction as his opponent moved and then moving in quickly with brutal combinations. It didn't take long. A left hook put Ratliff down for the eight count. A second later he was up and Tyson was next to him with another swift left hook combined with a right cross that sent Alfonso down again. Pearl took a fast look at Ratliff's eyes and stopped the match at once.

Mike Gerard Tyson had secured his opportunity to fight for the world's heavyweight championship in only eleven weeks.

He was twenty years old.

On November 15, 1986, seven days before the biggest match of Mike Gerard Tyson's life, the WBC world heavyweight championship against titleholder Trevor Berbick, I went to see Tyson train at the Johnny Tocco's Ringside Gym in Las Vegas. When he saw me, he jumped with genuine happiness and hugged me. He'd been under a lot of prefight pressure, championship tension, and had been driving Rooney and Lott up the wall. They were staying with Tyson at a house in Vegas's Spanish Oaks section, a mile from the Strip. It was owned by Dr. Bruce Handelman, a member of the D'Amato-Cayton-Jacobs extended family. Tyson had been uncooperative and contrary and prone to wild mood changes. At the gym he tormented assistant trainer Matt Baransky, who stayed at the hotel to manage Tyson's army of sparring partners: James Broad, Mike Williams, Oscar Holman, Walter Santemore, Mike Jameson, and Licous Kirkley.

Tyson was sparring that day, and Jacobs wanted my opinion. Actually, watching Tyson spar was like seeing him in competition. He had no mercy for these men, whose main function was to help him stay sharp and in shape. Their job was thankless. It was in gymnasiums, I'd learned long ago, that fighters get their noses flattened, their faces cut, and their bodies worn. Tyson pounded his sparring partners as if he were a soldier caught behind enemy lines and they were the enemy bent on killing him. These six men were receiving the equivalent of combat pay for their one-sided wars, $1,000 a week. Broad was paid $1,500.

Tyson was like a tiger and looked real sharp, I told Jacobs. The one habit that concerned me was Mike's tendency to stay in close, holding on, an imperfection that could be easily remedied by Rooney. After the workout Mike and I decided to walk from the gym to the Las Vegas Hilton, two or three miles away. I didn't want to offer Mike any advice in public—especially in front of Rooney, who knew Tyson's strengths and weaknesses better than anyone. I'd seen a few other mistakes and mentioned them to Mike as we walked to the hotel. He said very little. At times we would stop while I illustrated some technical point.

Then he changed the conversation to what had become his favorite topic: women.

"You know something," he said, "I like to hurt women when I make love to them." He stopped, searching my face for a reaction. But there was none. "I like to hear them scream with pain, to see them bleed," he said as he put his right arm around me. "It gives me pleasure."

"Why?"

"I don't know."

"You mean to tell me that you don't have any idea why you do that to women?"

Mike shook his head.

"You want me to believe that you always thought this was just natural behavior? You're full of shit."

"José, I am that way and I don't know why."

"Well," I said, "did it ever occur to you that men who behave that way probably hate women; that deep down they simply don't like them?"

"You may be right. You're the first person to tell me that.... You know, you may be fucking right. Holy fucking shit!"

We'd almost reached the hotel. Tyson grabbed me by the arm and told me to stop walking. He wanted to talk in the open air where it would be harder to overhear, where he could yell and curse. It didn't matter to him that in the street passersby would stop to salute him and motorists would blow their horns. Cus D'Amato had been dead a little more than a year, and Tyson seemed to miss their long rap sessions. He was a young man who wanted to understand affection, passion, lovemaking. Most of his short life had been steeped in violence, dedicated to doling out pain, and he wanted to learn and hear more about the other side of himself. Playing psychologist was not one of my favorite pastimes, but I tried.

"Let's go back to the shit about me not liking women," he said as we leaned against a pillar. "You're the first person who probably hit it right on the head."

I made one last effort to change the subject, but he persisted. "Come on, man, expand on that shit."

"I'm no fucking psychologist," I said, "but I may say something you wouldn't like at all."

"Speak up."

"Some men who dislike women at an unconscious level," I said, "could be considered latent homosexuals."

"What the fuck is that?" He was smiling and probably had an idea of what that meant.

"A state of homosexuality that may never manifest itself overtly."

"Explain that. I don't get it."

"A fag by implication, not by actual acts of homosexuality. . . . If you are a latent homosexual, you will keep making love and hurting girls. And you may hate them, but you may never engage in lovemaking with a man."

There was a blank expression on his face, but he nodded as if he finally understood what I was saying. A photographer materialized out of the dry desert air. Tyson and I posed for some pictures and then went up to my room in the hotel.

Inside, he forced a tight-lipped smile and moved his head as if he was trying to say something but couldn't think of the right words. "Hey, man," he said finally, "if you only knew."

I told him to tell me what was on his mind. "If you don't tell me, I may imagine anything."

"Like what?"

"Like, you are a homosexual."

He laughed hard and gave me a brotherly punch in the chest, then kissed me on the cheek.

"Girls, pussy, butts, women's butts," he said, "that's what I like."

He wanted to tell me something else but didn't. It turned out he was being treated for gonorrhea that he'd probably contracted in Vegas.

This kid could have almost any woman he wanted, but he preferred to take risks with strangers.

A few days before, he'd been in his car inside a car wash with Lott and pulled down his pants. "Look at this," he said, revealing patches of dried pus on the front of his underwear.

Lott, hiding his concern, told him not to worry. "It's not that serious," he told Tyson. But back at the hotel, Lott rushed to his room and telephoned Jacobs.

"We have a small problem," Steve told him. "Mike seems to have an infection." After getting the details, Jacobs told Lott to take Tyson to the fighter's personal physician—immediately.

So a week before the fight, Tyson had needle punctures in his buttocks and antibiotics in his blood. I'd fought many times with penicillin in my system, mostly because of colds brought on by prefight pressures. I related my own experiences to him.

"Mike," I said, "you're just recovering from a serious eardrum infection that was treated with antibiotics. Too much of that shit could do you harm. Do you feel strong?"

"Chegui," he said to me, using my nickname almost sarcastically, "nothing and nobody is going to stop me from winning this fucking fight. I refuse, I refuse. The doctor said it would make me weak and I say he's full of shit 'cause I want that title so bad. There is no way I would give up that title."

"That's not the point."

"That's the only point."

"Yes, but when you—"

"*When*," he interrupted, "they raise my hand in the ring as the youngest heavyweight champion of the world, all of yous are going to be very proud of me. That's the fucking point, my friend."

Who could dispute that? Cus's spirit was with him, and I felt it would do more harm than good to argue the point further. After all, there was a rightness to what he was saying. In effect, he'd been quoting Cus's mind-over-matter theories. I took a long, hard look at Tyson and I saw Cus. His head and face somehow seemed to resemble Cus's, and there were similarities in the way the two walked and talked. It was not a mystical transfiguration. Cus and Mike were so close in body and soul that Tyson had adopted some of his mentor's physical peculiarities.

• • •

November 22, 1986, arrived too fast. It was the twenty-third anniver-sary of President John F. Kennedy's assassination, and most of the country was commemorating it with solemnity and sadness. But in this self-involved land of entertainment, gambling, and prostitution, it was all Tyson and WBC champion Trevor Berbick. The memories of Kennedy, Lee Harvey Oswald, and Jack Ruby did nothing to diminish the hoopla.

Mike had gotten up that morning somewhat restless. As usual, he'd eaten some fruit for breakfast and had gone back to bed, leaving the television on and videotape movie cassettes all over the floor. When I arrived in the afternoon, he was in the living room chatting with Lott. He was quiet and in a no-nonsense mood. The war of nerves was on. I took him out on the back porch and showed him some basic moves and punches I didn't want him to forget that night. He started to relax. At 3:30 P.M. Steve cooked some spaghetti that Mike ate with a large New York-cut sirloin steak from a nearby restaurant. Before he sat down to eat we embraced, and I assured him he had nothing to worry about.

Jacobs had called Lott from his suite at the Hilton just about the same time Tyson sat down to eat and told Lott not to forget to be at the hotel by 6 P.M.

"Don't worry," Steve said. "I'll be there just before six." Tyson went straight to bed and in a few minutes was fast asleep.

At five-thirty Lott started to pack. All of a sudden Tyson woke up hungry. "Steve," Tyson yelled, stretching his arms and making an animal noise, "I'm hungry. Make me some dinner." Lott ran into the kitchen and put more spaghetti on to boil and continued to pack.

"I couldn't say, 'Hey, Mike, your manager wants you at the arena in fifteen minutes. I can't cook now, it will take too long,' " Lott recalled later. "Neither could I call Jim and say, 'Boss, Mike wants to eat now, what should I do?' "

His instincts went with Tyson. Lott continued packing, periodically going back to the kitchen and fixing the food, which Tyson wolfed down. "We got there just a few minutes late," Lott said, "and nobody said anything except for some stares from Jacobs."

Mills Lane was the referee that night—good news for Mike, given his fighting style. Lane was a complete referee, a professional who allowed boxers to fight inside as long as there was some action. He understood, like most good referees, that the boxing fan paid to be entertained. Accordingly, when a bout became dull and boring, Mills demanded activity. That night's boxing crew—the fight doctor, the inspectors, the judges—was, in fact, as efficient as any I'd seen. And I'd always thought that Sig Rogish was one of the most knowledgeable boxing commissioners in the business. Rogish, who two years later would work hard to elect Bush president, was a conscientious overseer who skilfully blended political savvy with boxing knowledge.

I was talking with Rogish when the bell sounded. Tyson walked toward Berbick, his gloves snug against his cheeks, his torso in perpetual motion first to one side, then to the other, then down. Each movement was perfectly choreographed. Jabs jutted out with the force of Mack-truck pistons between Tyson's moves. Berbick moved and missed, in succession, a couple jabs, a left hook, and a right cross. Then he was hit with a stiff left jab that snapped his neck back. In only a few seconds Tyson was solidly established as the man in charge. I rushed over to Jacobs and embraced him in celebration. "It won't go past three," I told him. He put his right arm around me in acknowledgment, but his eyes were fixed on the ring. He wanted to see what I'd seen. "Mike is the new champ," I screamed.

Just before the bell, Tyson landed a right hand to the forehead that stunned Berbick. When Tyson sat down after the round ended, he and his crew—Rooney, Lott, and Baransky—knew the fight was not going to last long. They were all trying to be nonchalant but couldn't. The heavyweight championship was in reach, right under their noses.

The second round started not much differently from the first, and Tyson, perceiving the inevitable, marched in with relentless jabs, constantly moving his head to avoid being hit by a stray punch. Berbick knew what was about to happen, but he tried not to make it too easy for the challenger. He threw a fast, desperate jab, stepped to the side, and came in with a five-punch combination. Tyson, extremely relaxed and controlled, saw every punch and moved out of danger, bobbing and weaving in synch with each stroke. After the futile combination, Berbick's eyes were glazed with shock, broadcasting distress. Tyson forced the issue. Berbick went inside and bent his waist forward as if bowing. Tyson loosed a deceptive left hook that landed on Berbick's right temple, and the champion dropped to the canvas. As Lane started the count, Trevor attempted to straighten up but was caught in a torturous conflict between body and mind. Berbick's 230 pounds zigzagged from one side of the ring to another. He fell twice more, got up, and was prevented from falling out of the ring by the ropes. Berbick's last dance as champion had the look of a death rattle. Lane chased Berbick around and held the big heavyweight still, telling him it was over, that he was no longer champion.

I jumped into the ring, and Tyson was talking to himself. "I can't believe this, man. I'm the fucking champion of the world at twenty," he was saying. "Shit, the champion of the world at twenty. This fucking shit is unreal. Champion of the world at twenty. I'm a kid, a fucking kid." Then he embraced his boxing family one by one.

I knew how he felt, overcome with joy, happy beyond belief, stuck between tears and laughter. Back in 1965 when I knocked out Willie Pastrano to become the light-heavyweight champion of the world, the first Hispanic to capture a heavy division, I jumped aimlessly around the ring like a chicken with his head cut off, screaming at the top of my lungs.

Minutes later came the official announcement from Chuck Null, who said: "The winner by a TKO in two minutes and thirty-five seconds of the second round, and the new WBC heavyweight champion of the world . . . Mike Tyson."

For me, the announcement was anticlimactic, but that didn't diminish my enthusiasm. This happy ending—a ghetto kid having his destiny and fortune forever changed by the wonderful, magical world of boxing—was almost a cliché, but as I stood outside the ropes everything about it seemed unique, special, wondrous. I'd witnessed a moment in history that had been foretold back in New York, and I felt very much a part of it.

MIKE TYSON

Life, March 1987

by

Joyce Carol Oates

22 November 1986.

When twenty-year-old Mike Tyson enters the packed arena of the Las Vegas Hilton Convention Center, it is through a deafening wall of noise. A neutral observer would wonder: Is this young man already a champion?—a *great* champion? Of the nearly nine thousand people jammed into the arena—in seats as costly as $1,000 at ringside—virtually everyone has come in expectation of seeing not merely a heavyweight title fight that promises to be unusually dramatic but boxing history itself. If Tyson takes away the World Boxing Council heavyweight title held by thirty-three-year-old Trevor Berbick, as he has promised to do, he will become the youngest heavyweight champion in the sport's recorded history. He will fulfill the prophecy made by Cus D'Amato, his boxing trainer, mentor, and guardian, that he would one day break the record of another of D'Amato's heavyweight prodigies, Floyd Patterson, who won the title shortly before his twenty-second birthday in 1956.

Mike Tyson, a boy warrior, has become legendary, in a sense, before there is a legend to define him. And never has the collective will of a crowd—the very nearly palpable wish of a crowd—been more powerfully expressed than it is tonight in Las Vegas. With his much-publicized 27-0 record as a professional boxer, of which twenty-five victories are knockouts (fifteen in the first round, several within sixty seconds), with so much expectation centered upon him as the "new hope" of heavyweight boxing, Tyson recalls the young Jack Dempsey, who fought his most spectacular fights before winning the heavyweight title. Like Dempsey in the upward trajectory of his career, Tyson suggests a savagery only symbolically contained within the brightly illuminated elevated ring, with its referee, its resident physician, its scrupulously observed rules, regulations, customs, and rituals. Like Dempsey he has the power to galvanize crowds as if awakening in them the instinct not merely for raw aggression and the mysterious will to do but for suggesting incontestable *justice* of such an instinct: his is not the image of the Establishment-approved Olympic Gold Medalist Muhammad Ali or Sugar Ray Leonard (indeed, it is said in boxing circles that Tyson was cheated of a gold medal at the 1984 Summer Olympic Games by way of the of the politics of amateur boxing), but the image of the outsider, the psychic outlaw, the hungry young black contender for all that white America can give. In a weight division in which hard punching is the point, Tyson has acquired a reputation for being an awesome fighter, as much admired and feared among his coevals as Sonny Liston, George Foreman, and Rocky Marciano were in their times: he has been called a "tank," a "young bull," a "killer," a "block of granite"; a force primitive and irresistible as nature. As one observer noted, there is something of a comic-book quality about Tyson's fights—the violence is so exaggerated it has a surrealist air. Opponents are propelled across the ring, fall insensible into the ropes, or, fully conscious, lose muscular control in their legs; they lie without moving for what seems a very long time. The violence may appear primitive and surrealist but it is thoughtfully administered: the result, as Tyson explains carefully in his soft, earnest, boyish voice, of punches thrown with a "bad intention in a vital area." Cus D'Amato was, among other things, a "master of anatomy."

Tyson himself has spoken of the phenomenon of Mike Tyson in gladiatorial terms: the warrior's vow to fight to the death if necessary precludes and makes irrelevant all merely personal motives, all conventional rationalizations for what he does. Boxing is his life, his voca-

tion; his calling. The Roman boast of *munera sine missione* in the gladiatorial games—no mercy shown—would be perfectly logical to him.
And so mesmerizing has the young boxer become in his scant eighteen
months as a professional, his appearance in the ring tonight in Las
Vegas, his mere physical presence, captivates the crowd's attention to
the degree that the entrance of reigning WBC champion Trevor Berbick
goes virtually unnoticed. Even the blazoning recorded music is
abruptly and mysteriously silenced.

Mike Tyson—"Kid Dynamite" as he has lately been billed—exudes
an air of tension, control, fierce concentration. At five feet eleven
inches, he is short for a heavyweight and strikes the eye as shorter still;
his 222 ¼-pound body is so sculpted in muscle it looks foreshortened,
brutally compact. (Berbick, at 218 ½ pounds, stands six feet two
inches—not a large man by today's heavyweight standards—and will
have a daunting seven-inch reach advantage.) Indeed, Tyson is so muscular as to resemble a bodybuilder rather than a boxer, for whom
upper-body flexibility is crucial; his neck measures an extraordinary
nineteen inches—larger than any heavyweight champion's since the
circus strongman Primo Carnera. His hair is trimmed savagely short,
Dempsey-style, along the back and sides, as if it were done with a razor;
he wears not a robe but a crude white terrycloth pullover that looks as
if he might have made it himself and, as usual, no socks—"I feel more
like a warrior this way"; and though his managers Jim Jacobs and Bill
Cayton will be fined $5,000 by the Nevada State Athletic Commission
for the privilege, Tyson is wearing the black trunks that have become
his trademark. (Trevor Berbick, who usually wears white, preempted
black for *his* trunks—very likely because he resents the extraordinary
prefight publicity Tyson has engendered and the humiliating fact that,
though the young challenger has never met an opponent of Berbick's
stature, he is a 3-to-1 favorite to win tonight.) Tyson remains the object
of the crowd's rapt attention. He is pumped up, covered in sweat, ready
to fight. Though this is the hour—the very moment—to which the past
six years of his life have been subordinated, he gives no sign of nerves
and will say, afterward, that he was "calm" and "relaxed" in the knowledge that he could not fail.

As he gives Tyson final instructions, his trainer, Kevin Rooney—
himself a D'Amato protege—touches foreheads with him and kisses

him lightly on the cheek. (Strangers to boxing's eerie combination of violence and childlike affection are invariably startled by such gestures, as by the abruptness with which, after the final bell, boxers often embrace each other in mutual gratitude for the fight. But such behavior, as spontaneous as it is traditional, and as natural as it is apparently contradictory, lies at the very heart of boxing.) As soon as the bell sounds, opening round one, Tyson rushes out of his corner to bring the fight to Berbick. In these quicksilver seconds, when far more happens than the eye, let alone the verbalizing consciousness, can absorb, it is clear that Tyson is the stronger of the two, the more dominant; willful. He pushes forward unmindful of Berbick's greater age and experience; the fight is to be his fight. If boxing is as much a contest of psyches as of physical prowess, it is soon clear that Tyson, on the attack, throwing beautifully controlled punches, is the superior boxer; and he is fast— unexpectedly fast. "This kid don't let you do what you want to do," Berbick's trainer Angelo Dundee will say after the fight. "He created the pressure and my guy didn't react to the pressure . . . He throws combinations I never saw before. When have you seen a guy throw a right hand to the kidney, come up the middle with an uppercut, then throw a left hook? He throws punches . . . like a trigger." (This in significant contrast to Tyson's less effective performances against Jose Ribalta in August 1986 and James "Quick" Tillis in May: the improvement, in so brief a period of time, is remarkable.) For those of us who have been watching preliminary bouts for the past two and a half hours, including a perfectly controlled but lackluster if not contemptuous performance by former WBC champion Pinklon Thomas, the quality of Tyson's fighting—one might say Tyson's *being*—is profound. The impact of certain of his body blows is felt in the farthest corners of the arena; the intensity of his fighting is without parallel. As an observer notes, Tyson's punches even sound different from other boxers' punches. In the ring, in the terrible intensity of action, Tyson is both sui generis and as stylized as the heraldic, struggling figures painted by George Bellows in such famous oils as "Stag at Sharkey's" and "Dempsey and Firpo." It seems suddenly possible that, as Cus D'Amato predicted, Tyson differs not merely in degree but in kind from his fellow boxers.

Early in the second round, Tyson knocks Berbick to the canvas with a powerful combination of blows, including a left hook; when Berbick manages to get gamely to his feet he is knocked down a second time with a left hook to the head—to be precise, to the right temple, a "vital area." (As Tyson will say afterward, he had come to "destroy" the champion: "Every punch had a murderous intention.") Accompanied by the wild clamor of the crowd as by an exotic sort of music, Berbick struggles to his feet, his expression glazed like that of a man trapped in a dream; he lurches across the ring on wobbly legs, falls another time, onto the ropes; as if by a sheer effort of will gets up, staggers across the ring in the opposite direction, is precariously on his feet when the referee, Mills Lane, stops the fight. No more than nine seconds have passed since Tyson's blow but the sequence, in slow motion, has seemed much longer. . . . The nightmare image of a man struggling to retain consciousness and physical control before nine thousand witnesses is likely to linger in the memory: it is an image as inevitable in boxing as that of the ecstatic boxer with his gloved hands raised in triumph.

At two minutes thirty-five seconds of the second round, the fight is over and twenty-year-old Mike Tyson is the new WBC champion. "I am the heavyweight champion of the world," he tells the television audience, "and I will fight anybody in the world."

The post-Ali era has finally ended.

Boxing is our most controversial American sport, always, it seems, on the brink of being abolished. Its detractors speak of it in contempt as a "so-called 'sport,' " and surely their logic is correct: if "sport" means harmless play, boxing is not a sport; it is certainly not a game. But "sport" can signify a paradigm of life, a reduction of its complexities in terms of a single symbolic action—in this case its competitiveness, the cruelty of its Darwinian enterprise—defined and restrained by any number of rules, regulations, and customs: in which case boxing is probably, as the ex-heavyweight champion George Foreman has said, the sport to which all other sports aspire. It is the quintessential image of human struggle, masculine or otherwise, against not only other people but one's own divided self. Its kinship with Roman gladiatorial combat—in which defeated men usually died—is not historically accurate but poetically relevant. In his classic Theory of the Leisure Class (1899), Thorstein Veblen speaks of sport in general as "an expression of the barbarian temperament," and it is a commonplace assumption for many boxers, particularly for young boxers like Mike Tyson, that in the ring they are fighting for their lives. (As Tyson said excitedly, following the Berbick fight, "I refuse to get hurt, I refuse to get knocked down, I refuse to lose—I would have to be killed—carried out of the ring. I would not be hurt.")

It should be kept in mind, however, that for all its negative publicity, and the sinister glamour of certain of its excesses, boxing is not our most dangerous sport. It ranks in approximately seventh place, after football, Thoroughbred racing, sports car racing, mountain climbing, et al. (It is far less systematically violent than professional football, for instance, in which, in a single season, hundreds of players are likely to be fined for the willful infraction of rules.) And in a time of sports mania unparalleled in our history, boxing remains the only major sport accessible to what is piously called "underprivileged" youth—the others are Establishment-controlled, sealed off from penetration by men with the backgrounds of Larry Holmes, Hector Camacho, Marvin Hagler, Mike Tyson.

It has always been, in any case, from the days of bareknuckle prize-fighting to the present, the sport that people love to hate. Its image of men pitted against each other in man-to-man warfare is too stark, too extreme, to be assimilated into "civilized" society. "You're fighting, you're not playing the piano, you know," welterweight champion Fritzie Zivic once said.

"Yes, I'm fighting for my life in the ring," Mike Tyson tells me. And, "I love boxing." And, a little later, "Am I a born boxer? No—if I was, I'd be perfect."

In person Mike Tyson exudes the air of an intensely physical being; he is guarded, cautious in his speech, wary of strangers, unfailingly courteous. His intelligence expresses itself elliptically, as if through a mask—though not the death's-head mask of the ring that so intimidates opponents. No doubt the referee's classic admonition, "Protect yourself at all times!" rings in his ears in situations like this—an interview, one of numberless interviews, thrust upon him in the ever-burgeoning phenomenon of Fame. (It is difficult to believe Tyson will ever be fully—narcissistically—comfortable in his celebrity as Muhammad Ali and Sugar Ray Leonard are in theirs.)

Tyson is a young man, a phenomenon, one might say, of paradoxical qualities: more complex, and more self-analytical, than he has seemed willing, in public, to acknowledge. With his boyish gap-toothed smile and his earnest voice he has disarmed speculation about his future as a precocious titleholder by telling reporters repeatedly that his life is simple: "You wouldn't believe how simple it is. I'm too young to worry about so many things. I let them worry." (Meaning that his professional affairs are handled—and handled, it would seem, with consummate skill—by managers Jim Jacobs and Bill Cayton of Big Fights Inc. and trainer Kevin Rooney.) He acquiesces to media descriptions of himself as a "boy champion"; he speaks, not, it seems, disingenuously, of being a "kid" whose career is a masterwork guided by others—primarily, of course, by the late Cus D'Amato. ("Cus laid the groundwork for Mike's career," Jim Jacobs tells me. "And when I say Cus laid the groundwork, I mean he laid the groundwork—for Mike's entire future career.") The young boxer's relationship to his handlers and to his "family"—an intimate though not blood-related constellation of men and women linked by way of D'Amato—allows him the freedom-within-discipline of the child prodigy in music whose teacher and parents zealously protect him from the outside world. And it is readily clear, speaking with Mike Tyson in the presence of Jim and Loraine Jacobs (my interview was conducted in the Jacobses' apartment in the East Forties, Manhattan, surrounded by boxing memorabilia that includes an entire wall of films and tapes), that he is fully aware of his good fortune; he understands that his emotional-professional situation is close to unique in the notoriously unsentimental world of professional boxing. He is loved by his family and he loves them—it is that simple, and that enviable. If in one sense, like other star athletes of our time, Mike Tyson is a child, he is also a fully, even uncannily mature man—a twenty-year-old like no other I have ever encountered.

"I'm happy when I'm fighting. The day of the fight—leading up to it—I'm happy," he says. In his black wool-and-leather sweater, black brushed corduroy trousers, a jewel-studded gold bracelet on his wrist, Mike Tyson looks very different from the man who "destroyed" Trevor Berbick seven days ago in Las Vegas; very different from the iconographic photographs of him that have appeared in various publications, here and abroad. (The Japanese are much taken with Tyson: his photograph has been on the cover not only of sports magazines but of movie and general-interest magazines. How to explain his popularity there, where he has never visited? Tyson smiles and shrugs. "Who knows?") Loraine Jacobs shows me a remarkable photograph of Tyson by Ken Regan of Camera 5 in which, in his boxing trunks, eerily shadowed and outlined by light, Tyson looks like a statue, or a robot—a high-tech fantasy of sheerly masculine threat and aggression. I ask Tyson what he thinks of his image—does it seem strange to him, to be so detached from a "Mike Tyson" who both is and is not himself—and Tyson murmurs something vaguely philosophical, like, "What can you do?" Yet it is clear that he too is fascinated by the phenomenon of Tyson; he remarks, a little later, thst it would be interesting if he could in some way be in the audience at one of his own fights, where the excitement is. In the ring, in the cynosure of action, the fighter does not experience himself; what appears to the crowd as an emotionally charged performance is coolly calibrated. If Tyson feels fear—which, he acknowledges, he does—he projects his fear onto the opponent, as Cus D'Amato instructed: but little emotion is ever visible on Mike Tyson's own face.

If Tyson is happy in the ring, unlike many boxers who come to dislike and dread their own life's work, it is perhaps because he hasn't been hurt; hasn't been seriously hit; has never met an opponent who was in any sense a match for him. (Do any exist? Right now? Tyson and his circle don't think so.) At the age of twenty he believes himself invulnerable, and who, watching him in action, would deny it? One of the fascinations of this new young titleholder is the air he exudes of "immortality" in the flesh—it is the fascination of a certain kind of innocence.

Asked after the Berbick fight why he is so concerned with establishing a record "that will never, ever be broken," Tyson said, "I want to be immortal! I want to live forever!" He was being funny, of course—he often is, making such pronouncements to the press. But he was also, of course, deadly serious.

Baptized Catholic, he no longer practices the faith but believes, he says, in God. As for life after death—"When you're dead, that's it." He is quick to acknowledge the extraordinary good fortune, amounting very nearly to the miraculous, that has characterized his life beyond the age of twelve, when, as a particularly unhappy inmate of the Tryon School for Boys in Johnstown, New York, a juvenile detention facility to which he was sent after committing burglaries and robberies in the Brownsville section of Brooklyn, he was brought to the attention of the elderly Cus D'Amato—a man who, judging by the testimony of numerous observers, seems to have had the mystical qualities of a Zen Master. But Cus D'Amato was a boxing trainer par excellence who had already cultivated another juvenile delinquent, Floyd Patterson, into a prodigy-champion heavyweight in the 1950s, and had discovered Jose Torres (world light-heavyweight champion 1965-66 and current head of the New York State Boxing Commission) as an amateur boxer in Puerto Rico. The story is that, having observed the untrained thirteen-year-old Tyson box a few rounds in the gym he run above the police station in Catskill, New York, D'Amato said to a Tryon School boxing coach: "That's the heavyweight champion of the world. If he wants it, it's his."

This is the stuff of legend, of course. Yet it happens to be true. The precocious criminal-to-be Tyson's earliest arrests were at the age of ten—he is taken up by one of boxing history's greatest trainers; is released into D'Amato's custody and, two years later, is officially adopted by him; lives, trains, most importantly is nourished, in Catskill, New York, in a fourteen-room house shared by D'Amato and his sister-in-law, Camille Ewald—far from the corrosive atmosphere of the black ghetto, in which, judging from his record, the young Mike Tyson would have been doomed. "Cus was my father but he was more than a father," Tyson says. "You can have a father and what does it mean?—it doesn't really mean anything. Cus was my backbone. . . . He did everything for my best interest. . . . We'd spend all our time together, talk about things that, later on, would come back to me. Like about character, and courage. Like the hero and the coward: that the hero and the coward both feel the same thing, but the hero uses his fear, projects it onto his opponent, while the coward runs. It's the same thing, fear, but it's what you do with it that matters." (Jim Jacobs tells me afterward that much of what Mike says is Cus D'Amato speaking; much of what *he* says is Cus D'Amato speaking.) Quite apart from his genius as a boxing trainer, D'Amato appears to have been a genius of a spiritual sort, if "genius" is not an inappropriate term in this context. Like a devoted religious elder he instilled in Tyson, and no doubt in others of his young boxer acolytes, qualities of an abstract nature: self-denial, discipline, will, integrity, independence, "character." It was D'Amato's belief that a fighter's character is more important ultimately than his skill: a perception proven, in the ring, only in the most arduous of fights—one thinks of the virtually Shakespearean struggles of the first Ali/Frazier match, the 1941 Louis/Conn match, the Leonard/Hearns. Most importantly, D'Amato instilled in Tyson that most invaluable and mysterious of gifts, an unwavering faith in himself. "He said I would be the youngest heavyweight in history," marvels Tyson. "And what he said turned out to be true. Cus knew it all along."

Jim Jacobs, D'Amato's devoted friend, a boxing manager of enormous reputation and prestige and the archivist of twenty-six thousand boxing films, says that D'Amato's word regarding Tyson's promise was enough for him: there was no one in the world whose judgment he trusted more than Cus D'Amato's. "When Cus told me that Mike Tyson was going to be heavyweight champion of the world, that's all I had to hear." So internalized is D'Amato's voice, and his instructions regarding the nurturing of the young heavyweight, Jacobs says that when he thinks about what he is doing, he has only to "press a button in my head and I can hear Cus talking to me. What I am doing is precisely and exactly what Cus told me to do."

If Tyson looked upon D'Amato as a father—Tyson's "real" father seems never to have figured in his life—it is evident that D'Amato looked upon Tyson as a son. In an interview for *People* shortly before his death, D'Amato told William Plummer that the boy meant "everything" to him. "If it weren't for him, I probably wouldn't be living today. See, I believe nature's a lot smarter than anybody thinks. During the course of a man's life he develops a lot of pleasures and people he cares about. Then nature takes them away one by one. It's her way of preparing you for death. See, I didn't have the pleasures any longer. My friends were gone, I didn't hear things, I didn't see things clearly, except in memory. . . . So I said I must be getting ready to die. Then Mike came along. The fact that he is here and is doing what he is doing gives me the motivation to stay alive." Though D'Amato died of pneumonia in November 1985, aged seventy-seven, approximately a year before

Tyson became the youngest titleholder in heavyweight history, he seems to be alive, still, in Tyson's soul. One man's faith in another can go no further.

Yet it would be imprecise to say that Mike Tyson is D'Amato's creature solely. His initial social shyness masks a quick, restless intelligence; he is not without humor regarding even the vicissitudes of his early life. Of his years as a child criminal—during which time, as the youngest member of a gang, he was frequently entrusted with holding a gun during robberies—he has said, "Please don't think I was really bad. I used to rob and steal but other guys did worse things—they murdered people." At times Tyson lived on the Bedford-Stuyvesant streets, slept in abandoned buildings like a feral child. When he was arrested, aged eleven, and sent to the Tryon School for Boys, no one could have guessed how his life, ironically, had been saved. He was violent, depressed, mute; one of the most intractable of the "incorrigible" boys. When he broke loose it required several adult men to overpower him. One official recalls having seen him dragged away in handcuffs, to be locked in solitary confinement.

Mike Tyson's story reminded me of those legendary tales of abandoned children so particularly cherished by the European imagination—Kasper Hauser of Nurnberg, the "wild boy" of the Aveyron. Such tales appeal to our sense of wonder, mystery, and dread; and to our collective guilt. These children, invariably boys, are "natural" and "wild"; not precisely mute but lacking a language; wholly innocent of the rudiments of human social relations. They are homeless, parentless, nameless, "redeemable" only by way of the devotion of a teacher father—not unlike Tyson's Cus D'Amato. But even love is not enough to save the mysteriously doomed Kasper Hauser, whose story ends as abruptly and as tragically as it begins. And the "wild boy" of the Aveyron loses the freshness of his soul even as he acquires the skills of language and social intercourse.

There is nothing nostalgic, however, about Tyson's feelings for his past. Many of his boyhood friends are in jail or dead; both his parents are deceased; he has a sister and a brother, both older, with whom he appears to be on friendly but not intimate terms. If he returns to his old neighborhood it is as a visitor of conspicuous dimensions: a hero, a "boy champion," a *Sports Illustrated* cover in the flesh. Like Joe Louis,

MIKE TYSON

Sugar Ray Robinson, Larry Holmes, et al., Mike Tyson has become a model of success for "ghetto youth," though his personal code of conduct, his remarkably assured sense of himself, owes nothing at all to the ghetto. He is trained, managed, and surrounded, to an unusual degree, by white men, and though he cannot be said to be a white man's black man he is surely not a black man's black man in the style of, for instance, Muhammad Ali (whose visit to Tyson's grammar school in Brooklyn made a powerful impression on him at the age of ten). Indeed, it might be said that Mike Tyson will be the first heavyweight boxer in America to transcend issues of race—a feat laudable or troubling, depending upon one's perspective. (In the light of which, a proposed match between Tyson and the zealously overpromoted "White Hope" candidate Gerry Cooney would have interesting consequences: allegiances are likely not to break down along cursory color lines.)

He will do what he can, Tyson says, to promote blacks, but he does not intend to become involved in politics. He will visit schools, make public appearances, do anti-drug commercials for the FBI and the State of New York. If his replies to questions about black consciousness—its literature, art, history—are rather vague, it should be said that his replies to most questions that deal with culture in a larger sense are vague. Tyson dropped out of Catskill High School in his senior year—"I hated it there"—to concentrate on his amateur boxing in clubs and Golden Gloves competitions under the tutelage of D'Amato; and at this point his formal education, such as it was, seems to have ended. He has virtually no interest in music—"I could live without music." He shrugs aside queries about art, dance, literature; his reading is limited to boxing books and magazines. With Jim Jacobs's library of twenty-six thousand fight films at his disposal he watches old fights with an almost scholarly passion—surely this is unusual, in a practitioner? (Jim Jacobs assures me it is.) For entertainment Tyson watches videos of karate movies, horror movies, occasionally even children's cartoons: no serious dramas, and no movies about the lives of fictionalized boxers. I am spared asking him the obligatory question about the preposterous *Rocky* movies.

It should not be assumed, on the evidence of the above, that Mike Tyson is not intelligent; or that he is intellectually limited. On the contrary, I sensed in him the prodigy's instinctive husbanding of the self: he dares not allow his imagination freedom in areas only peripheral to the cultivation of his talent. Because he is an unusually sensitive person—sensitive to others' feelings, not merely to his own—he does not want to be forced to expend himself in feeling, or in thinking; except of course on his own terms. The awareness of life's tragic ambiguity that serious art provides—the perception, as Henry James describes it in the preface to *What Maisie Knew*, that no themes are so human "as those that reflect for us, out of the confusion of life, the close connection of bliss and bale, of the things that help with the things that hurt, so dangling before us for ever that bright hard medal, of so strange an alloy, one face of which is somebody's right and ease and the other somebody's pain and wrong"—would be disastrous for the warrior boxer. When, the story goes, Alexis Arguello (the great champion of the featherweight, junior lightweight, and lightweight divisions) met Roberto Duran (the great champion of the lightweight and welterweight divisions) and proffered his hand to shake, Duran backed away and screamed, "Get away! You're crazy! I'm not your friend!" To acknowledge friendship, let alone brotherhood, always makes it difficult to kill—or to provide for spectators the extraordinary mimicry of killing that boxing of the quality of Mike Tyson's involves. Life is real and painful, and steeped in ambiguity; in the boxing ring there is either/or. Either you win, or you lose.

The brilliant boxer is an artist, albeit in an art not readily comprehensible, or palatable, to most observers. The instruments of his art are his own and his opponent's bodies. That it is, in a sense, a contemplative art contemplated, dreamt-of, for weeks, months, even years before it is executed—is a proposition important to understand if one is to understand the boxer. ("It's a lonely sport," Mike Tyson, who is surrounded by people who love him, says.) Obsession is not greatness but greatness is obsession, so it is no accident that, in his ambition to be not only the youngest titleholder in heavyweight history but (I would guess) the greatest titleholder of all time, Tyson is always, in a spiritual sense, in training. His admiration for past boxers—Stanley Ketchel, Jack Dempsey, Henry Armstrong, Kid Chocolate—and, not least, Roberto Duran, of whom he speaks with genuine awe is the admiration of the shrewd apprentice for his elders, not necessarily his

betters. When I ask Tyson to assess his heavyweight contemporaries, men he will be meeting in the ring in the next few years, he again becomes purposefully vague, saying he doesn't think too much about them: "That would drive me crazy." Pinklon Thomas, Gerry Cooney, Carl Williams, Tyrell Biggs, Bert Cooper—he'd rather change the subject. And this instinct too is correct: the boxer must concentrate upon his opponents one by one, each in turn: in the collective, they cannot be granted existence. I am reminded of a diary entry of Virginia Woolf's to the effect that she does not dare read her serious rivals. "Do I instinctively keep my mind from analysing, which would impair its creativeness? . . . No creative writer can swallow another contemporary. The reception of living work is too coarse and partial if you're doing the same thing yourself" (20 April 1935).

Similarly, Tyson does not want to think overmuch about fatal accidents in the ring. He takes it for granted that he will not, indeed cannot, be hurt—"I'm too good for that to happen"; on the subject of an opponent's fate at his hands he is matter-of-fact and pragmatic. He is a boxer, he does his job—throwing punches until his opponent is defeated. If, as in the infamous Griffith-Paret match of 1962, in which Paret, trapped in the ropes, was struck eighteen unanswered blows by Griffith, death does occur, that is no one's fault: it can be said to be an accident. "Each of you takes the same chance, getting into the ring," Tyson says in his soft, considered, alternately slow and hurried voice—one of the voices, perhaps, of Cus D'Amato. "That you might die. It might happen."

I ask Tyson what he was thinking when the stricken Berbick tried to get to his feet and he says quickly, "I hoped he wasn't hurt," and adds, "It was a deliberate punch, to the head—a bad intention in a vital area." The anatomical areas Tyson has been taught to strike with his sledgehammer blows include the liver, the kidneys, the heart, and, as in Berbick's case, a certain spot on the temple which, if struck hard enough, will cause a man to drop immediately to the canvas. He will be fully conscious, as Berbick was, but paralyzed. Helpless. Down for the count.

And Tyson is confident that he himself cannot be hurt—in any serious, permanent way?

"That's right. I can't be. I'm too good."

Following the accidental death of one of the Flying Wallendas some years ago, a surviving member of the family of famous aerial-trapeze performers told the press that none of them had any intention of quitting. "All of life," he said, "is just getting through the time between acts."

So too with the fighter who loves to fight; the man whose identity is so closely bound up with the ring that it might be said he has none, publicly speaking, outside it. His creative work is done only in the ring and only at certain designated times. Taped, it becomes permanent; it *is* himself—or all that posterity will know of him.

The extraordinary upward trajectory of Mike Tyson's career—twenty-eight professional fights in eighteen months—has been the result of discipline and concentration so fierce as to resemble monastic devotion. Now that he is a titleholder, and a celebrity, and no longer a hungry young contender, Tyson's sense of himself has irrevocably altered; though he has yet to unify the heavyweight title—to do so, he will have to beat "Bonecrusher" Smith for the WBA title and the elusive Michael Spinks for the IBF title—he is already being called, and, in excited moments, calls himself, the heavyweight champion of the world. He has outdistanced his contemporaries—the new young generation of boxers that includes such Olympic Gold Medalists as Tyrell Biggs, Mark Breland, Paul Gonzales, Meldrick Taylor, and Pernell Whittaker, he is the first among them to win not only a title but enormous popular success. "When I was a kid I wanted to be famous—I wanted to be somebody," Mike Tyson says. And: "If someone right now is going to be famous, I'm glad it's me." But fame and the rewards of fame are, in a very real sense, the counterworld of the boxer's training: they represent all that must be repressed in the service of the boxer's real, as opposed to his merely public, career. When boxers retire it is primarily because of the terrible rigors of training, not the risks of defeat, injury, or even death in the ring. (The boxer who is generally credited with having trained hardest is Rocky Marciano, who commonly spent upward of two months preparing for a fight. And when Marciano decided to retire, undefeated, at the age of thirty-three, it was because the sacrifices of the training camp outweighed the rewards of celebrity: "No kind of money can make me fight again," Marciano said.) The existential experience of the fight itself—spectacular, amplified, recorded in its every minute detail—is not only the culmination of the formidable training period but, in its very flowering, or fruition, it presents the boxer-as-performer to the world. Very likely this physical expenditure of the self (Tyson typically refers to it as "matching my boxing skills against my opponent's"), this bedrock of what's real, casts the remainder of life into a light difficult to assess. Life outside the ring is real enough—yet is it *really* real? Not public display as such but the joy of the body in its straining to the very limits of ingenuity and endurance underlies the motive for such feats of physical prowess as championship boxing or aerial-trapeze work. The performer is rewarded by his performance as an end in itself; he becomes addicted, as who would not, to his very adrenaline. *All of life is just getting through the time between acts.*

Since Mike Tyson is a young man gifted with a highly refined sense of irony, if not a sense of the absurd, it cannot have escaped his attention that, much of the time, in public places like the expensive midtown restaurant in which our party has dinner following the interview, or the reception two weeks later in a private suite in Madison Square Garden before the Witherspoon-Smith elimination match, he is likely to be the only black in attendance. He is likely to be the youngest person in attendance, and the only man not dressed in a suit and tie. Above all he is likely to be the only person with a gold tooth and a homemade tattoo ("Mike" on his right bicep); and the only person who, not many years before, was so violent and uncontrollable ("I went berserk sometimes") he had to be forcibly restrained. But when I mention some of this to a fellow guest at the Garden reception the man looks at me as if I have said something not only bizarre but distasteful. "I doubt that Mike thinks in those terms," he says. Not even that Tyson is the only black in this gathering of well-to-do white people, an observation that would appear to be simple fact? But no, I am assured: "Mike Tyson doesn't think in those terms."

Following a brief speech by the gentleman who runs Madison Square Garden, Tyson is presented with a ceremonial gift: a glass paperweight apple symbolizing New York City. He is photographed, he smiles genially, expresses his thanks for the paperweight, stands looking at it, for a moment, with a bemused expression. When, afterward, I ask Tyson how he likes being a celebrity—since, after all, he wanted to be famous—he says, "It's okay." Then: "Most of the time these things drive me crazy." I observe that he has learned to smile very nicely for photographers, and he responds with a violent parody of a celebrity smile: a death's-head grimace that is fierce, funny, self-mocking, inspired.

Four weeks later, still being photographed—this time by photographers for two magazines simultaneously—Tyson is back in training in Catskill, New York, in a third-floor walkup gym above Catskill Police Headquarters on Main Street. The gym is small, well-weathered, romantically shabby; owned and operated by the city of Catskill but leased for $1 a year to the Cus D'Amato Memorial Boxing Club, a non-profit organization. In the spareness of the gym's equipment as in the sentiment that so clearly accrues to its homeliest features, it is the very antithesis of today's high-tech high-gloss athletic clubs. It contains only a single ring and a few punching bags; its ceiling is high and blistered, its lights antiquated. Its peeling walls are covered with newspaper clippings, announcements of the Catskill Boxing Club, photographs and posters of great champions (Louis, Walcott, Charles, Marciano, Patterson, et al.), reproductions of magazine covers. Mike Tyson's entire career is recorded here, in miniature, and, beneath the legend WE MOURN HIS PASSING, there are numerous clippings and photographs pertaining to the late Cus D'Amato, who once presided over the Boxing Club. Tyson prefers this gym to any other, naturally: it was here he began training, aged thirteen, and here that D'Amato's spirit still resounds. The gym is as indelibly imprinted in Tyson's imagination as any place on earth, success has consecrated it in turn.

No athletes train more rigorously than boxers, and no present-day boxer is more serious about his training than Mike Tyson. Indeed, for the first eighteen months of his career he seems to have kept in condition more or less as the legendary Harry Greb did—by fighting virtually all the time. Today Tyson has done his morning roadwork—"three to five miles; I like it then 'cause I'm alone"—and is now going through the exercises that constitute "preliminary" training. (In Las Vegas he will work with at least five sparring partners. As Jim Jacobs explains, the sparring partners need time to recover.) Dressed in a black leotard and blowsy white trunks he moves from "work" station to station, closely attended by his trainer, Rooney, whom he clearly respects, and for whom he feels a good deal of affection, perhaps, at least in part, because Rooney is himself a D'Amato protege—a welterweight who once boxed on the U.S. Boxing Team—and even shared one or two cards with Tyson, when he was already Tyson's trainer.

The drills are fierce and demand more concentration, strength, and sheer physical endurance than any fight Tyson has yet fought. Rooney has set a timer made up of two bulbs, red and green, to monitor each drill, the red telling Tyson to pause, the latter to resume. First he jumps rope, as if in a kind of trance, the rope moving too swiftly to be seen; the spectacle of a man of Tyson's build, so light on his feet, so seemingly *weightless*, has a preternatural quality. Next the heavy bag: Rooney wraps his hands with white tape, Tyson puts on gloves, pushes the bag with his left, then pummels it with combinations as it swings back to him. Rooney stands close and after each flurry the two confer, even as the heavy bag still swings treacherously in and around them. As he launches his hooks Tyson leaps from point to lateral point with extraordinary agility—as if his upper body remains stationary while his lower body moves in sharp angles out of which solidly anchored punches are shot. These are blows of such daunting power it is difficult to comprehend how they could be absorbed by any human being . . . any fellow creature of flesh, bone, and blood.

Rooney is game to try, at least for a while, wearing padded mitts over his hands and forearms; then they move on to the "slip" bag, where Tyson bobs and weaves, eluding his invisible opponent's best-aimed blows to the head. Last, the speed bag. In the blurred and confusing action of a fight it is not so readily clear, as it is in the gym, that Tyson's relative shortness (he is considered a "little" heavyweight) is really to his advantage. Most of his opponents are taller than he, if not invariably heavier, so that they are obliged to punch at a downward angle, utilizing only their shoulder and arm muscles; while Tyson can punch upward, utilizing not only his shoulder and arm muscles but his leg muscles as well—and these muscles are massive. By crouching, he can make himself shorter, and yet more elusive. (As Jim Jacobs has explained, "People speak of a 'height advantage' when what they're really referring to is a 'height disadvantage.' If a boxer is good, and shorter than his opponent, the advantage is his, and not his opponent's. The same thing holds true with the fallacy of the 'reach advantage'—a boxer has a 'reach advantage' only if he is superior to his opponent.") But the strangest, most dazzling thing about Tyson's boxing style is really his speed: his incredible speed. How, one wonders, can he do it? Weighing what he does, and built as he is? And will he be able to keep it up, in the years to come?

"Eat, sleep, and train," says Kevin Rooney. "Mike loves to train."

But: "I'm tired," Tyson says several times, in a soft, nearly inaudible voice. (He is still being photographed.) In his black leotard, towel in hand, he is literally drenched in sweat; exuding sweat like tears. One can see how much easier fighting has been for him than the regimen Rooney has devised—so many of Tyson's fights have lasted less than five minutes, against opponents lacking the skill to so much as raise a welt on his face, or cause him to breathe hard. And this training session is only the beginning—on February 3 he leaves for Las Vegas and four weeks of "intensive" training.

He showers, dresses, reappears in jeans, a white tuniclike jacket, stylish tweed cap, brilliantly white Gucci sports shoes—surely the only shoes of their kind in Catskill, New York? When we're photographed together in a corner of the ring he complains in my ear of the hours he has endured that day alone, facing cameras: "You can't believe it! On and on!" Fame's best-kept secret—its soul-numbing boredom—has begun to impress itself upon Mike Tyson.

Catskill, New York, is a small town of less than six thousand inhabitants. Its well-kept wood-frame houses have that prewar American look so immediately appealing to some of us—the very architecture of nostalgia. Like Main Street, with its Newberry's Five-and-Dime, Joe's Food Market, Purina Chows, the Town of Catskill town hall a storefront facing the police station, and the village offices—clerk, treasurer, tax collector—in the same building as the Catskill Boxing Club. Parking here is five cents an hour.

Mike Tyson lives two or three miles away, in one of the largest and most attractive houses in town, the home of Mrs. Camille Ewald, Cus D'Amato's sister-in-law. The house is at the end of an unpaved, seemingly private road, immaculately kept outside and in, yet comfortable—"I've lived here for seven years now," Tyson says proudly. He leads me through a kitchen and through a parlor room gleaming with trophies he doesn't acknowledge and we sit at one end of an immense living room while, from varying distances, a photographer (from Japan) continues to take candid shots of him he doesn't acknowledge either.

Life in Catskill is quiet and nourishingly routine: up at 6 A.M., to bed at 9 P.M. Daily workouts at the gym with Rooney; a diet of meat, vegetables, pasta, fruit juice—never any alcohol or caffeine; a modicum, in this semirural environment, of monastic calm. But there are numerous distractions: last week Tyson addressed a junior high school in New York City, under the auspices of the Drug Enforcement Agency, and tomorrow he is due to fly to Jamaica for a boxing banquet at which, however improbably, Don King is going to be given a humanitarian award—"But I'm not going; I'm too tired." He speaks soberly of the responsibility of celebrity; the fact that fame requires, of its conscientious recipients, a degree of civic servitude. The awareness weighs upon him almost visibly.

With equal sobriety, and a mysterious conviction, Tyson goes on to say that friends, certain friends—"some of them the ones you like best"—can't be relied upon. "They want to be your friend, or say they do, then the least thing that goes wrong—" He makes a dismissive gesture. "They're gone." I suggest that this can't be the case with people he has known a long time, before he became famous, like Jim and Loraine Jacobs, and Tyson's face brightens. The Jacobses will always be his friends, he agrees. "No matter if I lose every fight from now on, if I was knocked down, knocked out—they'd always be my friends. That's right." He seems momentarily cheered.

Tyson's prize possession in Catskill is a young female dog of an exquisite Chinese breed, Shar-Pei, with an appealingly ugly pug face, rippling creases of flesh on its back, a body wildly animated by affection. He'd always wanted one of these dogs, Tyson says, but hadn't been able to afford it until now. "In China they were bred to hunt wild boars—that's why they have those wrinkles on their backs," he explains. "So when the boar bit into them they could twist around to keep on attacking." As Tyson speaks fondly of this uniquely evolved creature I am reminded of Tyson's own ring strategy—his agility at slipping an opponent's blows, ducking or leaning far to one side, then returning with perfect leverage and timing to counterpunch, often with his devastating right uppercut. The "little" warrior dramatically overcoming the larger. . . . He loves this dog, he says. For the first time today he looks genuinely happy.

On our way out of the house, Tyson shows me the dining room in which he ate so many meals with Cus D'Amato. The room is handsomely furnished, flooded with sunshine on this clear winter day. "Cus sat here," Tyson says, indicating the head of the table, "—and I sat here. By his side."

When Santayana said that another world to live in is what we mean by religion, he could hardly have foreseen how his remark might apply to the sports mania of our time; to the extraordinary passion, amounting very nearly to religious fervor and ecstasy, millions of Americans commonly experience in regard to sport. For these people— the majority of them men—sports has become the "other world," preempting, at times, their interest in "this" world: their own lives, work, families, official religions.

Set beside the media-promoted athletes of our time and the iconography of their success, the average man knows himself merely average. In a fiercely competitive sport like boxing, whose pyramid may appear democratically broad at the base but is brutally minuscule at the top, to be even less than great is to fail.

A champion boxer, hit by an opponent and hit hard, may realize the total collapse of his career in less time than it takes to read this sentence. Boxing is not to be seized as a metaphor for life, but its swift and sometimes irremediable reversals of fortune starkly parallel those of life, and the blow we never saw coming—invariably, in the ring, the knockout blow—is the one that decides our fate. Boxing's dark fascination is as much with failure, and the courage to forbear failure, as it is with triumph. Two men climb into a ring from which, in symbolic terms, only one climbs out.

After the Berbick fight Tyson told reporters he'd wanted to break Berbick's eardrum. "I try to catch my opponent on the tip of the nose," he was quoted after his February 1986 fight with the hapless Jesse Ferguson, whose nose was broken in the match, "because I want to punch the bone into the brain." Tyson's language is as direct and brutal as his ring style, yet, as more than one observer has noted, strangely disarming—there is no air of menace, or sadism, or boastfulness in what he says: only the truth. For these reasons Mike Tyson demonstrates more forcefully than most boxers the paradox at the heart of this controversial sport. That he is "soft-spoken," "courteous," "sensitive," clearly thoughtful, intelligent, introspective; yet at the same time—or nearly the same time—he is a "killer" in the ring. That he is one of the most warmly affectionate of persons, yet at the same time—or nearly—a machine for hitting "sledgehammer" blows. How is it possible? one asks. And why? Boxing makes graphically clear the somber fact that the same individual can be thoroughly "civilized" and "barbaric" depending upon the context of his performance. "I'm a boxer," Tyson says. "I'm a warrior. Doing my job." Murder, a legal offense, cannot occur in the ring. Any opponent who agrees to fight a man of Tyson's unique powers must know what he is doing—and, as Tyson believes, each boxer takes the same chance: matching his skills against those of his opponent.

The fictive text against which boxing is enacted has to do with the protection of human life; the sacramental vision of life. *Thou shalt not kill* (or main, wound, cause to suffer injury) and *Do unto others as you would have them do unto you* are the implicit injunctions against which the spectacle unfolds and out of which its energies arise. The injunctions are, for the duration of the "game," denied, or repressed, or exploited. Far from being primitive, boxing is perhaps the most highly regulated and ritualistic of sports, so qualified by rules, customs, and unspoken traditions that it stands in a unique, albeit teasing, relationship to the extremes of human emotion: rage, despair, terror, cruelty, ecstasy. It is an art, as I've suggested, in which the human body itself is the instrument; its relationship to unmediated violence is that of a musical composition to mere noise. There may be a family kinship between Bach and aleatory "music," but the kinship is hardly the most significant thing about either.

But what, one wonders, is the purpose of so extreme an art?—can it have a purpose? Why do some men give themselves to it so totally, while others, as spectators, stare in rapt fascination—and pay so much money for the privilege of doing so?

Wallace Stevens's insight that the death of Satan was a tragedy for the imagination has no validity in terms of the curious aesthetic phenomenon that is professional boxing. In the boxing ring, elevated, harshly spotlighted, men are pitted against each other in one-on-one mirrorlike combat in order to release energies in themselves and in their audience that are demonic by the standards of ordinary—or do I mean noncombative?—life. The triumphant boxer is Satan transmogrified as Christ, as one senses sitting amid a delirium-swept crowd like the one that cheered Mike Tyson on to victory. Yet, even before Tyson began to fight, even before he entered the ring, the crowd was fixed upon him emotionally. (As the crowd was fixed, more evenly, upon Marvin Hagler and Thomas Hearns in their April 1985 match, shrieking as soon as the men appeared and scarcely stopping until the fight itself was stopped after eight very long minutes. Ecstasy precedes stimulus and may, indeed, help bring it into being.) For many, Mike Tyson has become the latest in a lineage of athletic heroes—a bearer of inchoate, indescribable emotion—a savior, of sorts, covered in sweat and ready for war. But then most saviors, sacred or secular, are qualified by a thoughtful "of sorts." In any case, it's Tyson's turn. A terrible beauty is born.

Materials used in the preparation of this article: Elliot J. Gorn, "The Manassa Mauler and the Fighting Marine: An Interpretation of the Dempsey-Tunney Fights," *Journal of American Studies*, Vol. 19 (1985); Nigel Collins, "Mike Tyson: The Legacy of Cus D'Amato," *The Ring*, February 1986; Jack Newfield, "Dr. K.O.: Mike Tyson—Cus D'Amato's Upfinished Masterpiece," *Village Voice*, 10 December 1985; John McCallum, *The Heavyweight Boxing Championship: A History* (Radnor, Pa.: Chilton Book Co., 1974); and articles in *The New York Times* by Dave Anderson and Phil Berger.

HAPPY BIRTHDAY, INGRATE

New York Daily News, June 30, 1988

by

Michael Katz

Happy Birthday, Mike Tyson. You say you're now the former heavyweight champion of the world and I want to believe you. You say you're quitting, just as I reported last week. I didn't believe you then, I don't believe you now. But I want to. I'm not going to ask you to change your mind—because there's no one I want to see you fight. And I won't miss you—because outside the ring you've become a disappointment.

You say your life is hell, the only place you feel comfortable is in the ring and then you say you're quitting the ring.

In the ring, sure, you were a great fighter. Maybe you could have been the greatest. But you were never going to be The Greatest. You're no Muhammad Ali, who was a man of the people, a man of great soul.

Don't lecture me about the "woman you love." You're 22 today and you don't know the first thing about love. A woman you love, you don't hit. A woman loves you, she doesn't make you choose between you and your family, you and your friends.

You've turned your back on too many people who were kind to you, who got you out of the ghetto and tried to get the ghetto out of you. You call them "Jews in suits," which offends me, though I seldom wear suits. You're beginning to sound like Don King. You claim to be a boxing historian, yet you deny your own history and now you're saying you have no future.

Remember Jimmy Jacobs? You cried at his funeral. Where was your wife at this trying time? In the offices of Merrill Lynch—where Jimmy and Bill Cayton had set up an account that only you could touch—stomping around with your beloved mother-in-law, demanding "my money." Remember Lorraine Jacobs, Jimmy's wife, who treated you like the son they never had? If you do, why haven't you called her since the funeral?

Remember Cus D'Amato? He adopted you as a son to keep you out of trouble, force-fed you boxing and philosophy, tried to turn you not only into a fighter, but into a socialized human being? Your wife says he's a "ghost" and she doesn't appreciate living with ghosts.

Remember Steve Lott? You lived in his pad for 2 ½ years. He dedicated his life to you. Even now, he uses the word "love" to describe his feelings for you. Who was it, your wife or your mother-in-law, who asked you to kick him out of the camp? You didn't even want to do it yourself, asked Kevin Rooney to do your dirty work. Kevin Rooney is a stand-up guy. How come Robin and Ruth haven't tried to get rid of him yet? Or have they?

Remember Bill Cayton? You were never close to him. Understandably. He wasn't one of the guys you hugged. He did his work for you in the cold-hearted conference rooms. All he ever did was join with Jimmy in making you rich and famous in what must be one of the best jobs of managing a fighter in history. You know boxing history. You know what a lucky puppy you've been. Heavyweight champion at 20, a millionaire at 21. Go ahead, sue him and Jimmy's widow.

Remember Feb. 12, 1988? You were in the offices of the New York State Athletic Commission when you signed the contract extensions. Remember how the commission lawyers, taking your side, explained to you that if Jimmy died, Bill would be your manager and Lorraine would get half their cut? How if Bill died, Jimmy would be your manager and Doris Cayton would get half their cut? Remember how glad you were at the time that these people who love and honor you would be taken care of?

You blame me for your troubles, do you? Me and the rest of the

Tyson with Jim Jacobs

press for "embarrassing your family"? Hey, it was your wife who told NBC that Bill Cayton had to go. It was your sister-in-law who called *Newsday* to say how you beat your wife. Who's embarrassing whom? Why do you think they did that? Because they have your best interests at heart? You say it's because Bill Cayton put them up to it? Are you punch- drunk? I don't remember anyone hitting you. Let us assume Bill Cayton put a detective on your women. For argument's sake. You think it would be because he wants or needs your money? Or because he might be worried about you?

Frankly, I don't give a damn about your wife and her acting or Harvard Medical School careers. That's your business and hers. But don't talk about love until you understand the difference between love and obsession. And that would be my birthday present, if somehow it could be delivered.

Understanding. Because once you understand love, you might find peace in your life. You might then be able to convince your wife that she need not feel insecure, that the ghost of Cus does not mean her any harm. You might be able to reconcile your old family with your new one and live happily.

You were a great fighter Mike Tyson. Happy Birthday.

AT RINGSIDE WITH MADONNA AND SEAN

St. Petersburg Times, January 21, 1989

by

Harry Crews

"Do something, Lou," Madonna Louise Ciccone said, leaning forward on the seat, her lean little body tight with impatience.

Lou, a beefy-shouldered, balding bodyguard with a tendency to sweat, turned from where he sat in the front seat beside the driver and regarded her pleasantly, nothing showing in his face.

Stretch limousines were out by the hundreds—drunken dream fish, silver and schooling there in the late afternoon light in front of the Trump Plaza Hotel and Casino in Atlantic City, N.J., where on this June 27 Iron Mike Tyson and Michael Spinks were about to go at each other in the convention center for the pleasure of Madonna and Sean Penn and me and 20,000 other souls, plus untold millions around the world via satellite.

"G-d d—it, do something," Madonna said again.

What Lou was supposed to do was not entirely clear. We were in a stretch-limo gridlock. That fact did not seem to occur to Madonna. She had arrived. She knew where she wanted to go, what she wanted to do and she was not prepared to wait for anybody or anything. She doesn't know wait. She doesn't know later. She knows now.

AT RINGSIDE WITH MADONNA AND SEAN

Madonna left Rochester, Mich., for New York at the age of 18 with nothing but a suitcase and a heart scalded by ambition to be somebody.

She came with a million other nobodies in the annual pilgrimage to the brutally indifferent, dirty, savage shrine of power that is Manhattan.

A decade later, she was married to a handsome, hot-at-the-box-office, totally unpredictable actor named Sean Penn, had more money than she could ever count, a house in Malibu, an apartment on Central Park and renown to rival that of any other face and name on the planet. She also still had a heart scalded by ambition, a heart unsated and insatiable that will be lusting for action when the first shovelful of dirt drops on her coffin.

So don't talk to Madonna about waiting and later. Hovering in the air about her every act and utterance is the proposition never articulated but always present: Show me the damn wall I have to get through to get to the place I want to be and I'll take the wall down with my teeth and fingernails if necessary. It is not always a lovely thing to see.

But she is always a lovely thing to see. Her skin is diaphanously thin over the fine bones of her face and white as only skin can be that has never courted the sun. Her eyes under a wide, smooth forehead are direct and of a color indeterminate and changing, by turns deep violet with specks of green and gold, or heavy blue shading into a hue difficult to name. Her hair is thick and dark, with a healthy luster when the light catches it just right.

The magic is in the planes of her face and the way she moves. Her bone structure is such that at any angle—looking slightly to the side or down or up—her chin, the fine bridge of her nose, the flat high cheeks all collaborate to produce an unexpected and seductive beauty.

We are approaching the ballroom of the convention center now, where we are invited to a private party given by Donald Trump. A crush of people is pressing down on the walk leading to the building. Double lines of men wearing orange jackets emblazoned with the legend "Trump Security" try to restrain the crowd and keep the walk open.

As the car pulls to a stop and Madonna becomes visible through the window, a great roar bursts from the collective throat of the crowd. It is a sound one would expect to hear at a football game or a lynching.

"My f—ing fans," Madonna said, and the word "fans" was a greater obscenity in her mouth than the adjective modifying it.

Kevin Rooney wraps Mike's hands

For the first time, I noticed the incredible number of men and women—certainly more than a hundred—with cameras of one kind or another slung from their necks and shoulders. As if on signal, all the cameras raised and popped in a great flash of light as Madonna stepped from the car to take Sean's arm. I felt a very real threat and animosity from the crowd, which seemed to be made up entirely of hair, teeth and hysteria in more or less equal parts.

Perhaps my uneasiness showed in my face, because just before Lou threw himself into the throng converging on the car, he looked at me and said, "It'll be better inside. Stay close."

I stayed close, but it was not better inside. It went from hair, teeth and hysteria all the way to nightmare.

I don't think Madonna or Sean could tell you what the ballroom looked like. Certainly I could not, blinded as I was by flashbulbs.

Because when we went inside, the howling mob of photographers broke through Trump Security and came in with us. Madonna's bodyguard was in the lead and we followed. But Lou did not know where to go to get away from the sea of popping flashbulbs. I tried to tell myself that we were not in a lynch mob, that these people were only taking pictures, trying to do a job. But it was difficult to believe when I was taking shots to the kidneys and being bashed about the head and shoulders with flailing cameras. The three of us reminded me of nothing so much as bee-stung dogs, dashing blindly about with an angry hive of stinging bees in hot pursuit.

Finally we ducked out a back door and into an elevator Lou commandeered, and we went down one floor where we stayed in the elevator with Lou positioned in the open door. Somewhere along the way we had picked up a woman who was a Trump Casino employee. Madonna was beside herself with anger.

"Why were those f—ing people allowed in where the guests are?" she demanded.

"They weren't supposed to be, but. . . ."

"Where am I supposed to go? What am I supposed to do? I can't believe Donald Trump. This is outrageous."

The woman left us to try to find Madonna a room where we could stay while we figured out what to do. In the meantime, Lou, sweating bullets by now, stood in the elevator door fighting off people trying to use it, while Madonna said unkind things about Trump, including speculations about his ancestry.

The woman, full of apologies, returned. "There's not a room in the hotel, not one. But I've got a conference room you can sit in."

As we were leaving, Warren Beatty and Jack Nicholson—Nicholson with a bottle of beer in his hand and wearing his trademark dark glasses—started into the elevator.

"Man, you can't go up there," Sean said.

"The hell I can't," said Nicholson.

"It's a madhouse," Sean said. "They've let photographers in."

"Come on," said Nicholson. "Let's go to the party."

Instead of the party, we went down back corridors and back stairwells and sat in a little conference room where Madonna munched on popcorn until fight time.

At the fight I couldn't help noticing that Nicholson and Beatty sat quietly chatting and smiling about 10 seats away from us while Lou fought off photographers and Madonna told anyone who got close enough to ask for an autograph to bug off. Of all the celebrities at ringside—and everybody I'd ever heard of seemed to be there, including Jesse Jackson, Tom Brokaw and Richard Pryor—Madonna's picture was the one on the "wanted" poster. And she was not enjoying it—any of it—and had not enjoyed it since we had arrived.

Suddenly Trump appeared, hustling between the seats toward Madonna.

"I have better seats for you," Trump said to Madonna and Sean. He bent to touch Madonna's shoulder. Had he heard about her outrage over the photographers and the ruined party? I couldn't imagine what better seats would look like anyway. We were seven rows from the ring apron as it was.

"We can't go," Madonna said. "I have a guest." Trump looked at me, wondering, I'm sure, who the hell I might be.

"Go ahead," I said. "This is a great seat. I'll be fine."

Still Madonna refused. "We can't. He's my guest," she said to Trump.

Trump touched my shoulder. "Come on. It's all right."

So the three of us, with Trump leading the way, went down to the aisle directly on the ring. Trump waved is hand and a gofer in a tuxedo appeared with two chairs. Trump said I could sit two rows behind them, which God knows was fine with me. But Sean and Madonna were having none of that, either. Sean took Madonna on his lap, and Madonna motioned for me to take the chair beside them.

Later I told her it would have been fine to have left me where I had been sitting initially.

"Would you have left me if I had been your guest?" she asked.

"Well, no, but. . . ."

"I don't leave my guests either."

I'm obviously prejudiced in the matter, but I thought that a class bit of action I would have neither expected nor predicted.

As the whole world knows by now, the fight lasted 91 seconds of the first round, taking considerably less time than it took to introduce the celebrities at ringside. When Spinks went down we went out, led by the indefatigable Lou. But the photographers knew where Madonna had been sitting and had her staked out. The pushing and shoving and popping of flashbulbs was horrendous as we fought our way out to the sidewalk. To wait for the car and escape, we were forced to take refuge in a kitchen. When the steel doors were slammed and secured behind us, the sudden silence was like going under water.

And out of the dim recesses of the kitchen came six or seven young men, all black or Hispanic, wearing garbage-spattered aprons and walked-over shoes.

"Could I have your autograph?" one of them asked, holding a napkin and a well-chewed pencil out to Madonna.

She stood there, harassed, tired, regarding the napkin for a moment and then said, "Sure. Of course."

She and Sean then proceeded to write their names on Styrofoam cups and napkins and whatever else the young men produced. They were the first and last autographs they gave that evening. Later, I asked her why.

"These guys that work back in the kitchen don't get to see a hell of a lot. They're just back there doing a bad job. They sure as hell didn't see the fight, did they? And they weren't like most people wanting an autograph, coming up to you and demanding it. It's that impertinence that bothers you more than anything else. And I didn't get that feeling from them, not at all."

We waited around in the hot, dirty kitchen for another 15 minutes or so, the mob outside bouncing off the doors, before Lou managed to have the car brought around. On the three-hour ride back to Manhattan, Madonna put on a tape and dozed with her head in her husband's lap. At my hotel I thanked them and said good night. It was 3 A.M. As I watched the taillights disappear down the deserted street, it occurred to me that I had not heard her laugh or seen her smile during the entire evening. Nothing could diminish my own pleasure of attending a championship fight, and I had delighted in their company, finding both Sean and Madonna to be good, decent people who had shown me courtesy and kindness, but for them the entire evening had seemed an unrelieved ordeal—the price they had to pay for who they were and what they had achieved.

FROM BAD INTENTIONS

1989

by

Peter Heller

Many of Tyson's friends will joke that Mike Tyson behind the wheel of a car is more dangerous than Mike Tyson in the ring. Teddy Atlas recalls Mike's mounting the sidewalk and hitting a mailbox while trying to drive the first used car Cus D'Amato bought for the teenage fighter. Jay Bright laughingly said he hides behind trees when Mike gets in the car to drive. D'Amato once told his young fighter, after taking a drive with him, "Mike, I'll never have to use a laxative again." Tyson had no luck with cars, even when he wasn't driving. Before he and Robin were married, following an argument, she got into his Mercedes 560SL and slammed it into the rear of his Rolls-Royce, damaging both vehicles. On this rainy morning in Catskill, the BMW was parked on the grass. Tyson turned on the ignition, hit the gas pedal and the wheels began spinning in the wet grass and mud. Camille came out on the porch to try to tell him there was a telephone call for him. At that moment, the wheels suddenly grabbed and the car shot forward out of control. It lurched about 30 feet, and the right front bumper slammed into a chestnut tree at the edge of the property. It bounced off the tree, sustaining heavy damage to the front end, then came to a stop in some shrubs a short distance away. When Camille got to the car, Tyson appeared to be unconscious. His head was slumped back, his eyes closed. She slapped him a few times, and when he came to, asking her, "Camille, what happened?" "You hit a tree," she told him, and then he drifted off into unconsciousness again. Jay Bright phoned for an ambulance, which came from Catskill in about ten minutes. Tyson, according to one of the attendants, was still unconscious, although his pulse, breathing and blood pressure were normal. They rushed him to Catskill Hospital, but a short time later it was decided to move him to the larger Columbia-Greene Medical Center about fifteen minutes away in Hudson, New York, where a CAT scan could be performed.

Meanwhile, Ruth Roper and Robin Givens were notified in New York City about the accident and immediately began the two-hour drive to Catskill. Tyson had wanted Robin to spend a few days with him there while he trained and before they both left for the Soviet Union, but she had opted to stay in the city to attend the U.S. Open Tennis Championships which were under way. Before starting out for Catskill, Roper had told Camille they would want to transfer Mike to Columbia-Presbyterian Medical Center in Manhattan, where they felt he would receive better diagnostic treatment.

When Camille went to see Mike at the hospital in Hudson, around one o'clock in the afternoon, the fighter was fully conscious and in good spirits, though rather embarrassed by the mishap and the fuss. Camille told him that Ruth and Robin wanted him transferred to New York City, but Mike said he wasn't going anywhere until he had something to eat. He was starving, and food was his major concern at that moment. Jay Bright went to a Chinese restaurant and brought him a large quantity of fried rice and beef with broccoli, which the champion ravenously consumed. Mike joked with Camille about what a "nice Labor Day weekend" it had turned out to be, with him in the hospital, and the two laughed about it.

His spirits brightened further when Robin arrived later in the afternoon, along with her mother and their public relations representative. By then, Tyson had undergone a CAT brain scan, an EEG and an EKG, and Bill Cayton had been informed by Columbia-Greene doctors that Mike was "absolutely okay." Shortly after 7:00 P.M. with local newspaper and TV cameramen waiting outside, Mike was brought out, strapped to a stretcher, looking bewildered and embarrassed, and placed in an ambulance for the trip to Manhattan. In response to a question, he nodded and quietly acknowledged that he was feeling fine. Robin got in the back of the ambulance with him, and as photographers jockeyed for position to take pictures through the ambulance window, she blocked their view with her hand until a towel was placed across the window to curtain off the view. Earlier in the afternoon, there had been an unpleasant shouting match between Robin and trainer Kevin Rooney, when he arrived at the hospital to visit Tyson. Robin had tried to prevent him from getting into Mike's room, but he had brushed past her and gone in to see his young charge.

Shortly after 9:00 P.M., Tyson's ambulance arrived at Columbia-Presbyterian Medical Center in Manhattan, where reporters, photographers and TV cameras were waiting. As Tyson's stretcher was taken out of the ambulance, Givens became involved in another scene, shouting at the newspeople to "leave him alone, nothing's the matter, give the guy a break." No one was bothering Mike, just taking his picture, but Givens suddenly jumped right over her husband's stretcher, which was momentarily on the ground, and lunged at a TV cameraman, pushing him until he admonished her to "Take it easy, lady." Thus she became the focal point of the next day's TV newscasts and newspaper photos.

In the hospital, Tyson was once again subjected to a battery of even more sophisticated tests. Late that night, the Assistant Professor of Neurology at the hospital, Dr. Carolyn Britton, told the media that Mike had "suffered minor trauma to the head and chest wall" as the result of banging into the steering wheel when he hit the tree. She said he would remain in the hospital to undergo further observation and diagnostic testing, but his condition was "quite stable" and he was "neurologically normal."

The next day, Mike was isolated in a private room on the ninth floor, with security guards posted to protect his privacy. The two women compiled a list of approved visitors to Mike's room. Bill Cayton and Kevin Rooney were not on it. They had made it clear many times that the people who had been with Mike all along, from the beginning, were not part of their group. Even Cus D'Amato, who, despite some errors in judgment had done more for Mike Tyson than anyone else, was no longer in favor with the two women. Robin had said in the past she was "tired of constantly hearing about an old dead man I never knew," and said she didn't want her life infringed upon by the "ghost" of Cus D'Amato. The past meant nothing to these women. They were calling the shots now. Bill Cayton tried as gracefully as possible to excuse the fact that he was turned away when he tried to visit Mike, but Rooney was enraged. So were others, including Broadway and film star Danny Aiello and photographer Brian Hamill, who were also unceremoniously rejected when they arrived at the hospital. All had known Tyson from the early days and were friends in the true sense with no ulterior motives. Aiello and Hamill were personally turned away by Robin, who gave them a curt "no," without explanation or even cursory thanks for dropping by.

The list of those who could enter the inner sanctum and visit Mike was a joke. It included, besides Roper and Givens, Roper's assistant and henchwoman, Olga Rosario, Peter Parcher and Steven Hayes, the two attorneys retained by Roper to represent Tyson, Donald Trump and his wife, Ivana, and Howard Rubenstein, Trump's public relations man, who had, not accidentally, been retained by Roper and Givens to represent them as well as Mike. "Mrs. Trump!" exclaimed Danny Aiello. "We've known Mike since he was a kid. Trump knows him for half an hour," he told Pete Hamill.

Roper spoke touchingly of her daughter's loyalty. "Robin is hanging in there with her man, as usual," she said. "When he gets bruised, she hurts." Don King, on the outside looking in, offered his opinion that something was evidently wrong with Mike, he was confused, and those around him, suggested the benevolent promoter, shouldn't be so concerned about Mike fighting and making money. Instead they should be interested in his welfare as a human being, said the noted humanitarian King. Sugar Ray Leonard put forth the opinion that "there is something bothering Mike, probably something that stems back to when he was a kid." Larry Holmes said Tyson needed some guidance and good advice, and sent Mike a telegram offering to help if Mike wanted to talk to him. Muhammad Ali said he had never gotten in trouble while champion, but said Mike was "still young and he's got a few little faults and habits, which we all have, that have got to be corrected. He's in a position now where the world is watching him, and I think after a few mistakes he'll realize that. . . . If he wasn't famous and he wasn't where he was, he wouldn't make the news. But he's popular."

On Tuesday, Tyson underwent further testing. It was determined he could be released within a day or two, but Dr. Britton then said the words that Jarvis Astaire and Mickey Duff didn't want to hear. She said Mike had been unconscious for about twenty minutes following the accident, and he had suffered some temporary amnesia. His doctors recommended that he should not train for thirty to sixty days, making an October date at Wembley an impossibility. In London, Jarvis Astaire acknowledged that both October 8 and the back-up date of October 22 were now out of the question. He said there was no choice but to implement the contingency plan of moving the fight indoors to a much smaller venue, the Wembley Arena, and a tentative date of December 16 was set. Astaire made it clear there would be no stepping aside by Bruno to allow Tyson to fight an interim challenger. "Bruno is the nominated next challenger," he said. "We have a contract for Tyson to fight him, and that is what will happen. . . . If anything, this should give Frank encouragement. The invincibility of Tyson has taken a bit of a blow. Once he gets over his initial disappointment, Frank is going to fancy his chances even more. Psychologically, what's happened must worry the champion."

Back at the hospital, Tyson was getting petulant and restless. The security guards assigned to him described him as a "big baby," complaining all the time and watching television constantly, throwing the white hospital gowns at nurses and attendants and telling them he only wore black.

The front page headlines all week had riveted people to the Tyson story: "Iron Mike KO'd in Crash," "Car Skid KO's Tyson," "Iron Mike Faces Brain Scan," "Tyson's Bout [vs. Bruno] KO'd," "Alone at the Top, Tortured Tyson Has Nowhere to Turn," "Tyson-Bruno Off, Doctor Says Champ Needs Time to Recover." But the New York *Daily News* headline on the morning of Wednesday, September 7, set off more reaction, controversy, claims and counterclaims than any Tyson had previously had in the three years since he first hit the news: "EXCLUSIVE: TYSON TRIED TO KILL SELF," said the paper's front page in two-inch bold black letters. The subheading said, "Friends Reveal Suicide Threat." The story, written by columnist Mike McAlary, was, to say the least, sensational. It claimed that on Sunday morning, Tyson, whose mind "was racing and tortured," called Givens in Manhattan and told her, "I'm going to go out and kill myself. . . . I'm going to crash my car." The story says Tyson then went to the BMW and hit the gas pedal without putting on his seat belt, and "aimed the car into a tree." McAlary presented an entire dossier of allegations, among them that the previous Thursday Tyson "had threatened to kill Givens," and that the next day, "according to . . . friends," two shotguns were delivered to Tyson. "I'll kill you and then me," McAlary reported Tyson as saying to Robin.

According to McAlary, when Givens arrived at the hospital upstate on Sunday afternoon, Tyson said to her, "I told you I'd do it . . . and as soon as I get out of here, I'll do it again." McAlary said for several weeks Roper and Givens had tried unsuccessfully to get Mike to see a New York psychiatrist, Dr. Henry McCurtis, who was the Director of Psychiatry at Harlem Hospital and who specialized in the treatment of athletes suffering from stress. While in the hospital, Tyson had at last spoken with Dr. McCurtis. Although the psychiatrist would not discuss Tyson with him, McAlary's "sources" told him that Dr. McCurtis believed "Mike Tyson should be committed for psychiatric evaluation." The reporter went on to reveal, "Only a small circle of people know what is said to be Tyson's problem, that he has a chemical imbalance that prods him to violent behavior. . . . As a child, the champ reportedly took medication for this affliction. But then he became a boxer and quit the medication. His old trainer, Cus D'Amato, believed that he could control Tyson by keeping him in the ring. But . . . evidently there is no controlling his demons. . . . The people with knowledge of Tyson's problems include Donald Trump and public relations man Howard Rubenstein. Tyson's lawyers—Peter Parcher and Steven Hayes—also understand the situation. . . . They are more interested in the fighter's future than his next fight." McAlary included Givens and Roper among those truly concerned for Tyson's well-being, painting Cayton and Rooney as money-grubbing and interested only in milking every last dollar from Tyson: "The nonfight people were trying to help the heavyweight champion of the world save his life. The second set—the fight people, Cayton and Rooney—were trying to save a meal ticket."

The writer further portrayed Givens as the long-suffering wife, saying she was "distraught" when she entered Mike's hospital room, while depicting Tyson as a monster. "The Tyson marriage that you see on television—the smiling pictures you see on gossip pages—is a lie. Mike Tyson, his friends and relatives say, is a wife-beater. They say he has learned to hit his wife with the bottom of his hand, boasting that this is a blow that when delivered correctly leaves no mark.

"The champion is also said to be big on choking," McAlary wrote. "He grabs Givens by the neck, friends say, and shakes her. . . . Mostly, Tyson curses his young wife. He does this in public. He also takes phone calls from girlfriends in front of his wife." McAlary then states that two months earlier Tyson and Givens had vacationed at Donald Trump's hotel on Paradise Island in the Bahamas. While there, Tyson got into a fight with both his wife and her friend, Lori McNeil, one of the premier professional women's tennis players, who was also at the hotel. "Tyson is reported to have smacked both women," said the sensational *Daily News* story. "According to friends of the couple," wrote McAlary, "Givens suffered a black eye and swollen jaw. She spent most of her vacation waiting for the bruises to clear."

Those who bought the *Daily News* that morning certainly got their money's worth. Tyson could not believe it when he saw the paper. He called Camille in Catskill and rhetorically asked her, "Who the hell said I was committing suicide?" Reaction was swift. Respected columnist and author Pete Hamill wrote: "I have only one response to this story. Bull." Pat Putnam, of *Sports Illustrated* magazine, wrote, "The story made for juicy reading, but there was a problem: It was a plant, and an artless, bubble-headed one at that." One by one, those who really knew Tyson reacted. Bobby Stewart said, "I dispensed the medication [at the Tryon school], probably most of them[the boys] were on medication at the time, something to slow them down. Mike was not on anything." Teddy Atlas said Mike was not on any medication while at Catskill, something he certainly would have known about as the fighter's trainer, friend and housemate. Kevin Rooney also confirmed this and called the story "bullshit." Bill Cayton termed the *Daily News* story "obviously a plant . . . outrageous . . . a pack of falsehoods and untruths . . . despicable lies." All those who knew Tyson treated the allegations of attempted suicide as a joke, pointing out that a person doesn't run a car thirty feet across a wet lawn into a tree if he's trying

With Robin Givens and Ruth Roper

to kill himself. As for McAlary's charge that Tyson wasn't wearing his seatbelt, it wasn't necessary—the BMW, as Mike well knew, was equipped with an inflatable bag safety feature in the front seat. The collision into the tree wasn't even of sufficient force to release the air bag!

Donald Trump was unavailable for comment. Award-winning sports columnist Jerry Izenberg wrote in the New York *Post* that the McAlary piece was "a calculatedly leaked story—apparently from one of the attorneys his wife's family chose for [Tyson] and he described the entire situation as "an emotional tug of war over [Tyson] in which the participants are engaged in a deadly game of media roulette with a bullet in every chamber. . . . With no place to hide, no place to think things out and no place for Mike Tyson to catch his breath . . . unless the heavyweight champion gets the one-on-one help he so desperately needs with absolutely nobody else involved, it is a story with a frighteningly predictable ending."

Tyson's sister went to visit him at the hospital the day the story appeared. She said Mike laughed about the suicide report and told her, "I wouldn't even know how to do it." In a telephone interview with sports reporter Carl White, Tyson said the story was "ridiculous. . . . They're trying to make a freak show out of my life, to say I would try to kill myself. Nobody has more, better reasons to live than I do. . . . No one loves living more than I do. . . . I have way too much butt to kick in the ring to try to kill myself out of the ring . . . why does my wife have to be a bad person? We're both basically good people. We're high-strung but we're basically good people." Tyson added, "I love my wife. I don't beat on my wife. I'm never going to leave my wife. My wife's never going to leave me."

On Friday night, September 30, much of the country sat transfixed as Mike Tyson, Robin Givens and Ruth Roper allowed the ABC News program "20/20" to come into their New Jersey mansion and put the young couple's personal life under the microscope of the television camera's lens. The interviewer was Barbara Walters, who had carved out a reputation for being able to secure hard-to-get interviews and make people reveal things about themselves they would not tell other interviewers. In this instance, Walters's skills at eliciting information were hardly necessary. Givens was ready and willing to air the dirty laundry for everyone to see. Walters, good friends with Donald Trump and thus able to get access to the Tyson family, was willing to provide Givens with the forum to discuss the family's personal problems.

Speaking with Walters individually, Ruth Roper said she had become a "surrogate mother" to Mike, that she loved him like a son, that she wasn't trying to control him or his money, but that "people who earn a living through Michael" found her close relationship with him intimidating. Walters then asked, "Like Bill Cayton?" to which Roper replied, "Yeah, like Bill Cayton, to be very direct." Don King's involvement as an instigator in the whole Tyson mess was never explored by Walters. In a separate interview taped with Cayton at his office and inserted in the program, Walters asked him whether he was concerned that if Tyson had to take psychiatric medication to control his emotions he might not be able to box. "If Mike Tyson needs medication," replied the manager, "I want him to take medication. Whether he boxes or not is of no great interest to me." "You make money from him," shot back Walters. "I have money," the millionaire Cayton pointed out to her. "I don't need Mike's money."

Walters did a one-to-one interview with Tyson, during which he told her, "I'm not a psychopath or a maniac or anything. . . . I've seen some doctors and I have a very slight illness that I had all my life, just being extremely hyper. . . . I'm a moody person by nature. . . . At times I raise hell, yeah, and I like to raise hell because that's basically my nature, coming from my background." Tyson denied the reports that he hit Robin. "My wife and I have arguments," he said. "I grab my wife and hold my wife, I shake my wife up, but I never struck my wife."

The interview with Tyson, which was taped several days before broadcast, had concluded when Givens, who did not participate, approached Barbara Walters and said to her, 'You're not getting the story straight." She volunteered to tell the truth, and so the camera rolled again, and with Mike at her side, without speaking up once to contradict her, Givens said of their marriage, "It's been torture. It's been pure hell. It's been worse than anything I could possibly imagine . . . every day has been some kind of battle, some kind of fight, with managers, with members of the family. . . . The fights with [Mike] make me wonder why I'm going through the other fights, the other battles. . . . He's got a side to him that's scary. Michael is intimidating, to say the least. . . . He gets out of control, throwing, screaming, he shakes, he pushes, he swings . . . and just recently I've become afraid, very very much afraid. . . . Michael is a manic-depressive. He is. That's just a fact. . . . The type of disease Michael has . . . it's something he's had for a very long time. It went untreated, therefore it got worse." Givens insisted, though, that she loved him, that he wasn't a bad guy, he had a sense of humor, he was smart and gentle.

Walters asked Givens about the lack of a prenuptial agreement. "Why should there be?" replied the actress. "There's a certain sense of idealism that comes with being young that I wouldn't trade for any-thing in the world. We got married to be together forever, not to play for divorce." At this point, Mike jumped in and said, "I do have many millions. My wife would just have to ask for it and she has everything I have. If she wants it right now, she could leave right now, take every-thing I have. Just leave . . . she has the power to do that. She's still here, she tolerates my shit, and I love my wife." Mike said he was aware his illness had to be "taken care of," but he said he was not taking the Lithium his doctor had prescribed because "I'm handling myself very well." Givens concluded her remarks by giving credit to her always-present mother. "I don't know what Mike Tyson would be without my mother, what we would be. She's been the glue that's kept us together . . . and I do come with a package, that's how I am. My mom, my sister." Robin expressed her concern that if she and her mother left Mike he would be alone: "He would have gotten so bad that I think maybe one day he would have been more deliberate [than the car accident of two weeks earlier] and killed himself, or hurt somebody else."

Privately, Tyson had told Camille Ewald while staying in Catskill the previous weekend he was not taking the Lithium because he didn't like what the pills did to him, how they made him feel sluggish and dopey. "I like the way I am, the way I used to feel," he told her, and ignored persisting calls from his doctor reminding him to take the mind-controlling drug. Dr. Gene Brody, Mike's physician, had said repeated blood tests he'd given Mike had never revealed any "chemical imbalances" in Tyson's system.

Both Tyson's friends and impartial observers were shocked in the wake of the televised interview. Bill Cayton said he did not believe Mike was a manic-depressive but was turned down by Ruth Roper when he asked if Mike could be seen by an independent doctor— alone. "I feel it's imperative that Mike have at least one other psychiatrist examine him," said Cayton. "What are they [Ruth and Robin] afraid of? That they'll be contradicted?" Tyson's friends said there was a concentrated effort on the part of the two women to cut Mike off from all those previously close to him. They said the women constantly changed the phone number at the house so no one could reach him. Camille Ewald said Mike was "an emotional captive" who had confided to her the previous weekend at her house that he was very unhappy with his marriage. Jose Torres said Mike was not a manic-depressive, but a confused young man who had been manipulated and brainwashed. "Ruth Roper is a dangerous woman," he said. "She has complete control over Tyson." Other friends termed the entire affair a "diabolical plot" against Mike and were shocked that he could sit quietly stroking his wife's neck while she aired all their private business, true or untrue, on national TV. They said Mike appeared to have been drugged, perhaps with a dose of Lithium, before the interview. They felt he had been humiliated by his wife and mother-in-law for their own self-serving ends.

Slowly, as the feedback filtered to him over the weekend and it dawned on him just what had taken place, Tyson grew enraged. He knew he had taken a prescribed combination of Thorazine and Lithium before Barbara Walters and her TV crew arrived at the house. On Sunday morning, Tyson's rage erupted. In an argument with Robin he picked up a sugar bowl and threw it across the room, smashing it. He then allegedly threw some chairs through the windows, while Givens ran to the phone to call Dr. McCurtis. While Mike continued his rampage, she and Ruth escaped from the house and drove to a nearby gas station, where they called their friend, Shelly Finkel, who had been at the house with Mike and the women the previous day, to celebrate Roper's birthday. They then telephoned the Bernardsville police, asking them to come to the house. When the police arrived, Givens and Roper returned. Dr. McCurtis phoned back and told the women to leave the house as soon as possible, advising them to arrange for emergency psychiatric evaluation for Mike. He also spoke to the police at the house and told them he was worried about the safety of Givens and Roper.

Tyson was calm when the police arrived, but became agitated again when Givens brought them into the house to show them the damage. He began to yell that he owned the house and everything in it, that it was none of anybody's business if he wanted to break his own things. Givens and Roper packed their bags, preparing to leave for Roper's apartment in Manhattan. When they left the house, Tyson came outside and began to confront them once again, and another shouting match developed. Tyson then turned his attention to the police, telling them in the language of the streets that he did not want them on his property. "Fuck you all," he shouted. "Fuck you cops, you scum. Get the fuck off the property, and fuck off." With that, he got into his Mercedes and drove off.

Givens did not file a formal complaint, so no arrest was made, but she did go into the Bernardsville police station and give a detailed seven-page statement about what had transpired, thus establishing an "on-the-record" account of the incident.

Meanwhile, Tyson arrived in Manhattan, trying to meet up with his fellow boxer and friend Mark Breland, who was managed by Finkel. He missed their rendezvous. Mike had telephoned his sister, Denise, and made her promise him that he would be buried next to their mother. She became concerned and called Bernardsville police, asking them to return to the house and break in if they got no answer. When they got to the house, however, Tyson's friend, Rory Holloway, answered the door and said that Mike had left. Tyson's bother, Rodney, speaking from Los Angeles, also expressed concern to Mike Katz of the *Daily News* about Mike, describing Ruth and Robin as "manipulative."

On Monday morning, Givens flew to Hollywood to resume taping her TV show. That same morning, October 3, something very unexpected happened. Mike Tyson paid a visit to his estranged manager, Bill Cayton, and his estranged friend, Steve Lott. He ran up the stairs to Cayton's private office and embraced his manager, the first thaw in their relationship since the death of Jim Jacobs nearly seven months earlier. He hugged Steve Lott as well, and they all sat down to talk. Mike was warm and outgoing. He told Cayton he was anxious to get back into the ring and fight. He didn't mention the previous day's incident at his home. Cayton said he would go ahead with plans to have Mike meet Frank Bruno in London on December 17. First, however, he wanted Mike to undergo complete neurological and psychiatric evaluations, just to be sure.

The next day Tyson was examined by Dr. Abraham Halpern, Clinical Professor of Psychiatry at New York Medical College, who gave him a clean bill of mental health. "I saw Mr. Tyson and, from a clinical standpoint, he showed no signs of a major mental disorder. Certainly there's no sign of a manic-depressive condition or psychosis," Halpern said, adding that he had spoken with Dr. McCurtis and that McCurtis had said he had never diagnosed Mike as being manic-depressive. "Dr. McCurtis spoke of a mood-regulatory disturbance," reported Dr. Halpern, "and that's a far cry from a major mental illness such as manic-depression." He said Dr. McCurtis had examined Mike once, but got most of the information about his behavior from Ruth and Robin. Mike had been put on the Lithium by Dr. McCurtis on "a trial basis" to "stabilize" his moods, a treatment Dr. Halpern termed "not unreasonable," although not necessary. "He needs to be goal-oriented again," Dr. Halpern said. "He wants to box, and the training would be most therapeutic right now." He did suggest Mike should see a psychotherapist, "somebody to talk to that he trusts to relieve his pressures," and added that Mike "misses his wife terribly and he loves her." If, indeed,

Dr. McCurtis had never diagnosed Mike as manic-depressive, then it was Givens and Roper who decided to use that term to describe Mike's condition. When the neurological experts confirmed Mike was showing no signs of injury from the car accident, Bill Cayton said "All systems are go" for the Bruno fight in December. Tyson flew to Detroit for the weekend to see Mark Breland fight. Then he would head for Catskill to begin training.

By now, although Mike was still obsessively attached to Robin, the people closest to him could hold their peace no longer. Jay Bright said the people "who know Michael and who genuinely care about him are disgusted by what they saw on that show. To see his wife emasculate him on national TV like that was offensive and vile." Camille Ewald said, "If that was my wife sitting next to me saying those things I would have choked her." And Ewald now had much more to say. Roper and Givens were angry with her because, like Cayton, she had wanted Mike to be examined by other doctors besides Dr. McCurtis. She now revealed that when Mike began earning large purses, Jim Jacobs had arranged for Camille to be paid house expenses by Mike, such as phone, electricity, repairs, taxes, an amount coming to thousands of dollars a year, nothing to Tyson, nor did Mike have any objections about taking care of the woman who had cared for him (and silently put up with, as he termed it, "my shit"). When Roper came on the scene, everything was paid through the company she formed, Mike Tyson Enterprises. Roper and Givens told Ewald they thought it was only fitting, since she was an old woman and Mike was paying the bills, that she should leave the house in Catskill to Mike in her will. To tighten the vise on Ewald, they stopped sending her expense checks. At one point, Kevin Rooney had to bail her out when her telephone was about to be disconnected for nonpayment by the phone company. "I don't think we should pay the bills," Roper told Ewald over the phone in September, "unless Mike will be inheriting the property." Ewald became angered with Roper when the mother-in-law asked why Mike was paying for the house upkeep and not Cus's other fighters, Jose Torres and Floyd Patterson. Ewald told her it was because Torres and Patterson never lived in that house. When he learned what was happening, Bill Cayton took over payment of the house bills.

Ewald also said Roper had refused to pay thousands of dollars in outstanding bills to the private limousine company that chauffeured Tyson, because the company refused to report back to her every place they drove Mike, every stop he made, who he went to see.

With Tyson willing and anxious to fight, Bill Cayton outlined a plan for him that in the space of twelve months would earn him $50 million gross. It would start in December with the scaled-down (due to the move indoors) purse of $6 million against Bruno in London; then in Rio, during Carnival in February, $9 million for an easy defense against Brazil's Adilson Rodriguez; in April, $5 or $6 million for a mandatory defense in the United States against number one IBF challenger Carl Williams; followed by a bout for perhaps $10 million in Milan's soccer stadium against Italian challenger Francesco Damiani in June; then would come The Big One, the next "super fight," late in the year, a closed-circuit and pay-per-view $20 million payday for Tyson against undefeated world cruiserweight champion Evander Holyfield. Tyson would finish the year in Japan, which desperately wanted him for another performance, against forty-one-year-old former heavyweight champion George Foreman. The only thing Bill Cayton had not taken into consideration, the one thing that would rend all these plans asunder, was the sudden reentry into Mike Tyson's life of Don King.

WHEN AN OGRE LOOKS FORLORN

from *McIlvanney on Boxing,* February 18, 1990

by

Hugh McIlvanney

The assassin's swagger with which Mike Tyson intimidated other men also served to keep his own demons at bay and now he knows it will never come as easily again.

Deep down in a private world that has always been filled with flitting shadows, is Tyson responding to humiliation in Tokyo with snarling defiance or does he realise that, even if the loss of his heavyweight championship to James 'Buster' Douglas is temporary, something more basic has gone forever?

The career of an ogre of the ring tends to be a one-way street with a cliff at the end of it. Sonny Liston and George Foreman were demythologised with startling suddenness, although George is currently doing an effective job of hoisting his ageing and overweight body back up the rock face to riches.

But Liston and Foreman were both undone by Muhammad Ali, who confronted them with the greatest arsenal of gifts the heavyweight division has ever seen. Tyson, at 23, had his dreams of invincibility pulverised by an opponent whose credentials suggested beforehand that he had the same chance as a trout being dropped into a bathtub with a hungry pike. If there is a Richter Scale for sporting earthquakes, what happened in Japan last Sunday would have to be considered two or three points clear of any other shock in twentieth-century boxing.

Don King's scandalous attempts to minimise the devastation could only exacerbate in the end the damage done to the principal victim, Mike Tyson. It was predictable that King would mount blustering protests about the length of time Douglas was on the canvas after he was left in a sprawling daze by a classic right uppercut from Tyson in the last seconds of the eighth round. The promoter tried to harry the notoriously malleable officials of the World Boxing Council and the World Boxing Association into accepting the monstrous contention that by failing to be precise in his counting the referee had permitted a knockout in the eighth which invalidated a total demolition of Tyson in the tenth.

Of course, the referee's voice is all a fallen fighter is obliged to heed and, in any case, the battered Tyson could not escape the raw truth of what he had been through. All the hustler's rhetoric from King did was draw a merciless bombardment of contempt and indignation from across the world and by the time he and Tyson turned up together at a press conference in New York on Tuesday they had no option but to acknowledge James Douglas as the legitimate, undisputed champion.

King's conciliatory tone in Manhattan had nothing to do with an uncharacteristic upsurge of decency. Looking for fair play from him is like asking a wolverine to use a napkin. The former racketeer's survival instincts had told him that he had gone too far, that even amid the incorrigibly sleazy standards which constantly prevail outside the ring in professional boxing his conduct was being exposed as despicable and he had better pull back from the brink—if only to protect his investment.

The investment sat alongside him, wearing dark glasses to conceal the left eye that had been blinded by an ugly ball of swelling for several rounds before Douglas completed his historic destruction in the tenth. There was good reason for Tyson to be subdued, almost plaintive, in the hotel next to Grand Central Station (all he wanted was the rematch, he insisted mildly, and then he would put everything right) but what many of us are anxious to know is why he was nearly as subdued from the moment he entered the ring in Japan.

As someone whose experience of the fight has been restricted to the

Buster Douglas defeats Tyson

two-dimensional testimony of a television screen, I have no right to over-vehement interpretations. But after hours with the video machine I am left with the bemusing impression that the Tokyo Dome housed a contest between two ringers. Maybe both men's fingerprints should have been taken before the start to confirm that they were who they purported to be.

James Douglas was certainly unrecognisable as the often dispirited journeyman who scuffled around the heavyweight division throughout the 1980s, incorporating serious blemishes into his record. Being stopped by David Bey, Tony Tucker and the spectacularly unfamous Mike White was bad enough but there was probably even more embarrassment in an eight-round draw with Steffan Tangstadt, a Norseman who could scarcely pillage a hairdressing salon. And in gathering these negative references, Douglas occasionally invited suspicion that his appetite for conflict was less than voracious.

Yet courage and commitment were outstanding among the array of pugilistic virtues he brought to his meeting with Tyson. One theory is that a tornado of tragedies that has swept through Douglas's personal life recently has given him a new perspective about the hardships of his business, convincing him that he had learned to cope with more desperate hurt than Mike Tyson could inflict on him. There is no doubt that he had become increasingly formidable in the run-up to his challenge, winning six fights in a row and five of them inside the distance, but his performance in Tokyo amounted to an almost miraculous raising of his game.

The 29-year-old from Columbus, Ohio, was a remarkable heavyweight last Sunday, big (16 ½ st and, at 6 ft 4 in, five inches taller than Tyson), fast, determined and skilful. Douglas did not just beat Tyson. He administered a terrible hiding, one that made the scoring of the American judge Larry Rozadilla (88 points to Douglas, 82 to Tyson at the end of the ninth) only the merest touch excessive and made that of his Japanese counterparts look like manifestations of dementia. Masakuzu Uchida had the scores level after nine and Ken Morita had Tyson one point ahead, which indicates that he would have given Pompeii the verdict over Vesuvius.

That Douglas was far ahead before landing the punches that ended the fight should not be disputed. The real question concerns the identity of the man he beat. My anxiety to give full credit to someone who tossed every dismissive prediction back in the forecasters' teeth cannot rid me of the conviction that the real Mike Tyson never showed up in Tokyo.

His face offered strangely soft lines instead of the usual sculpted menace and his body, too, lacked tautness. Where previously he had prowled through preliminaries with contained but vibrant truculence, here he looked simply morose. There was no ominous flexing of the neck and shoulder muscles, no hint of smouldering aggression in the eyes. He looked as if he might be sick and he fought that way, without fire or rhythm, devoid of the skipping liveliness that normally makes his footwork deceptively competent and the spontaneous adjustments of range and timing which make his fierce blows connect. Some of us have long been convinced that his squatness and limited reach would make him vulnerable one day to a tall, crisp-punching opponent of true quality (convinced that the young Ali for one would have outclassed him) but Tokyo was surely a misrepresentation of his own tremendous assets.

A pathetically amateurish corner did not help but mattered less than the debilitating influence of his private life and the rust encouraged by having just 93 seconds of ring action since the Bruno fight in February 1989. Most damaging of all, perhaps, has been his alliance with Don King, who has precipitated decay in practically every fighter with whom he has been associated. King gives no evidence of really believing in boxing, or in fighters come to that. His obsession with his own grotesque persona and with labyrinthine wheeling and dealing seems to make him a ruinous contagion.

If Tyson means to rehabilitate himself for the rematch with Douglas that could be contrived by paying Evander Holyfield to postpone the challenge he was due to present on 18 June in Atlantic City, he should start by distancing himself from King. But he may find that even more difficult than quietening the clamour of doubts that must now be raging in his head.

FROM THE INNER RING

1995

by

Rudy Gonzalez with Martin A. Feigenbaum

To the memory of Camille Ewald

There was one obstacle which Don King hadn't anticipated as the Tyson marriage travelled down its rocky but still intact road into mid-1988. A very big factor had been looming in the wings but now was definitely coming into the picture. Donald Trump was at the summit of fame and power. Atlantic City was booming, and its star was the larger-than-life New York developer known as "The Donald." The Taj Mahal, a huge palace casino, was the crowning jewel of his many well-known properties.

Donald Trump had been involved with HBO for some time putting together professional boxing matches in Atlantic City. Several had Mike Tyson on the heavyweight card, Tyrell Biggs on October 16, 1987, and in 1988, Larry Holmes on January 22 and Michael Spinks on June 27. The very powerful Donald Trump was getting too involved in the world of professional boxing for Don King's taste. And in that world, Mike Tyson was the biggest game in town. Robin Givens connected Tyson with the Trumps. She had been palling around with Ivana Trump for awhile. The Trumps became very chummy with the Tysons, eventually inviting them to spend an extended period of time on their 225' yacht, the *Trump Princess* which was tied up behind the Trump Regent Hotel.

Don King began searching for a wrench to throw into that disturbing Trump-Tyson friendship. And because he always saw the big picture, King also was looking for a way to eventually dump Givens and her mother. And what better weapon to employ for these tasks than the services of Mike Tyson's closest friends. He found those friends in Rory Holloway and John Home.

Bill Cayton had been keeping a wary eye on Holloway for some time. From the beginning, the training team and Tyson's co-managers made it clear to me that they believed Holloway was a bad influence and threat to their fighter's career. They knew Holloway took Tyson out for late night forays into the club scene. They also knew that Holloway ran with a bad crowd back in Albany. There wasn't much I could do except try and keep my boss out of trouble.

Tyson enjoyed visiting Holloway in Albany, and I must have taken him there several dozen times during the first two years I worked for him. I suspected that my boss liked the escape factor. When life's stresses got to him, Tyson liked to hit the road to upstate New York. Although his parents owned a small grocery store, Holloway wasn't doing much of anything when I met him. Tyson helped him out financially, sending him a weekly "paycheck." With this money, and by living with his parents, Rory Holloway drove a brand-new automobile and sported a Rolex watch. However, in the very near future, another source of funds would make Rory Holloway an overnight millionaire.

Like Robin Givens, Rory and I didn't get along very well either. Again, the feeling was mutual. Once, during May of 1988, MT wanted to fly out to Los Angeles to track down his wife. She was supposed to have returned to Bernardsville two days before after completing a shoot for *Head of the Class*. The studio hadn't been able to locate her, and MT was furious. Holloway already was in Los Angeles at the time and suggested he and Tyson hook up. I was chauffering them around in a rental limo which we had picked up at the airport. Holloway suggested that we head for The Comedy Club. When we arrived, MT told me to park the limo and come inside with them.

"Don't let that nigger come with us," Holloway protested. "What're you still doing with that stringy-haired motherfucker anyway? With all the niggers out there without a job, why you keep hanging around with that fool?"

Tyson got pissed at his friend. "Rory, don't tell me what to do! Rudy's been with me for a long time. Leave him alone."

Inside, as usual, I stood near MT, keeping an eye on things so he wouldn't be hassled. A tall, skinny black guy named John Horne came on stage to perform. He reminded me of Jimmy Walker from the TV comedy *Good Times* but, unlike Walker, Horne wasn't funny. Rory Holloway knew Horne from back in Albany, and Horne later had relocated to California. Although Holloway appeared "surprised" to run into his old friend at The Comedy Club, it was likely that Holloway already knew Horne would be there that night.

After his performance, Horne "realized" Holloway was at a table with Mike Tyson and hurried over.

"Hey, man!" he said, slapping Holloway's back, "What're you doing with Mike Tyson!"

They bullshitted for awhile, catching up on things. I could see the dollar signs flashing in Horne's eyes as he kept staring that evening at Tyson's gold jewelry and diamond Rolex watch. After awhile, Tyson was able to locate Givens, and we headed for a restaurant where she was waiting for him. Everything turned out very lovey, dovey that night between MT and his wife.

Tyson wanted to drive with his wife cross-country back to New Jersey. He had a black Ferrari Testarosa which had been sitting in an LA parking lot for months. As a married man, with his life now centralized in Bernardsville, he wanted to bring all his important possessions to the estate. Givens didn't like the idea of a long drive so Tyson told me to bring the Testarosa. Over a period of four days, I got a lot of curious and envious stares whenever I pulled in to fill up for gas along I-70.

One morning not long after that, Tyson was eating his daily bowl of Captain Crunch. The chef could be whipping up shrimp or lobster omlettes, but Tyson wouldn't even look at them until he first had his ritualistic bowl of "CK" without milk. MT mentioned that he would be driving into the City with Givens for the day and for me to just hang out at the Bernardsville estate. Soon after they departed, I got a page from Rory Holloway.

"Yo, Rudy, I need you to do me a personal favor. I want you to pick up a friend of mine and bring him to my place."

"Yeah, who is it?"

Holloway told me it was John Horne, and I thought to myself, "Oh, yeah, the comedian who's not funny." I knew Tyson would have wanted me to accomodate his close friend, so I agreed and left a note telling MT where I had gone. Holloway gave me instructions to go to Kennedy Airport. Horne was waiting for me, standing by the curb dressed in old jeans, sneakers, an LA Raiders t-shirt, and carrying a small duffel bag. When I pulled up in the $400,000 limousine, Horne's eyes bugged out. He literally was sniffing the rich leather seats during the drive to Albany.

After a four-hour drive, we pulled into the driveway of Rory Holloway's house. Holloway came out to greet us, hugging his buddy from California.

"Don't leave, Rudy. Give me a few minutes."

I was feeling anxious waiting around for these two after the long drive to Albany, especially because it was going to take me another four hours to return to Jersey. Tyson could reach me anytime through the Skypager, but I didn't like the idea of being pulled away from my regular duties. Finally, Holloway and Horne emerged from the house and jumped into the back of the limo.

"Take us to New York," said Holloway. "32 East 69th Street in Manhattan. And step on it. I need to get there fast."

I wasn't very happy about being told to make this additional trip, delaying further my return to Bernardsville.

"This is two tons of very expensive steel. I'll do my best."

"Just step on it, Rudy," Holloway said coldly.

MT didn't like reaching for buttons so he had installed a voice-activated intercom in his sound-proofed Rolls Royce limousine. Holloway and Horne didn't know about the system so I decided to get some revenge by eavesdropping on these two. They kept babbling excitedly about their meeting in the City, but I couldn't determine what it was about. They kept repeating that they "had to make it work."

We only stopped once during the trip, a rest stop on the highway, where my passengers grabbed some food at McDonald's. Then it was on to 32 East 69th Street between Madison and Park Avenues. We pulled up to a beautiful brownstone with two huge flags in front, one the stars and stripes, the other a crown with the name "Don." I realized

The Billion Dollar Hand

we had arrived at the offices of Don King Productions. Holloway told me to wait for them outside, and he and Horne entered the building. A few moments later a Rolls Royce sedan pulled up behind me. Don King, dressed in jeans and leather jacket, got out, his signature hair at attention, carrying a briefcase.

I waited there for three hours and watched the sun go down. I had been calling the mansion in Bernardsville repeatedly, but there was no answer. Because the estate was only forty minutes away, I was upset but not nervous as I was waiting around in upstate New York at Holloway's house.

I'll never forget the wide grins which Holloway and Horne were wearing when they finally descended the steps of Don King Productions. They piled into the limo, asked me to take them back to Albany, and quickly raised up the partition separating us. Now I was really pissed. I was looking at eight hours roundtrip before I would be back at Bernardsville. I thought about clearing this return trip first with MT. While I was considering what to do, I decided to again eavesdrop on my passengers by way of the voice-activated intercom.

"You believe that we just made the biggest deal in boxing history!" Horne was screaming. "We made it so fast and easy! Can you believe the nigger gave us one million in cash just to get the nigger to the table?" Horne kept squealing like an excited pig. "I can't believe it! I can't believe it!"

Holloway lowered the partition. "Where's Mike?"

When I told him that he probably was back in Jersey after a day of shopping in the City with Givens, Holloway ordered me to forget Albany and take them straight to Bernardsville. Then Holloway grabbed the phone in back and started trying to reach Tyson at the mansion. We arrived just as Tyson and Givens were unloading a large number of bags and packages.

Holloway ran over to MT. "Mike, Mike, we did it, we did it!" he said excitedly. They started walking toward the limo, Holloway hugging him and whispering in his ear.

"Mike, Mike!" Horne yelled, waving wildly at Tyson from inside the limo.

John Horne didn't know Mike Tyson at all, yet he was acting like he was an old friend. Horne noticed my expression.

"What are you looking at?"

"Nothing," I said. "What's the matter?"

Horne raised the partition as MT and Holloway approached.

"Why are you staying in the car?" Tyson asked me.

"Sir, there's somebody still inside."

"Who the fuck's in my limo?"

"It's John Horne, my boy from LA," Holloway beamed, shepherding Tyson into the back of the Rolls. "Take us to 221 East 62nd Street," he said.

I turned around to see what MT wanted me to do.

"Rudy, just drive the fucking car," Holloway snapped, raising the partition.

Because I didn't hear anything else, I started the limo and pulled out of the Bernardsville estate, heading toward Manhattan, noticing that Tyson had turned off the voice-activated intercom.

At 62nd Street between Second and Third Avenues, we pulled up to a striking four-story brownstone building with several security cameras. To my surprise, Don King opened the door. My passengers went inside while I waited for them to return. At about 10 p.m., I was standing next to the Rolls when a taxi pulled up behind me. Two men in suits carrying briefcases got out. They climbed the stairs to the front door and rang the bell. In a few moments, Don King answered and ushered them inside.

I don't know why but Don King glared over at me, with a look that gave me the chills, and then slammed the door. I had a feeling at that moment that there was something really wrong going on inside. Four hours later my three passengers left Don King's residence, and we headed back to Bernardsville. After that night, and until close to the end, Rory Holloway and John Horne stuck to Mike Tyson like he was their personal life-support equipment.

John Horne never returned to live in LA after that day I had picked him up at Kennedy Airport. He and Rory Holloway stayed in an apartment nearby and also with MT many times as houseguests. Whenever possible, they would hang out with MT until late into the night, then seek him out early the next morning. There was a very noticeable change in the conversations I started hearing on a daily basis around the Bernardsville mansion. Now it seemed like everything was a racial issue. Holloway and Horne began continuously pounding Mike Tyson with a "black rap." The white man, Bill Cayton, was using him and stealing his money. And his white trainers, Rooney, Lott, Baransky, didn't give the champion the same respect they would give to a white fighter. Instead, they treated him like a child and kept him on a very tight leash.

Holloway and Horne began cranking up another "rap" to lay on Mike Tyson. They started working to destroy his relationship with his TV actress wife. It wasn't clear at that time that their marriage would fail. The Tysons had become close to the Trumps, and MT seemed to enjoy this friendship, spending a good deal of time on the *Trump Princess* anchored at the marina. The more friends they shared, the better chance their marriage would have to survive. But Holloway and Horne were trying to get Tyson in a certain frame of mind: Robin Givens is taking your money while she's out sucking somebody else's dick.

These campaigns represented two very big gambles for Rory Holloway and John Horne. There had been, and still were, many white people intimately woven into Mike Tyson's human experience. Nobody had been more important to him than Cus D'Amato, except perhaps his own mother, Lorna, and his sister, Denise. And Tyson had great love for his adoptive mother, Camille Ewald, and great affection for his "brother" Jay Bright. Despite his fame and fortune, he had never turned his back on The White House in Catskill, New York. It was still his home, and the attic bedroom was still his bedroom, where he had many fond memories, where he spent hundreds of hours watching Jim Jacobs' collection of boxing films.

Even though the training team, Kevin Rooney, Steve Lott, and Matt Baransky, whom D'Amato had assembled to propel Mike Tyson to the summit of professional boxing, was very strict with him, he knew they cared about his welfare in every respect. Tyson had become very close to co-manager Jim Jacobs, a man who spent many hours counseling him after D'Amato's death. Although Tyson never developed that closeness with Bill Cayton, he was grateful to both of his co-managers for their careful and conservative management of his business affairs. And, of course, Mike Tyson was very much in love with Robin Givens, the girl of this young man's dreams, once believed beyond his reach, now permanently at his side.

But there was a method to the madness, this very big gamble by Rory Holloway and John Horne. And the method had been designed and patented by Don King.

Rory Holloway and John Horne were taking over so much by the early summer that they now ordered me to chauffeur them around. At the same time, there was a new and frequent visitor to the Bernardsville estate, Don King. Bill Cayton, aging and ailing, didn't know about this transformation in Mike Tyson's life.

Holloway and Horne used Givens' criticisms of Tyson's eating habits to their advantage, making fun of him for letting the bitch talk down to him. They also were aware that in front of him Givens would savor sumptuous meals prepared by the gourmet chef while he was relegated to the greaseless, tasteless foods prescribed for him while he was training. Kevin Rooney worked closely with the chef, ensuring that Tyson's caloric intake was carefully monitored. Tyson usually got very small portions of meats and vegetables, mostly turkey and carrots. It was no wonder MT wolfed down his food like an animal. He was always starving.

"Is this all you're getting?" I used to ask him at the beginning before I understood the dynamics of the training diet for a heavyweight fighter like Tyson.

"I know, shit! Can you fucking believe this Rudy?"

That's why he needed his Captain Crunch every day. His "CK" made him feel full, and his trainers wouldn't bother him about it, so he consumed it dry by the boxful.

One day, while Robin Givens was in Los Angeles filming *Head of the Class*, MT and I were driving around when he asked me to call Holloway on the cellular so they could catch a movie together. Holloway said he would meet Tyson at Victor's Cafe, a Cuban restaurant in Manhattan. I waited outside while Holloway and Horne sat with MT and had lunch. I could see them through the window, and they were laughing a lot. After awhile, they piled into the limo.

"You know, that bitch's doing you wrong, MT," Rory said. "She's sleeping around. Why you need her?"

"But I love her."

I could hear Holloway and Horne giggling and making fun of his response. They told him he was a fool, that she had to be sucking somebody else's dick because that was the reality of Hollywood. I had been noticing an evolution in MT's attitude ever since Holloway and Horne had been sticking to him like superglue. He was paying a lot more attention to their comments. Once they knew they had his ear, their comments about Robin Givens got increasingly vulgar. Tyson had assigned me to stay with Givens as much as possible, but I had never seen her flirting with anybody else or doing anything to raise my suspicions. As Holloway and Horne were well aware, if somebody tells you something *over and over* enough times, you're *eventually going to believe it*. That's the method used by all successful tyrants. Later I would learn that Don King, an enthusiastic student of the Nazi movement, particularly the propaganda techniques employed by Josef Goebbels, was the real force behind Horne and Holloway's constant bombardment of Tyson with these "raps."

It wasn't long before Horne and Holloway pulled out all the stops to make Tyson a single man again. They orchestrated things so that there always would be a lot of women hanging around whenever Robin Givens was out of town. And Ruth Roper was in the dark because she went everywhere with her daughter. So there came a point in time when Tyson "groupies" were just about anywhere Holloway and Horne could get away with it, if not in Bernardsville, then at least in the privacy of the limousine. While Holloway had Tyson on a nostalgia trip, back to their wild days in the Albany club scene, Horne became responsible for organizing group sex.

During the last three months of their marriage, things rapidly went downhill between the Tysons. There were times when Robin called the Bernardsville mansion from the set of *Head of the Class* and heard music blasting and girls screaming in the background. Givens would rant and rave to her husband about his wild partying while she was out of town. But after enough megadoses of the "rap" laid on MT by Horne and Holloway, his response to Robin Givens became standard: "I don't give a shit. I'll do what I want."

By the end of the summer of 1988, Don King's master game plan, instead of being a very big gamble, started looking like a sure thing. For several months, two forces independently had been hard at work to

The old team

achieve one of King's goals, the elimination of the Tyson tradition. First, Givens and Roper had been wearing down Mike Tyson with their "rap" about white people controlling his career and money, and they in fact already had secured certain concessions from Cayton. Second, Holloway and Horne followed them, incessantly bombarding Tyson with the same "rap."

Not long after Robin Givens had humiliated Mike Tyson and announced in Los Angeles that she was filing for divorce, he fired Kevin Rooney, the man whom Cus D'Amato hand-picked to oversee his training. Rooney tirelessly had worked to take the fighter to the top of his profession and also had tried to be a good friend along the way. In late November of 1988, Tyson had seen Rooney on TV where the trainer gave the impression that having Don King to deal with was going to be worse than Givens. The next day, Kevin Rooney, who didn't have a written contract, who had worked for years on the strength of a handshake, was out. Steve Lott, the second trainer, had been fired sometime before. And an official battle had broken out between Cayton and King, who was promoting Tyson fights without authority from Cayton. He was just doing it. Pieces of the Tyson tradition, a solid rock for a number of years, were falling to the ground.

Mike Tyson never mentioned to me that he was going to fire Kevin Rooney or anybody else. Whether he made these decisions or simply just communicated them, I really don't know. By this stage, his mind was so messed up by all the negative forces working around him that he "just didn't want to know anything." For a time he had been refusing to take calls from Rooney, Lott, and Cayton, the people upon whom he most needed to rely to protect his best interests. But he was too busy with his new life filled with intrigue provided by Rory Holloway and John Horne who had convinced him that his white intimates were doing him harm. Almost overnight, Mike Tyson was doing the exact opposite of what he had been doing when I first came aboard in May of 1987.

At the same time, the Horne-Holloway force had been firing numerous torpedoes, trying to sink the Tysons' marriage. It didn't take many. During those eight months, Givens and Roper pretty much already had sown the seeds of marital failure by their money-grubbing attitude and the disrespect they displayed toward Mike Tyson. Thus, another Don King goal was close at hand.

Emboldened by the way things were spinning out, Don King decided he safely could fire one of his own missiles and land a direct hit. Before she filed for divorce in Los Angeles, Robin Givens returned to Bernardsville with her mother. At that time, the Tysons still were close to Donald and Ivana Trump. "The Donald" invited the Tysons to spend an entire week aboard the *Trump Princess* so I chauffeured them, along with Holloway and Horne, to Atlantic City where we spent time on both the yacht and at Tyson's Ocean Club penthouse.

One afternoon, Givens went out shopping alone while we stayed in the penthouse watching television. Holloway and Horne also were there. Tyson was wearing his favorite white t-shirt that said "Iron-Man Mike" which he wouldn't part with no matter how ratty it had gotten over the years. One of my jobs was to make sure that the t-shirt was with us wherever we were travelling or training.

We got buzzed by security from downstairs that Don King had arrived and wanted to come up, and Tyson said it was okay. King said that he had a big promotion going on in Atlantic City that month and wanted Tyson to get involved and go to a press conference. But MT wasn't interested because he was going to spend time hanging out with the Trumps. The two couples had planned to take the *Trump Princess* to the Bahamas for a few days. Don King got wound up when Tyson refused to assist him with his program.

"Goddammit, Mike, you've got to do this! There's millions of dollars involved!"

Don King needed a lot of hype for the upcoming fight, and getting Mike Tyson in front of the cameras would ensure there was plenty. But Tyson held firm, he just wasn't interested because it wasn't one of his fights. King's demeanor and voice changed from irritation to rage.

"I'm tired of your shit with Trump!" King boomed. "Goddammit, Mike, while you're out with Trump on the boat, why don't you ask him why he's *fucking* your wife!"

With that, Don King stormed out of the penthouse apartment. Tyson had the remote in his hand and suddenly threw it violently against the fifty-inch screen, breaking the control. I got scared because I had never seen MT vent his anger like that, except in the ring. The mere thought that his wife was having sex with "The Donald" was unbearable for him. I went to the kitchen to get out of the way. The manner in which Don King had blurted this thing out about Donald Trump and Robin Givens made it sound very believable. Tyson headed for the master bedroom and slammed the door. Fifteen minutes later, Robin sauntered into the penthouse carrying several bags from her shopping trip.

"Mike, I'm home!" she announced.

A few moments later I heard a big smack. As I raced out of the kitchen, I saw Givens on the ground, packages all over the floor. Tyson had let fly an open-handed left to the cheek. MT then stormed out of the apartment just as the maid came in. We tried to help Robin up, but she was dazed, her face still glowing from the smack. When she got to her feet, she started after MT, trying to catch him before he descended in the express elevator. Unable to reach him in time, she came back sobbing and very upset. I tried to explain what had happened, but she didn't want to hear from anybody. When Ruth Roper walked in, Givens screamed to her mother that "I'm not going to take it anymore!" and "This is it!"

John Horne appeared and asked me if I knew where MT had gone.

"If I know him, he's heading for New York."

"Get the limo!" Horne ordered. "You're taking me and Don King to New York."

I got dressed and pulled the Rolls Royce limousine out of the garage to pick up my passengers. Just then, MT pulled up in the red Lamborghini Countach. I got out to see how he was doing.

"Where you goin' with my limo?" Tyson demanded to know.

When I told him, he ordered me to return it to the garage. "You and me are going to New York in the Countach."

Tyson went inside the Ocean Club to use the bathroom. I got behind the wheel of the Lamborghini and waited for him. Moments later Don King and John Horne appeared at the front door. When they saw me, they started screaming because I didn't have the limo ready for them. Just then, Tyson returned from his trip to the bathroom.

"Don't you yell at him!" MT shouted, jabbing a finger in their direction. "Get your own fucking drivers!"

We left King and Horne in front of the Ocean Club, jumping up and down and yelling like a couple of spoiled brats who didn't get their way, and hit the street in the direction of the Jersey Turnpike. After a few minutes, MT changed his mind and told me to head for the Bernardsville estate instead of the City, put on the headphones to his Walkman, closed his eyes, and listened to rap music the entire trip. After we reached the mansion, MT raced upstairs and went on a terrible rampage, breaking furniture and smashing paintings. He also tore up a lot of Robin's clothes. I begged him to stop, but it was no use so I went downstairs and told the staff to leave our boss to himself. After about an hour I didn't hear anything so I went back up to assess the situation. Like I had seen so many times before, Mike Tyson was asleep, not on the bed, but leaning against its side. I covered him up, and he slept through the night.

The next morning, Robin Givens arrived accompanied by Rory Holloway and John Horne. She went upstairs while Holloway and Horne took me aside.

"You work for Don King, not MT," Holloway told me.

"You shouldn't have left us in the street, motherfucker," Horne added.

I tried to hide my intense dislike for these two assholes and said calmly, "I'm confused. I thought Bill Cayton is MT's manager."

Holloway hesitated, then said: "Yeah, whatever."

The next thing that happened was that we heard furniture being tossed out of the master-bedroom window. Robin already had called 911, reporting domestic violence. Soon the local police showed up. They interviewed Tyson who by that time was calm and rational. Because there was no need to arrest him, the patrolmen left as quickly as they had come. Soon after that, Givens descended the staircase with two bags and asked me to take her to Kennedy Airport so she could catch a flight to LA. John Horne jumped in and said he would take her because he had to go to New York anyway. A few days later, Marvin Mitchelson, Robin Givens' attorney, made the announcement that divorce papers had been filed.

Robin Givens left a huge wake of doubt and insecurity behind her when she stormed out of the Bernardsville mansion, and Mike Tyson's life, forever in early October of 1988. The year had started off with great promise for Tyson's personal life. He had the girl of his dreams permanently at his side, and there would be a baby, making them a true family. By June, he knew the joyful sounds of a newborn would not be filling their cavernous home. And his dream girl, while she had taken huge sums of his money, had openly disrespected him and his friends and, worse, had been "doing The Donald," a rich and famous white guy whom Tyson thought he could trust. Now, as the year came to a close, more darkness fell over Mike Tyson's life from which he still has not seen day.

Mike Tyson's life video was turning into a blockbuster movie with a happy ending. But as Don King watched this videotape, he wasn't seeing *It's A Wonderful Life* but rather *Nightmare On 69th Street*, the street where Don King Productions was located. Mike Tyson, managed by Jim Jacobs and Bill Cayton, had been a thorn in DKP for almost two years, knocking out all of its fighters and capturing the unified heavyweight crown. For Don King, the man who supposedly controlled the world of professional boxing, a world where fabulous sums of money were to be made overnight, not controlling Mike Tyson was excruciatingly unbearable and totally unacceptable.

Don King finally saw the opportunity in 1988 to press the rewind button on the video and erase and record over key portions of the Mike Tyson life experience. By manipulating Givens and Roper, and by employing mercenaries Holloway and Horne, Don King was able to

November 22, 1986

retitle and rewrite the script. The new screenplay was "Team Tyson," replacing the previous title, "The Tyson Tradition." The original cast, Cus D'Amato, Camille Ewald, Jay Bright, Jim Jacobs, Bill Cayton, Kevin Rooney, Steve Lott, and Matt Baransky, all were to be eliminated. Now there would be only the following main characters listed in order of importance: Don King, Don King Productions, Don King's family, John Horne and Rory Holloway. It wasn't going to be "lights, camera, action" at the filming of "Team Tyson." There were no lights in this Don King "production" as the plot revolved around a foolish and deceitful "rap" designed to keep Mike Tyson in the dark about the most important things in his life.

After John Horne wedged his way into Tyson's life, he utilized Holloway and his long-standing friendship with MT to convince him that "Daddy King" was the saviour. In fact, Don King arranged for a very downcast and lonely Mike Tyson to be baptized in Cleveland, Ohio at the Holy Trinity Baptist Church. The baptism took place on November 27, 1988, presided over by the Reverend Henry Payden, with the assistance of the Reverend Jesse Jackson, while Tyson's new "father figure" proudly looked on. A few days after the ceremony, Mike Tyson fired Kevin Rooney.

Meanwhile, Horne was relentless, rapping constantly to MT that the white man was "evil," and that "you're a nigger, and you've got to hang out with niggers. Let's rock the world because we're a bunch of bad-ass niggers who don't need the white man. We're not going let the white man get away with enslaving us again." This was classic *The World According To Don King*. King knew, valued, and employed the fundamental technique used by the Nazi propaganda machine: *if you repeat something to the masses enough times, they eventually will believe it and act upon it*. In a *New York Daily News* article, former world heavyweight champion Larry Holmes said of Don King: "He treated me like a sucker, but I respect him for getting away with it. You know he's the best. He sells black. Don King is the black KKK, a black supremacist."

John Horne and Rory Holloway filled a huge, gaping hole in Mike Tyson's existence after Robin Givens packed up and left, his dream girl and dream life gone in a flash. He couldn't understand how the marriage could get so messed up so quickly. As a married man, his social life had seemed more fulfilling. After the divorce, MT often would walk around the Bernardsville mansion by himself, dazed, confused, lonely, and vulnerable. In this condition, and without benefit of effective assistance of his counsel, D'Amato, Jacobs, or Rooney, much of this silly "rap" started to make sense to him. It was a perfect time to start rolling the cameras for the first scene in "Team Tyson." And it didn't involve discipline and training. These no longer were priorities, and in fact were excused by the end of 1988. Tyson was convinced by those around him that there was no real threat to his crown. While Don King battled with Bill Cayton for control of the fighter, Horne and Holloway replugged Tyson into "the street" where crime and violence were glorified. They weren't just doing the regular club scene and staying out all night. Rather, they started getting Tyson to hang out with a "gangsta'-rap" crowd in New York and Los Angeles. Horne and Holloway goaded their famous friend to demonstrate just how "bad" he was wherever they went, resulting in a lot of negative press for Mike Tyson.

Part of the plan orchestrated by Don King was to distance Tyson from long-standing friendships which included people from all races, nationalities, and religions. Horne and Holloway constantly were telling him that his old friends "just wanted his money." Soon, King, Horne, and Holloway were convinced they had gotten Mike Tyson just where they wanted him. If Mike Tyson could turn his back on Kevin Rooney, he could turn his back on anybody. Sadly, Tyson began pushing Camille Ewald, his "mother," out of his life. He stopped making frequent visits to his old home in Catskill. The times we did go back to The White House, Tyson would run up to Camille, give her giant bear hugs, sweep her off the ground, and swing her around. "Put me down, Michael!" she would protest because she already was in her eighties and could easily be broken into pieces by Tyson. But Camille loved this powerful show of affection and acted like a little girl whenever she saw MT pulling into the long driveway of The White House.

After greeting Camille, MT would check up on his five dogs, among which were three "royal blood" shar-peis, gifts from the Japanese emperor. Tyson didn't like small dogs, but these were Camille's favorites. And then there were the several hundred pigeons of all types, fliers, tumblers, homing, long-haired. Tyson would walk into the pigeon coop before entering the house. Another ritual was to make sure to bring Camille the famous cheesecake from Junior's bakery on Atlantic Avenue in Brooklyn. I remember how she used to fawn over MT around the clock whenever he spent time back in Catskill. If Tyson were laying on the couch, she would put a pillow under his head. Camille loved cooking meals for a big crowd. She also had a thing about making real hot chocolate, the kind from thick bars. Many times it gave Tyson a bad case of diarrhea, but he never let her know.

When we stayed at The White House, I would notice that there was a daily ritual. Camille and MT would disappear into the den which she had maintained exactly like Cus D'Amato had left it the day he died. They would close the door and speak privately for about an hour, not to be disturbed under any circumstances. They would talk about Cus' advice to Tyson over the years and about what was going on with his life these days. And there was another constant topic, Camille's criticism of MT's constant speeding and growing collection of traffic tickets. She found out that he had gotten two tickets in one night and had to do some community service, going around to Catskill-area schools, lecturing about the dangers of speeding. These same students later would see us outside with the twelve-cylinder five-hundred horsepower Lamborghini, giving us looks of "yeah, right."

"You're going to kill yourselves," she used to warn us. "Why don't you buy normal looking cars?"

Tyson wanted Camille to learn how to drive so she wouldn't be so dependent on others. He told me to teach her how to drive, and she finally did obtain a license. Then Tyson bought her a white Range Rover.

Camille Ewald had a talent for bringing out the "son" in Mike Tyson. Even though he could have bought the local hotel, MT always stayed in his small attic bedroom where he had spent hundreds of hours watching fight films, the screen a sheet tacked to the wall, of some of history's greatest, Dempsey, Marciano, Johnson, Louis. Many of Tyson's techniques, such as the "peek-a-boo" style, were harvested from the wealth contained in these films.

For a brief time after the divorce, before Tyson almost completely turned his back on her, Camille tried to help him heal from the tremendous hurt he was feeling. But his confidence shaken by his failed marriage to a beautiful actress, Tyson started devoting his time exclusively to "gang bangers," street girls from the hood. Horne and Holloway never let Tyson forget that Givens and Trump were out of his league and had treated him as such. I remember the time when MT had the chef hide a tennis bracelet, studded with very large diamonds, in an omlette which Tyson served his wife in the master bedroom. Horne and Holloway got their "friend" into a mentality where romance was for pussies. Tyson was on an emotional rollercoaster, and he began acting very badly toward a lot of people about whom he used to care. He also started showing signs for the first time of losing interest in his career.

Mike Tyson consistently had been fair to me, probably because I had continued to be very professional, respectful and courteous, and always kept my distance. I never acted like I was a part of his inner-circle. Perhaps if I had started calling him "Mike," he would have fired me, but I still was calling him "sir." Meanwhile, Horne and Holloway continued to treat me like shit. They tried everything they could think of to get MT to fire me, but it was one of the very few things they never could accomplish. This made them hate me even more. In fact, Tyson kept adding to my responsibilities and duties after Robin Givens left,

123

depending on me more and more to keep his life organized. He trusted me and knew I got results. I now was taking all his phone calls, managing the staff, and scheduling his private appointments and public appearances. He also relied on my judgment in selecting his wardrobe.

The next match was on February 25, 1989, against Great Britain's Frank Bruno at the Las Vegas Hilton. It was my first trip to the neon city. Tyson's corner had new people. By now, Rooney, Lott, and Baransky were gone, and Aaron Snowell was the new first trainer. It was obvious that it was not the same Mike Tyson who entered the ring that night. In the first round, Bruno connected with two hooks which made MT stagger. Although by the fifth round he had disposed of Bruno, it was obvious that his lack of training was taking its toll. His performance was sloppy, failing to effectively employ his trademark techniques which had made him heavyweight champion, patience, cunning, rapid side-to-side moves, and rapid combination strikes.

When we returned to the East, Mike Tyson didn't want to continue living at the Bernardsville estate. He wanted to remove every item from the mansion because they reminded him of his failed marriage. He wanted to strip the mansion bare, leaving it an empty shell, much like his life was at that time. Robin Givens was notified and made arrangements to pick up a number of things. I sent the balance to storage.

As his chauffeur, waiting hours for him as he used to stroll aimlessly around the empty mansion, I probably was the only person to know how much Tyson continued to suffer deep inside. He always had been in love with Robin Givens and blamed himself for many of the problems leading to the breakup of his marriage. Mike Tyson was the heavyweight champion of the world, undefeated in thirty-six professional bouts, but he had lost the battle to keep his first marriage together.

The Ocean Club in Atlantic City again became our home base. Tyson wasn't training during this time, the next fight, against Carl Williams, not scheduled until mid-summer. With Kevin Rooney out of the picture, no time was being spent polishing Tyson's techniques. My boss still would run in the morning, but there was nobody coaching him. Mike Tyson had become his own trainer.

What *was* getting a thorough workout during this period was Tyson's social life. With Horne and Holloway around all the time serving as cheerleaders, Tyson started partying around the clock. To avoid the risk of another deep wound, like the one he had suffered with Robin Givens, Tyson now was seeking only brief encounters with women, not romantic relationships. The club scene provided a revolving door for sex, picking up women and doing the *wild thing*, gang-banging in the back of the limo, then dropping the girls off back at the clubs. I soon realized that John Horne never took advantage of the plentiful pussy passing through the rear of the limo. However, Tyson pal Eddie Murphy frequently would join up with Tyson to hit the club scene and participate in the gang-banging. I once risked asking Murphy for his autograph which I was going to give to my mother who adored him. I should have known better because he never yet had acknowledged my existence. "Hey, don't bother me with that shit, man," he said, pushing the paper out of my hand. After that night, I never again have asked a celebrity for an autograph, nor have I ever wanted to be photographed with one.

As we headed into the summer of 1989, it was unclear who officially controlled the career of Mike Tyson, Don King or Bill Cayton. The Carl "Truth" Williams fight was coming up on July 21 at the Atlantic City Convention Center. This was going to be the second and only other fight of 1989. There literally were both Cayton and King people in Tyson's corner that night when Tyson knocked out the "Truth" in the first round.

Tyson really wasn't interested in getting involved. He really didn't care to know anything about Don King or Bill Cayton, or anyone for that matter, at this point. To him every thing already had turned into bullshit a long time ago. As far as he was concerned, he wasn't going to do anything until taking on the number one contender, Evander Holyfield. His thinking was: "Fuck it. I'll just hang out for awhile."

After the Williams fight, Mike Tyson wanted a change. He spent a lot peaceful time with friends from his old neighborhood. On Christmas Eve of that year, I took him to the house of that close childhood friend from Brownsville known as "Ouie." When we first arrived at Ouie's house, as usual I remained outside with the limo. Apparently, MT still was so preoccupied with everything that was going on around him, and so relieved that again he was going to spend time with an old friend, that he forgot I was outside waiting for further instructions. I remained there for three days.

Sitting by the fireplace with Ouie, MT travelled back to the old days and, in so doing, found a brief refuge from the darkness of "The Kingdom." They didn't talk about money or contracts or upcoming fights, and they didn't do the club scene. A lot of family and friends stopped by, it seemed sometimes by the busloads, during this time at Ouie's. Tyson enjoyed visiting with everybody and playing with the kids. He felt comfortable in this atmosphere, really chilling for the first time since I could remember.

For awhile we didn't hear anything from Don King or John Horne. They were busy in Japan trying to promote a fight between Tyson and James "Buster" Douglas. On the third day of waiting for MT to emerge from Ouie's house, I got paged by John Horne. He and Don King were back in the City and wanted to speak with Mike Tyson. I went up to the front door and knocked. Ouie answered and I told him about the page. A couple of minutes later, Tyson appeared at the door.

"Shit, Rudy! You've been sittin' here for three days in the fucking car?"

"Sir, Don King and John Horne are looking for you."

"I don't want to talk to them. Say you don't know where I'm at."

I called Horne back and asked for a number where they'd be at so that, in case I reached MT, he could call them. Horne gave me the number for the cellular phone in Don King's limousine. After awhile, Horne called Tyson's own cellular phone. MT handed it to me. He was worried that they were going to track him down at Ouie's place. Therefore, I related to Horne that we were on the road near a certain exit of the Long Island Expressway, sending him on a wild goose chase away from Ouie's house. However, Tyson still was worried that they eventually would show up.

"Shit, man, I've gotta' get outta' here," he said, pulling on some clothes.

As we sped along the Expressway back toward the City, Don King's limousine passed us, then dropped back. A few seconds later, the car phone rang.

"Goddammit, Rudy!" John Horne screamed. "You better stop that limo!"

"Don't stop, Rudy!" Tyson shouted. "Keep going!"

I accelerated but King's limousine, headlights annoyingly flashing at us, was bearing down hard.

"What do I do, sir?"

"Lose them!"

I jumped the limo onto an embankment and hung a u-turn, almost flipping the limo over. Now we were headed east back toward Long Island. I looked over and saw King's limo still heading west. Don King had his head stuck out of the window, his hair spiked straight up like a porcupine, shaking a fist angrily at me. The car phone and my beeper went off simultaneously, MT laughing uncontrollably in the back. I wondered what would have happened if I had wrecked this expensive automobile. After a dozen rings, Tyson finally answered the phone.

"What, Don, what? Fuck, no, I'm not going to Japan. I'm fighting Holyfield!"

Mike Tyson was supposed to fight the premier challenger, Evander Holyfield, in Vancouver, British Columbia in two months. But the Buster Douglas fight Don King was promoting in Japan would make DKP a lot of money. For Mike Tyson, earning a few million more wasn't a priority. He already had wealth. Tyson wanted to fight and defeat the number one contender as soon as possible because that's what a champion was *supposed* to do. He hung up on Don King.

"Don't answer the fucking phone no more. Take me to the the apartment in the City."

As I waited in front of the Marlborough House at 245 East 40th Street in Manhattan, I wondered how the rest of the night was going to shake out. It wasn't long before Don King's limo pulled up, and King and John Horne jumped out.

"You're fired!" King shouted at me. "And your games are over, motherfucker!" He turned to Horne. "Take the keys from the limo and throw that motherfucker out!"

I locked the doors before Horne could reach me. He started banging on the windows, screaming "Open the fucking door, give me the fucking keys!" I sat there listening to the radio and ignored him. Horne finally gave up and went inside the building. About two hours later, MT, King, and Horne came outside. Tyson got into the limo.

"We're going to fucking Japan," he told me. "So we've gotta get ready."

Tyson had been transformed in this short time, becoming submissive to the wishes of King and Horne. It was as if they held some special power or control over him which could take away his will to resist whatever they wanted him to do.

I drove back to Bernardsville where MT wanted to pick up a few items that remained there, including luggage and a steamer trunk which had belonged to Robin Givens. Then Tyson told me to head for the Catskills for one of the few visits he made to The White House after things started going badly. We stayed there for three days, then made the trip back to Manhattan. We arrived at DKP on East 69th Street and the darkness of The Kingdom.

Having come down with a severe case of the flu running around the Catskills, I stayed in the City while Team Tyson took off for Japan to participate in promotions and to train for the February 11, 1990, Buster Douglas fight at the Tokyo Dome. After I had chauffeured everybody to the airport, I went to see my mother. It was the first time I really had spent any time with her since May of 1987 when I went to work full-time for Mike Tyson. Sometimes I would be only a few blocks away from her building in Spanish Harlem, but working for Mike Tyson was a twenty-four-hour job. I never wanted to violate Tyson's trust by doing personal things. I would call her a lot and always say: "Mom, I'll see you soon." By now my father had been released from Sing Sing and was back living with my Mom. So I was able to spend a couple of weeks with them both. I had been to see my Dad a few times, usually taking one of my girlfriends along who thought it was "cool" to visit a big prison like Sing Sing and to have a father who was a convicted drug dealer doing hard time.

When Tyson called from Tokyo, he told me that I could use his apartment at the Marlborough House. I recovered from my flu very quickly, put the limo in the garage, and pulled out the black Ferrari. Tyson also owned a rare Lamborghini "jeep," originally built for the King of Saudi Arabia. It had a 200-gallon fuel tank, was bullet-proof, and had room for four passengers and six bodyguards. It was designed to do 200 m.p.h. over the desert. Made of $\frac{3}{4}$" steel, it was so heavy it couldn't be towed. Sometimes I would drive that "jeep" around the City if there was a lot of snow on the ground. It was such an unusual and exotic vehicle that the "jeep" once had been loaned to the crew filming an episode of *Miami Vice*. These two weeks before I joined Tyson in Japan was going to be my first vacation in three years. By now

I was a "celebrity" in my old neighborhood, and I enjoyed being a "big shot" for a few days, cruising around town in the Ferrari with my old buddies.

Don King was milking the Japan trip for every penny he could get, having organized each day of Mike Tyson's schedule for the purpose of raking in the bucks. It didn't matter that the hectic pace wasn't in Tyson's best career interests. Somebody said King was going to haul in $100 million during this Japanese promotional tour. King had Tyson running all over the country, and by the time I got there, my boss was exhausted. Everywhere MT and his crew went there were multitudes of people taking pictures. Tyson was used to locking himself inside the gym in preparation for a fight. This wasn't possible anymore now that Don King had taken over. Rather, Tyson's workouts in Japan had become public spectacles. With all the curious onlookers everywhere we went and trained, I felt like we were in some kind of "freak show." We had been to Japan before, the Tony Tubbs match on March 21, 1988, but MT had trained in the States and only spent a short time away from our home base before the fight. Now, Tyson was spending more than a month before the Douglas fight doing promotions to make DKP a ton of money. As consolation, whenever there was free time at the hotel, MT was banging geisha girls.

Adding to the problems was the matter of diet. Tyson was having some very real problems with the local food. He was having frequent bouts of diarrhea, and his weight was fluctuating a lot. Our hosts were very gracious and eager to please, but it was made known to Tyson that refusing to eat dishes offered to him during the promotions would be considered an insult to the Japanese. Once we were eating a particular dish and later found out it was rattlesnake. Tyson also ate some blow-fish which made him very sick. When he once requested a bowl of fried rice, he was served beautifully-sculpted but very tiny cubes.

"We're gonna die of hunger," I used to say after too many "displays" like this. On this issue, I didn't feel like keeping my mouth shut. We started checking out the local American fast food, like McDonald's, but it didn't taste like anything we were used to back in the States.

Unable to take it any longer, and with the fight still weeks away, one day MT said: "Man get me Chef Early. I need some crunchy fried chicken, potatoes, and grits."

The next day, the tall, distinguished black chef arrived with a large supply of chicken, ribs, and steaks. Tyson was delighted to see his "James Brown-of-soul-food" cook. Chef Early had been hired by Tyson when his predecessor didn't cooperate about having enough Captain Crunch on hand. With that in mind, his first day on board Chef Early brought with him a hugh supply of the cereal. Tyson always used to say: "Where's my CK man, gotta' have my CK." We used to fight over the prizes in the cereal boxes. Sometimes me and Anthony would steal them before our boss got to the table, and he would hunt us down to get them back.

Chef Early wanted to use the facilities in our Tokyo hotel. Apparently, this was an insult to the hotel's chefs, causing a big stir. After negotiations were conducted, and apologies duly tendered, the Japanese conditionally surrendered. The kitchen was handed over to Chef Early as long he agreed to teach them the art of soul-food cooking. This was so they would be ready to better serve the famous fighter the next time he came to Japan. We ate like kings once Chef Early got things going in the kitchen.

It was in Japan that Mike Tyson learned about the benefits of aged ginseng root. We went to a farm where high-quality product was available, and MT spent $5,000 for some very old ginseng root. Apparently, it made you burn calories faster, and it sure made MT sweat a lot. Ginseng root also supposedly detoxified the system in the process. After he drank a tea made from dissolving the root in boiling water, Tyson pissed black with a very funky smelly-feet odor. But he also felt very good afterwards. When we got back from Japan, Tyson continued to purchase aged ginseng root and drank three cups of the tea each day.

It was getting close to the match date, and Tyson still hadn't gotten into a real fight-training mode. All the training so far had been to play to the cameras. Don King kept assuring the undefeated champion that there was nothing to worry about. Douglas was a bum who couldn't possibly beat the world champ. The odds-makers had it made a whopping 42-1 long shot. Tyson kept insisting that he should be fighting the only real contender, Evander Holyfield. He wanted to dispose of Holyfield as soon as possible. And Don King kept trying to convince him that Holyfield wasn't a *contender*. Holyfield *wasn't* a contender because he was controlled by Dan Duva and *not* Don King. As DKP kept revving up the jampacked promotional pace in Japan, Tyson started shifting his interest away from the Douglas fight and in the direction of getting more blowjobs.

Whether on a level playing field on February 11, 1990, Buster Douglas was a real contender against Tyson will never be known because two days before the fight the field tilted. Buster Douglas' mother, Lula, had died a few days before. And the mother of his young son had just learned she had a life-threatening kidney disease. While Tyson was cavorting around Japan for weeks with Don King, his image spread every day all over the TV and press, Buster Douglas had been training back in the States. Now, as he readied for the fight, Douglas, sitting in a Tokyo hotel, was a very lonely man with a one-way-ticket to nowhere. Nobody even had cared to photograph the challenger at his weigh-in the day before the fight. Oscar de la Hoya had surprised the boxing world when he won a gold medal. He had promised his own mother he would put a gold medal around her tombstone. A hungry man has an advantage over a man with a full stomach.

Unexpected things began happening right from the first bell. Douglas started landing rights on Tyson like nobody ever had witnessed before. At the end of the second round, Douglas hit Tyson with a hard uppercut to the chin. Tyson recovered ground in the third with a big left body punch. Douglas wasn't shaken because he soon wobbled the champ with a chopping right, causing Tyson's left eye to begin swelling. In the eighth, Tyson landed one of his classic uppercuts which knocked Douglas to the canvas with six seconds left in the round. The referee, Octavio Meyran Sanchez, started counting two beats behind the knockdown timekeeper. Keeping his attention on Meyran's hands, as he was supposed to do, Douglas waited until the nine-count before he rose. The bell then ended the round. This was going to cause one of the biggest controversies in boxing history at the end of the match.

In the next round, Douglas pushed Tyson into the ropes and landed four big punches. Tyson was shaken, his head flopping backward, his left eye completely closing. At 1:23 into the tenth, Douglas hit Tyson with a right uppercut, two more punches, then a chopping left hook which dispatched the champion to the floor. Never having been knocked down in his professional career, Tyson stretched out his right glove and swept it along the canvas. Finding his mouthpiece, he was so dazed that he put it in backwards, and struggled to his feet, falling into Meyran's arms. The fight was over.

This was a hugh disaster for Don King. Suddenly, he no longer controlled the heavyweight champion of the world. This meant that the eventual pay-per-view match with Evander Holyfield, worth an estimated $70 million, wasn't going to happen according to plan. Now the championship fight would be between Holyfield and Douglas, two non-champs. By being greedy, first wanting to reap millions by promoting Tyson in Japan for weeks without training him properly and then putting him up against a non-contender, Don King inadvertently had dethroned his heavyweight meal-ticket and bushwhacked his own biggest payday yet. King had to mount an immediate campaign to have the match nullified as a result of the late eighth-round Meyran count against a floored Douglas. However, the tactic didn't work. James "Buster" Douglas officially was declared the new heavyweight champion of the world.

After the fight, Douglas told a TV interviewer that he had won the fight "because of my mother, God bless her heart." The papers called the fight "the biggest upset in boxing history." *Time* magazine declared "a story like this happens only in the movies. To be exact, it happens only in *Rocky* movies." Tyson's post-fight statement to the press simply was: "Greater fighters than I have lost."

THE MANLY ART OF SELF-DELUSION

The New York Times, August 4, 1991

by

Robert Lipsyte

When I was small, Joe Louis was the Champ and Franklin D. Roosevelt was the President. By the time I could read, they had both been hot-typed into media legend: The Brown Bomber was the role model for his race, humble, powerful and nonthreatening to whites, while F.D.R. was the bold aristocrat who used his power for the little people. They both adored their wives.

We know better now. Louis was psychologically disturbed, eventually institutionalized, perhaps because of the pressure of a double life. He was an abuser of alcohol, drugs and women of all colors. Roosevelt abused his power and cheated on his wife. The false images were created for the supposed good of the country. We needed historians to finally tell us the truth because journalists, mostly male and white, didn't want to jeopardize their access to the big league locker rooms.

Seasons end but the games don't change. If Mike Tyson wasn't jamming his way onto the front pages and the TV screens in an orgy of self-destruction, we would never have this live account of how one of the biggest and the baddest think an American Powerboy can act.

This is what it's about. Naked power. What you can get away with because you're a big boy, because too many people are afraid of you and dependent on you and hooked on a system of male entitlement that tolerates, if not encourages, a man forcing his way. The Presidents and the champions who used women like Kleenex were merely exercising an aspect of their power. They did it because they learned they could. And sports has been a primary classroom for such lessons. Especially the "manly" power sports of football and boxing.

Mike Tyson may finally be in serious trouble. Sometime in the next few weeks, a grand jury in Indianapolis will investigate an allegation that he raped a contestant in the Miss Black America beauty pageant in July. According to the prosecutor, the jury could presumably decide to charge him with the crime by Labor Day. Tyson is scheduled to meet Evander Holyfield in Las Vegas on Nov. 8 for the heavyweight championship of the world, the manliest nonelective office.

Consider the following notes of a born-again sportswriter still trying to figure it all out. It is not a psycho-history of major league sexual abuse and neither is it an advance conviction of Tyson nor an apology for his behavior. He has been streaking wildly for several years now, bullying and intimidating men and women on the street, crashing cars, impregnating women to whom he was not married. His life has become a rap song without reason or rhythm.

Even if his current problems—the Indianapolis story includes an allegation from last year's pageant winner that he sexually harassed her during a photo opportunity—are all a cry from the heart, an attempt to declare spiritual bankruptcy, even to break free of Don King, the convicted killer who controls Tyson's boxing career, there can be no justification for rape. If he is guilty, he should be, as none other than the Rev. George Foreman recently declared, "put in a cage."

But if you think that Tyson is just a street kid who got too big too quick and then lost it, you have not been paying attention. This is how we condition our sports heroes and, by extension, so many political and business leaders brought up on the varsity syndrome of winner take all, winning at any cost, violence as a tool, aggression as a mark of masculinity.

In a recently published book, "Boys Will Be Boys: Breaking the Link Between Masculinity and Violence" (Doubleday), Myriam Miedzian, a Columbia University scholar-in-residence, maintained that in the testosterone-high worlds of football and national security, men are rarely demoted or even chastised for mistakes that emerge from a zeal for overkill. In an interview, she was even more specific about football players.

"They are taught to hurt people," Miedzian said. "Empathy has been knocked out of them. If they don't see the guy across the line as a human being, how can they see a woman as a human being? As long as you rear boys to be tough, dominant, in charge, they simply won't be prepared for contemporary women."

American boys are primarily reared not to be girls, and the sports anecdotes supporting this are cliches: from the Little League coaches exhorting 9-year-old boys to be "men out there" to Coach Bobby Knight leaving sanitary napkins in the lockers of his Indiana players to make them more aggressive. Women are moms, wives, cheerleaders, groupies, in this view, the camp followers of sport. Zeke Mowatt's crudity to a female reporter in the New England Patriots' locker room was at once an inexcusable—and possibly actionable—response, and also the understandable expression of so many men who think that women are part of the game's equipment. They are there only to serve.

When Joe Louis asked Lena Horne, with whom he was then having a relationship, to keep score for him at a Hollywood golf benefit, the singer refused—she was entertaining troops that day. Joe hit her with a left hook. Then he started to choke her. In his 1978 autobiography, written with Edna and Art Rust Jr., Louis said that the only thing that saved Lena's life was an aunt in the next room who threatened to call the police. Louis was heavyweight champ at the time, enjoying brief matches with leading ladies.

Muhammad Ali's sexual adventures were so relentless, indiscriminate and indiscreet that they sometimes seemed less like traditional male "scoring" than the great man offering his body in the same generous spirit he posed for snapshots and signed autographs. Ali's press entourage, overwhelmingly male, seemed variously to feel that strong men had strong appetites, that they would behave similarly with such sexual access or that a story about Ali's escapades would lose them access.

As it turned out, it wasn't until Ali held a gratuitous news conference explaining a mix-up in Manila in which his current traveling companion was mistakenly presented to Ferdinand Marcos as his current wife that reporters reluctantly unrolled the sexual thread of the Ali yarn.

By that time, of course, we had learned that one of our most swaggeringly macho presidents, John F. Kennedy, had done risky business in the White House, smuggling in girlfriends while his wife traveled. In the recently published "Lone Star Rising" (Oxford University Press), author Robert Dallek reports that Lyndon Johnson's response to tales of J.F.K.'s womanizing was strictly competitive. L.B.J. claimed he had slept with more women "by accident" than J.F.K. had slept with on purpose. Powerboys keep score.

Dr. Wilbert McClure, a Boston psychologist and a former Olympic gold medal boxer, says he has never felt particular sympathy for the Powerboys, particularly the athletic ones, because "they are on a gravy train of breaks and resources, and only their egos get in their way."

But he says he understands that they don't always fully know what they are doing. "That look of innocence when caught is sometimes real," McClure said. "Rules have not been applied to them. They have been allowed to take what they want. The worst part of it is the message they send to others."

Such as younger athletes, Powerboys in training. In her well-regarded text "Fraternity Gang Rape: Sex, Brotherhood and Privilege on Campus" (New York University Press), Peggy Reeves Sanday of the University of Pennsylvania points out how frequently athletes are involved in group sexual misconduct against women.

Two recent local incidents bear witness. High school football players in Glen Ridge, N.J., were charged with molesting a retarded classmate and in Queens, members of the St. John's lacrosse team stood trial on charges of sexually assaulting a classmate. The lacrosse players, who said they had consensual sex with her, were found not guilty. But the larger issue, of why a group of young men, particularly attractive, strong, privileged athletes, would engage in such activity, has yet to be fully discussed.

It is something men rarely talk or write about, and women only recently. Professor Sanday touches upon it briefly. Within this team behavior of group serial sex, called "pulling train," are intimations not only of antiwoman aggression and homophobia (men who don't participate are called "fags") but a strand of homoerotic behavior. Within male sports, homosexuality is almost never mentioned.

It has been hard to deal with such subjects in any but the most raditionally "manly" ways. In the 19th century, sports was exemplified by "muscular Christians." Theodore Roosevelt opened the 20th century with a call for the "strenuous life." Ernest Hemingway's "grace under pressure" was another shibboleth for boys will be boys.

Our best-known contemporary Powerboy cheerleader, Norman Mailer, wrote: "Men who have lived with a great deal of violence are usually gentler and more tolerant than men who abhor violence. Boxers, bullfighters, a lot of combat soldiers, Hemingway heroes, in short, are always gentle men."

And novelist Joyce Carol Oates seems to have picked up the cant with her observation that the difference between the male boxer and the male fan is so great as to cast them as members of a different species, a difference perhaps as great as the difference between most men and most women. Oates saw Mike Tyson as the extreme example of that ultra manhood, a prehistoric creature rising from a fearful crevice in our collective subconscious.

However you view him, there is no doubt that Tyson is a person on the edge, a Psycho Pup acting out, a fearsome yet fearful Powerboy on a crash course. He is traveling with the likes of Rory Holloway, an old neighborhood friend with whom he once shared, according to Jose Torres's 1989 biography of Tyson, 24 women in a single night, and Don King, who now uses words like "racism" instead of fists to force his way.

Tyson was merchandised as the ultimate short-term Powerboy, and a ruthless tragic monster, as well. But since he lost his heavyweight title, and his self-control, he has been dismissed as just another messed-up street boy with too much gold and not enough brains. That's harsh, and, I think, unfair. But Mike Tyson does need to grow up. Maybe not to be a man, but to be a human being.

MIKE TYSON: TALES FROM THE DARK SIDE

M Magazine, January 1992

by

Phil Berger

Not long ago, as I walked through the lobby of Bally's casino in Reno, I saw a photo that stopped me in my tracks.

It was accidental art, a black-and-white closeup of Michael Gerard Tyson, made from a color original. It had been meant as a standard head shot, to be used to hype a closed-circuit telecast of Tyson's projected fight with heavyweight champion Evander Holyfield—the November 8 title match that was postponed in October after Tyson damaged his rib cage.

Anyway, a strange thing had happened in cooking down that pedestrian color shot to shades of gray. The picture turned into a stunning metaphor for the Tyson I had known since 1985, the year he began fighting professionally.

In that photo, one side of Tyson's face was hidden in a deep shadow that cast a broad hint of menace, while the other side, in light, portrayed him as alert, intense and forthright. The picture was a perfect expression of the schism in Tyson's nature that has made him so intriguing to the public and kept the boxing press more than a little busy for the last six years.

MIKE TYSON: TALES FROM THE DARK SIDE

Long before Tyson stood accused of raping a beauty pageant contestant in Indianapolis last July—for which he is scheduled to stand trial at the end of January—he seemed a fragmented figure, alternately exposing a dark, troubled aspect with a gentler, kinder side. This was the Tyson who routinely handed out $100 bills to derelicts and a day later espoused the virtues of punching the tip of an opponent's nose "because I try to push the bone into the brain."

In the beginning he was afforded the benefit of the doubt, as new heroes are. What an impression he made as he padded into the ring—always without a robe or socks, wearing black trunks and black high-top shoes, the no-frills gladiator, oiled and greased and ready to go. And he fought with a damn-all fury that registered on even the casual spectator and left his overpowered opponents, when asked what it was like to be hit by him, saying things like "He have a sledgehammer."

Yet in those early days, he seemed a user-friendly heavyweight. In part, that impression came from the lispy, whispery voice and from his habit of analyzing his brutal approach to the game in language that was crisp as a starched collar—an echo, some would say later, of the rhetorical style of Cus D'Amato, the veteran boxing trainer who became Tyson's mentor in the sleepy village of Catskill, New York. The rest had to do with the Cus-and-the-kid tale: old white guy takes a black hooligan and retools his felonious urges into the stuff of champions. We are all suckers, aren't we, for those boot-strap tales of reformed character?

In time, the tale would tarnish a bit as snoops in the press discovered that the reality was not quite so idyllic as the fighter's handlers wanted people to think. Tyson had had his share of problems in Catskill—trouble with teachers, "incidents" with coeds, even the occasional run-in with D'Amato himself. For those of us who covered Tyson, it didn't take long to combine those tales with our own impressions of him and then to wonder how well he would hold up if his career flourished and the clamor increased. By 1986, as he started to become big enough to appear on the *Today* show and on the cover of *Sports Illustrated*, it was clear he was struggling to cope with the furor he was creating.

After one bout in early 1986 he turned up at the postfight news conference in a pair of gaudy, triangular sunglasses and with an attitude to match. For reasons not clear to the newspeople there, he was surly and remote, almost challenging them to provoke him.

Yet a few months later I rode with him in a limo on the way to a TV appearance and, as we eased through New York traffic, he said, "From Brooklyn to the David Letterman show," his tone of voice suggesting incredulity at how quickly his career had turned him into a star. He was 20 years old.

There was never any accounting for his moods. The first time I interviewed him, in November 1985 in Catskill, he was articulate, expansive and interested. He was an engaging if shy figure. At one point, as I spoke with Camille Ewald, the woman in whose house D'Amato had raised him, he came into the room, sat on the arm of her easy chair and hugged her, saying, "Is Mr. Berger interrogating you, Camille?"

Yet some time later, in the Manhattan offices of his managers, Bill Cayton and Jim Jacobs—who had taken over as Tyson's mentor after D'Amato died in 1985—Tyson was antsy and so removed from the interview that he insisted on doing it while watching old fight films of Jack Dempsey on a small TV monitor. It was a curious interview, with Tyson's responses interrupted by his reactions to the events on the screen: "Wow! Boom! What was your question?"

His changeability would become routine in his relationship with the press and, it seemed, the world at large. Jacobs and Cayton made a point of accentuating the distance Tyson had traveled from his nasty origins in the Brownsville section of Brooklyn. They understood that if Tyson was ever to capitalize beyond the ring on his success, it was imperative that mainstream America feel comfortable with him. Although the public might marvel at the savagery with which Tyson dismantled opponents, it needed to be assured that he was, in a term sports executives love to use, "good people." Good people, and not another athletic creep.

That is why Jacobs and Cayton sought to defuse Tyson's first "incident," in June 1987, when he stole a kiss from a female parking-lot attendant in Los Angeles and then smacked her male superior for butting in. It cost Tyson $105,000 to settle that little problem and avoid the media circus that, his managers assessed, would have attended a lawsuit and trial.

In those days there was always a lurking sense of extremist edges to

Tyson. That was what attracted the public to him. They saw him as larger than life in the ring, and that roused curiosity about his life outside it. In time that translated to the big-time celebrity of supermarket tabloid tales and a visibility that attracted the predatory fringe.

I remember Tyson telling me once about the "strange people" who managed to get his unlisted phone number in Catskill. "They call and we talk to them: we're bored," Tyson said. "Girls call. Nuts call to say, 'We're related from another world.' There was this one girl who called. She tells Camille she needs money for an operation. She's been in a bad accident and is paralyzed. She sends pictures showing she's crippled. I look at them and tell Camille, 'She's not crippled.' And you know what? I end up seeing this woman on the TV show about America's most wanted criminals. Turns out she's a con."

A curious world it was for Tyson, source of perpetual curiosity and the target of a multitude of schemes. Yet from the other end of the telescope the view seemed nearly as odd—and grew more so when he found himself in a bad and conspicuous marriage to the actress Robin Givens in 1988.

A week after he married, he was jolly as he boasted to me of how he had—in his words—"suaved" Givens, saying this even as she sat, in a housecoat and with a sleepy expression, sipping early-morning coffee. But in a matter of months, he was snarling and cursing at the press one day, and the next breaking into tears as he spoke of D'Amato.

Then there was the day in New York when he greeted me icily at a shooting session for a Diet Pepsi commercial and an hour later saw me backstage and threw a bear hug on me and kibitzed. Could I account for either reaction? Hardly.

As the marriage came unglued, so did Tyson. You remember. There was the cockeyed bit of largess when he dented his $180,000 silver Bentley convertible and tried to give it away to a couple of New York Port Authority police officers. There was the early-morning street fight with heavyweight Mitch Green. There was the night Givens went on the TV show "20/20" and made Tyson out to be as volatile as Conan the Barbarian (and manic-depressive to boot) while he sat at her side with a sedated and dopey expression.

It was during this marriage that illusions about his combustible quality dropped away. That is why, I suspect, every transgression of his got big play from the news media. There was a sense now that Tyson was a clear and present danger to Tyson—that eventually he would land in the crapper.

The marriage lasted only eight months—from the civil ceremony in February to Givens's filing for divorce in October. But they were intense months—marked by turbulence and violence and ending in anger and rejection—that would have been traumatic for any 22-year-old man, and especially so for one living them in public view.

In January 1989, I bumped into Tyson at a 24-hour health club in Las Vegas. He was stepping from a shower after an hour on a stationary bicycle. We hadn't been in touch for a while. During the marriage, I and others in the boxing press had found access to the heavyweight champion, once relatively easy, suddenly denied by Givens and her mother, Ruth Roper.

Anyway, on this day Tyson gave me a cordial handshake, and as we chatted I mentioned how long it had been between interviews. He nodded, and we talked some more. Then, as he thought about the interview, he looked at me and said, "You gonna make me out to be some sort of psychotic killer?"

"No. A manic-depressive killer," I quipped.

A joke. But Tyson's intent expression didn't change. I gave a tiny smile to signal comic intentions and he relaxed. But that word *psychotic* had echoes that lingered, suggesting he was becoming increasingly weary of his fame. Of course, that was his moment's whim. The year of his marital mishap had been a year of mood swings.

John Hornewer, the attorney to a rising heavyweight contender named Lennox Lewis, happened to be on a Chicago street in 1989 when Tyson, his aides and his promoter, Don King, went shopping. "The whole group was in fur coats and they were in a store that had locked its doors to let them shop in private," Hornewer says. "Well, I got there as they unlocked the doors. King led the way. 'Out of the way,' he says. 'Here comes Mike Tyson, heavyweight champion and the greatest fighter of all time.' And the Tyson group kind of pushed its way through the crowd to a limo and off they went.

"I saw that and I thought back to March '87, the morning after Tyson defended his title against Bonecrusher Smith in Las Vegas. I came down to the hotel lobby and Tyson was standing there by himself. I congrat-

Mike Tyson vs. Mitch Green

ulated him on the victory. He didn't know me, but he gave me a big hug and said: 'Thanks for coming. I'm sorry I gave such a bad performance.' He seemed like such a happy, nice kid."

Those vignettes of Hornewer's capture the broad strokes of this contradictory soul—the vulgarian excess and the little-boy sweetness. Tyson's unsettled nature seemed to hold the increasing possibility that somewhere, sometime, he would detonate, and his sumptuous life would go up in smoke.

Tyson's combustibility was familiar enough to me by then and, given the strange, Dickensian route he had taken to the top, not so surprising, really. I mean, consider his hot rocket ride from obscurity.

In September 1980, Tyson—pickpocket, mugger, stick-up accomplice —was released from the Tryon School, a juvenile lockup in upstate New York, and paroled to D'Amato, who already had guided two fighters, Floyd Patterson and Jose Torres, to world titles.

D'Amato had been made aware of Tyson by a boxer acquaintance of his, Bobby Stewart, who happened to be a counselor at Tryon when the surly street punk from Brooklyn showed up. Tyson found out Stewart had been a fighter, and he persuaded him to show him the nuances of the manly art.

Stewart tugged the bureaucratic strings of the correctional system and got Tyson a day pass so he could haul him to Catskill, where D'Amato lived in Ewald's 14-room Victorian home, hard by the Hudson River, and where he taught boxing in a gym on Main Street. In sparring with Tyson, Stewart had absorbed enough of his punches to recognize the kid's uncommon power. Just watching. D'Amato detected the same seismic force. Quickly, passage to the free world was arranged, under D'Amato's auspices, and the inner-city delinquent hunkered down in bucolic Catskill. D'Amato's objective was simply to make him the heavy-weight champion of the world.

As comfortable as Tyson proved to be in the gym, he was keenly aware of being an outsider in the small-town setting. One evening, when he and another amateur boxer walked into an ice-cream parlor for a $1 cone, Tyson tipped the store owner $2.

"Why'd you tip so much?" his friend asked.

"Cause I could see he was afraid of me," said Tyson. "So I wanted him to know I'm a good guy."

A documentary film on D'Amato from this period includes a revealing scene of Tyson at 15, competing at the Junior Olympics in Colorado Springs, Colorado. Tyson, a defending champion, is seen in boxing gear, walking the street outside the arena with his trainer at the time, Teddy Atlas. As Atlas puts his arm around his fighter's shoulder, Tyson begins to cry. On the soundtrack, amid his snuffling, only snatches of Tyson's conversation can be heard. "Come a long way, remember?. . . . Everybody likes me . . . I'm proud of myself. . . ."

As Atlas later recalled: "What he was saying to me was that he had come a long way. 'People like me. I've done good. And people like to know me.' He was afraid of losing all that and he felt that if the guy beat him he *would* lose that."

By January 1989, Jacobs too had died and Don King had usurped Cayton as the guiding force behind Tyson's career. King's approach, for all his flamboyance, was like that of the managers before him—accentuate the positive and let the lawyers clean up the problems.

So when Tyson gave out Thanksgiving turkeys to the poor, or made donations to charity, or received an honorary degree, it tended not to be kept a secret. The public-relations axis of the Tyson enterprise would swing into action.

The irony here was that Tyson in private was far more generous than he was in these public shows of philanthropy. He bought jewelry, cars and more for friends of both genders. Rock Newman, the manager of heavyweight Riddick Bowe, wandered into the Gucci shop at Caesars Atlantic City on the morning after Tyson had knocked out Tyrell Biggs in October 1987, and noted the doors were locked while a group of young people were shopping inside.

"I counted 12 people," says Newman, "and they were: 'Give me two of these, two of those.' I said to a salesperson, 'What's going on?' She said, 'These people are guests of Mike Tyson. We're taking care of them, giving them what they want.' I watched. One person rang up $2,700 in 10 minutes."

Tyson himself quickly became an elite consumer. Under Givens he began dressing up and in time he would lavish as much praise on the style of Gianni Versace as he did on those gritty turn-of-the-century fighters he had studied under D'Amato and Jacobs.

After his divorce, he moved to Southington, Ohio, near King, and settled into a six-bedroom, 27,000-square-foot home on 66 acres, a place that had the lavish refinements only a man of monstrous success could afford. The living room had a 100-inch television screen and a 1,100-pound chandelier, and the balcony overlooking the room was bordered by brass railing.

"Brass and gold—if I was an architect, they'd be my trademark," Tyson said as he gave me a tour of the place.

Tyson's bed was covered with a fox-fur blanket replete with foxtails, and there were 72 pairs of size-13 shoes and sneakers in a walk-in closet that was the size of a small studio apartment. The recreation room had a slate-and-marble pool table that doubled as a craps table one night when Tyson won 60 grand from King.

But the most conspicuous show of wealth was in his driveway. Parked there were nine luxury cars—a Rolls-Royce, two Porsches, two Ferraris, a red Range Rover, a Lamborghini and two Mercedeses, including a four-door convertible that Tyson said was custom-made for him. When I noted the mileage on the odometers and did the arithmetic, the average came out to a little more than 4,000 miles of use per vehicle.

"Yeah," said Tyson. "I don't drive them much. I just like having them."

He said it with an affecting shyness, a boyish quality that strangers found endearing. The shyness was no put-on, but those who knew him better were aware of how fleeting his moods could be. A year after I saw the place in Southington, Tyson had occasion to drive from there to New York in one of those fancy cars of his. That morning, at a news conference for his fight against Holyfield, when asked about the journey, he called it "a fly ride," and then added: "It's one that you'll never have."

What prompted that sudden peevishness was not clear to his interrogators. It was Tyson being Tyson—mercurial, a man who resisted easy understanding.

By his last fight, against Donovan (Razor) Ruddock in June 1991, hardly a day passed in which Tyson's civility was not impugned. While in training he had punched an ABC-TV camera lens into disrepair, and during a news conference to promote the bout he talked to Ruddock with brutishness uncommon even among fighters. He said Ruddock was best suited to be his concubine. "You're a transvestite," Tyson said at one point. "You know you really like me. I'm going to make you my girlfriend June 28. I'll make you kiss me with those big lips."

Yet later I stumbled into an instance of good Mike. While watching Tyson train, I saw a retired fighter, Scott Ledoux, sitting with Tyson's sparring partners. Ledoux, 42 years old, was a heavyweight who fought in the late 1970s and early 1980s.

These days, Ledoux told me, he worked as a salesman for a freight company in Minneapolis. A year and a half earlier, Ledoux's wife had died of cancer. The medical care for her had left Ledoux and his two children in a financial pinch.

Tyson had heard about Ledoux's situation and invited him to training camp nearly two months before the fight with Ruddock. While Ledoux was fit enough, he was now just a middle-aged fighter.

"Mike used him once in sparring early on," Tyson's trainer, Richie Giachetti, said, "and realized it wouldn't work. But he told me, 'Richie, keep him on. Keep paying him.' " Tyson's sparring partners routinely get $1,000 a week.

"I'll tell you this about Mike Tyson," Ledoux said. "He's got a lot more heart than folks give him credit for."

A month later he was charged with rape.

In the tumultuous eight months of Tyson's marriage, there were plenty of clues that Tyson was wired for his own destruction. In fact, there were enough to incite the doomsayer's impulse in me as I finished a book on Tyson in that summer of 1988. As I wrote then: "A premonition crept upon [me] and wouldn't let go, that this was another Joplin or Hendrix—live fast and die. Dead or arrested before his time—that was the creepy intuition that played in [my] mind . . ."

Of course, the words flashed back at me this last July when news of Tyson's alleged rape of an 18-year-old contestant for Miss Black America moved on the wires. In September he was indicted in Indianapolis and two days later he was arraigned. That afternoon I was aboard the same flight from Indianapolis to Las Vegas that Tyson was on. One of the other passengers asked the flight attendant to get Tyson's autograph for him. "Tell him to sign it, 'To Steve,'" he said.

When the attendant returned with Tyson's signature on a piece of lined paper, the passenger turned to the man next to him and said, "If he gets 63 years, it'll be worth a lot more."

On Tyson's arrival in Vegas, fans waved and voiced encouragement as he moved through McCarran International Airport. "She's just trying to get famous off you, champ," one man kept shouting.

"You dick!" one woman screamed at him and then raced ahead to harangue him again.

A Las Vegas TV sportscaster shouted at him: "How come you only answer the soft questions, Mike?"

Tyson appeared indifferent to the tumult. He stood tall and looked calm. He answered reporters' questions on the move, giving pat responses—"I'm okay . . . Looking forward to the [Holyfield] fight . . . I'm innocent and will prove it"—before making it to the ever-present limousine that swept him away.

But a few weeks later, when I returned to Las Vegas for three days, Tyson seemed more restless, as though the pressures on him had turned his focus inward. Word was he had not expected to be indicted in Indianapolis—King supposedly had assured him he wouldn't be—and Tyson had been stunned and angry when it hadn't turned out that way. In any case, he wasn't exactly in a chatty mood when we met up.

His expression was bland. His answers were neutered of emotion and detail. His words were robo-speak. The idea that Tyson is unaffected by the chaos that often surrounds him doesn't hold.

Just what Mike Tyson did in room 606 at the Canterbury Hotel in Indianapolis last July 19 is not for me to say. Sometime in 1992, a jury will weigh the evidence and then judge him. He faces a maximum sentence of 63 years in prison if found guilty on all four counts in the indictment: rape, two counts of criminal deviate conduct (digital penetration and oral sex) and confinement.

Should Tyson end up doing time in Marion County, Indiana, I for one will not lapse into shock. In the summer of '88, when I imagined a grim ending for Tyson, I figured if it happened it would involve a woman.

After coming onto the boxing beat in 1985, I kept hearing stories that had as a common thread Tyson's playing women cheap. What was compelling was the diversity of sources who would mention, in passing, a nasty bit of misogyny involving Tyson—tales told mostly without my broaching the subject, unsolicited testimony that took on force in my mind.

A female photographer told me Tyson had walked up to her during a shoot and, without so much as a hello, had taken her breasts in hand and squeezed. A West Coast fight manager talked about overhearing Tyson at a post-fight party in L.A. propositioning women in the rawest, most direct way. Jose Torres, who had been a confidant of the fighter and later wrote a book about him, related to me conversations in which Tyson expressed pleasure at "hurting" women, through anal sex.

In 1988, Tyson's amateur trainer, Teddy Atlas, told me that Tyson had had problems with women as a teenager: "He'd verbally, and a little physically, force himself on girls in school. There were a whole bunch of incidents reported, incidents by young girls in school. They'd say no. He'd get emotional. Wasn't good emotion. He felt he had a right to act that way."

After Tyson was indicted, I called Atlas, who declined to add to his previous accounts of Tyson's problems with women for fear, he said, that it would harm Tyson's case in Indianapolis. But Atlas stood by what he had said, and corroborated, back in '88, including the details of a run-in with Tyson over an incident with Atlas's teenaged sister-in-law.

She told Atlas's wife that Tyson had put his hands on her in school. When Atlas found out, he confronted Tyson—with, it was rumored, a gun in his hand. "I had something in my hand—let's leave it at that," said Atlas in 1988.

After his marriage crumbled, Tyson became entangled in several incidents involving women. By his own admission, he was drinking heavily and feeling forlorn. In December 1988, after Tyson spent a night at a New York disco, Sandra Miller of Queens, and Lori Davis of Bay Shore, New York filed separate lawsuits charging that Tyson had fondled them. Miller eventually won a token $100; Davis settled her case.

In January 1989, at the Desert Inn Hotel and casino in Las Vegas, Tyson gave a deposition in his lawsuit to void his management contract with Cayton. There was a moment toward the end of the two days of testimony when lawyers for both sides conferred about dates for future depositions.

As I and several other New York boxing writers watched on a closed-circuit television in an adjoining room, Tyson began speaking softly to somebody just out of camera range. It was obvious he was trying to be charming. Then he began to gesture—poking a finger through a circle formed by his thumb and index finger. It wasn't hard for the newsmen to guess he was coming on to Joann Crispi, an associate of Cayton's attorney, Thomas Puccio.

A day earlier she had told me during a break that Tyson had asked her out. "I told him, 'I'm the opposition,' " she said. "He said, 'So what. You're not doing anything.' "

When the second day's depositions ended, reporters sought out Crispi, who confirmed that, yes, it was to her Tyson had been talking on the closed-circuit screen. "I want to fuck you," she said Tyson told her.

Even as I lay out these tales, I know there are stories that make a better impression for Tyson. I have spoken to girlfriends of his who beat the world *gentleman* like a tom-tom and insist the untold story is the boldness with which many women approach him. They say he is more victim than victimizer.

What I have glimpsed of Tyson's interactions with women has often been tame enough. One time, as I walked through a hotel lobby, I heard a theatrical throat clearing. When I looked up, there was a smiling Tyson, with a good-looking woman on his arm, extending his hand for a high five. Yeah, I suppose that word *boyish* would apply there, as it did one time back in June 1987, when he was asked how things were going and he blurted out, "I'm in love"—referring to Givens—and then he blushed.

Of course, there have always been skeptics who say the two sides of Tyson are really the same, that the sweet side simply reflects the ingenuity that certain jailbird sorts have for ingratiating themselves, and that the real Tyson has always been mean-spirited to the core.

In Marion County, the jurors who look into Tyson's behavior of last July will have more than an opinion about how dark his heart is. They will have the ability to bring consequences.

RAPE AND THE BOXING RING

Newsweek, February, 24 1992

by

Joyce Carol Oates

Mike Tyson's conviction on rape charges in Indianapolis is a minor tragedy for the beleaguered sport of boxing, but a considerable triumph for women's rights. For once, though bookmakers were giving 5-1 odds that Tyson would be acquitted, and the mood of the country seems distinctly conservative, a jury resisted the outrageous defense that a rape victim is to be blamed for her own predicament. For once, a celebrity with enormous financial resources did not escape trial and a criminal conviction by settling with his accuser out of court.

That boxing and "women's rights" should be perceived as opposed is symbolically appropriate, since of all sports, boxing is the most aggressively masculine, the very soul of war in microcosm. Elemental and dramatically concise, it raises to an art the passions underlying direct human aggression; its fundamentally murderous intent is not obscured by the pursuit of balls or pucks, nor can the participants expect help from teammates. In a civilized, humanitarian society, one would expect such a blood sport to have died out, yet boxing, sponsored by gambling casinos in Las Vegas and Atlantic City, and broadcast by cable television, flourishes: had the current heavyweight

RAPE AND THE BOXING RING

champion, Evander Holyfield, fought Mike Tyson in a title defense, Holyfield would have earned no less than $30 million. If Tyson were still champion, and still fighting, he would be earning more.

The paradox of boxing is that it so excessively rewards men for inflicting injury upon one another that, outside the ring, with less "art," would be punishable as aggravated assault, or manslaughter. Boxing belongs to that species of mysterious masculine activity for which anthropologists use such terms as "deep play": activity that is wholly without utilitarian value, in fact contrary to utilitarian value, so dangerous that no amount of money can justify it. Sports-car racing, stunt flying, mountain climbing, bullfighting, dueling—these activities, through history, have provided ways in which the individual can dramatically, if sometimes fatally, distinguish himself from the crowd, usually with the adulation and envy of the crowd, and traditionally, the love of women. Women—in essence, Woman—is the prize, usually self-proffered. To look upon organized sports as a continuum of Darwinian theory—in which the sports-star hero flaunts the superiority of his genes—is to see how displays of masculine aggression have their sexual component, as ingrained in human beings as any instinct for self-preservation and reproduction. In a capitalist society, the secret is to capitalize upon instinct.

Yet even within the very special world of sports, boxing is distinct. Is there any athlete, however celebrated in his own sport, who would not rather reign as the heavyweight champion of the world? If, in fantasy at least, he could be another Muhammad Ali, or Joe Louis, or indeed, Mike Tyson in his prime? Boxing celebrates the individual man in his maleness, not merely in his skill as an athlete—though boxing demands enormous skill, and its training is far more arduous than most men could endure for more than a day or two. All athletes can become addicted to their own adrenaline, but none more obviously than the boxer, who, like Sugar Ray Leonard, already a multimillionaire with numerous occupations outside the ring, will risk serious injury by coming back out of retirement; as Mike Tyson has said, "Outside of boxing, everything is so boring." What makes boxing repulsive to many observers is precisely what makes boxing so fascinating to participants.

This is because it is a highly organized ritual that violates taboo. It

154

flouts such moral prescriptions as "Thou shalt not kill." It celebrates, not meekness, but flamboyant aggression. No one who has not seen live boxing matches (in contrast to the sanitized matches broadcast over television) can quite grasp its eerie fascination—the spectator's sense that he or she is a witness to madness, yet a madness sanctioned by tradition and custom, as finely honed by certain celebrated practitioners as an artist's performance at the highest level of genius, and, yet more disturbing, immensely gratifying to the audience. Boxing mimics our early ancestors' rite of bloody sacrifice and redemption; it excites desires most men and women find abhorrent. For some observers, it is frankly obscene, like pornography; yet, unlike pornography, it is not fantasy but real, thus far more subversive.

The paradox for the boxer is that, in the ring, he experiences himself as a living conduit for the inchoate, demonic will of the crowd: the expression of their collective desire, which is to pound another human being into absolute submission. The more vicious the boxer, the greater the acclaim. And the financial reward—Tyson is reported to have earned $100 million. (He who at the age of 13 was plucked from a boys' school for juvenile delinquents in upstate New York.) Like the champion gladiators of Roman decadence, he will be both honored and despised, for, no matter his celebrity, and the gift of his talent, his energies spring from the violation of taboo and he himself is tainted by it.

Mike Tyson has said that he does not think of boxing as a sport. He sees himself as a fantasy gladiator who, by "destructing" opponents, enacts others' fantasies in his own being. That the majority of these others are well-to-do whites who would themselves crumple at a first blow, and would surely claim a pious humanitarianism, would not go unnoticed by so wary and watchful a man. Cynicism is not an inevitable consequence of success, but it is difficult to retain one's boyish naivete in the company of the sort of people, among them the notorious Don King, who have surrounded Tyson since 1988, when his comanager, Jim Jacobs, died. As Floyd Patterson, an ex-heavyweight champion who has led an exemplary life, has said, "When you have millions of dollars, you have millions of friends."

It should not be charged against boxing that Mike Tyson *is* boxing in any way. Boxers tend to be fiercely individualistic, and Tyson is, at the least, an enigma. He began his career, under the tutelage of the legendary trainer Cus D'Amato, as a strategist, in the mode of such brilliant technicians as Henry Armstrong and Sugar Ray Robinson. He was always aware of a lineage with Jack Dempsey, arguably the most electrifying of all heavyweight champions, whose nonstop aggression revolutionized the sport and whose shaved haircut and malevolent scowl, and, indeed, penchant for dirty fighting, made a tremendous impression on the young Tyson.

In recent years, however, Tyson seems to have styled himself at least partly on the model of Charles (Sonny) Liston, the "baddest of the bad" black heavyweights. Liston had numerous arrests to his credit and served time in prison (for assaulting a policeman); he had the air, not entirely contrived, of a sociopath; he was always friendly with racketeers, and died of a drug overdose that may in fact have been murder. (It is not coincidental that Don King, whom Tyson has much admired, and who Tyson has empowered to ruin his career, was convicted of manslaughter and served time in an Ohio prison.) Like Liston, Tyson has grown to take a cynical pleasure in publicly condoned sadism (his "revenge" bout with Tyrell Biggs, whom he carried for seven long rounds in order to inflict maximum damage) and in playing the outlaw; his contempt for women, escalating in recent years, is a part of that guise. The witty obscenity of a prefight taunt of Tyson's—"I'll make you into my girlfriend"—is the boast of the rapist.

Perhaps rape itself is a gesture, a violent repudiation of the female, in the assertion of maleness that would seem to require nothing beyond physical gratification of the crudest kind. The supreme macho gesture—like knocking out an opponent and standing over his fallen body, gloves raised in triumph.

In boxing circles it is said—this, with an affectionate sort of humor—that the heavyweight champion is the 300-pound gorilla who sits anywhere in the room he wants; and, presumably, takes any female he wants. Such a grandiose sense of entitlement, fueled by the insecurities and emotions of adolescence, can have disastrous consequences. Where once it was believed that Mike Tyson might mature into the greatest heavyweight of all time, breaking Rocky Marciano's record of 49 victories and no defeats, it was generally acknowledged that, since his defeat of Michael Spinks in 1988, he had allowed his boxing skills to deteriorate. Not simply his ignominious loss of his title to the mediocre James (Buster) Douglas in 1990, but subsequent lackluster victories against mediocre opponents made it clear that Tyson was no longer a serious, nor even very interesting, boxer.

The dazzling reflexes were dulled, the shrewd defensive skills drilled into him by D'Amato were largely abandoned: Tyson emerged suddenly as a conventional heavyweight like Gerry Cooney, who advances upon his opponent with the hope of knocking him out with a single punch—and does not always succeed. By 25, Tyson seemed already middle aged, burnt out. He would have no great fights after all. So, strangely, he seemed to invite his fate outside the ring, with sadomasochistic persistence, testing the limits of his celebrity's license to offend by ever-escalating acts of aggression and sexual effrontery.

The familiar sports adage is surely true, one's ultimate opponent is oneself.

It may be objected that these remarks center upon the rapist, and not his victim; that sympathy, pity, even in some quarters moral out-rage flow to the criminal and not the person he has violated. In this case, ironically, the victim, Desiree Washington, though she will surely bear psychic scars through her life, has emerged as a victor, a heroine: a young woman whose traumatic experience has been, as so few traumas can be, the vehicle for a courageous and selfless stand against the sexual abuse of women and children in America. She seems to know that herself, telling *People* magazine, "It was the right thing to do." She was fortunate in drawing a jury who rejected classic defense ploys by blaming the victim and/or arguing consent. Our criminal-justice system being what it is, she was lucky. Tyson, who might have been acquitted elsewhere in the country, was unlucky.

Whom to blame for this most recent of sports disgraces in America? The culture that flings young athletes like Tyson up out of obscurity, makes millionaires of them and watches them self-destruct? Promoters like Don King and Bob Arum? Celebrity hunters like Robin Givens, Tyson's ex-wife, who seemed to have exploited him for his money and as a means of promoting her own acting career? The indulgence gener-ally granted star athletes when they behave recklessly? When they abuse drugs and alcohol, and mistreat women?

I suggest that no one is to blame, finally, except the perpetrator himself. In Montieth Illingworth's cogently argued biography of Tyson, *Mike Tyson: Money, Myth and Betrayal*, Tyson is quoted, after one or another public debacle: "People say 'Poor guy.' That insults me. I despise sympathy. So I screwed up. I made some mistakes. 'Poor guy,' like I'm some victim. There's nothing poor about me."

REQUIEM FOR THE CHAMP

The Progressive, April 1992

by

June Jordan

Mike Tyson comes from Brooklyn. And so do I. He grew up about a twenty-minute bus ride from my house. I always thought his neighborhood looked like a war zone. It reminded me of Berlin—immediately after World War II. I had never seen Berlin except for black-and-white photos in *Life* magazine, but that was bad enough: rubble, barren, blasted. Everywhere you turned, your eyes recoiled from the jagged edges of an office building or a cathedral, shattered, or the tops of apartment houses torn off, and nothing alive even intimated, anywhere. I used to think, "This is what it means to fight and really win or really lose. War means you hurt somebody, or something, until there's nothing soft or sensible left."

For sure I never had a boyfriend who came out of Mike Tyson's territory. Yes, I enjoyed my share of tough guys and gang members who walked and talked and fought and loved in quintessential Brooklyn ways: cool, tough, and deadly serious. But there was a code as rigid and as romantic as anything that ever made the pages of traditional English literature.

A guy would beat up another guy or, if appropriate, he'd kill him.

But a guy talked different to a girl. A guy made other guys clean up their language around "his girl." A guy brought ribbons and candies and earrings and tulips to a girl. He took care of her. He walked her home. And if he got serious about that girl, and even if she was only twelve years old, then she became his "lady." And woe betide any other guy stupid enough to disrespect that particular young black female.

But none of the boys—none of the young men, none of the young black male inhabitants of my universe and my heart—ever came from Mike Tyson's streets or avenues. We didn't live someplace fancy or middle-class, but at least there were ten-cent gardens, front and back, and coin laundromats, and grocery stores, and soda parlors, and barber shops, and holy-roller churchfronts, and chicken shacks, and dry cleaners, and bars and grills, and a takeout Chinese restaurant, and all of that kind of usable detail that does not survive a war. That kind of seasonal green turf and daily-life-supporting pattern of establishments to meet your needs did not exist inside the gelid urban cemetery where Mike Tyson learned what he thought he needed to know.

I remember when the City of New York decided to construct a senior housing project there, in the childhood world of former heavyweight boxing champion Mike Tyson. I remember wondering, "Where in the hell will those old people have to go in order to find food? And how will they get there?"

I'm talking god-forsaken. And much of living in Brooklyn was like that. But then it might rain or it might snow and, for example, I could look at the rain forcing forsythia into bloom or watch how snowflakes can tease bare tree limbs into temporary blossoms of snow dissolving into diadems of sunlight.

And what did Mike Tyson ever see besides brick walls and garbage in the gutter and disintegrating concrete steps and boarded-up windows and broken car parts blocking the sidewalk and men, bitter, with their hands in their pockets, and women, bitter, with their heads down and their eyes almost closed?

In his neighborhood where could you buy ribbons for a girl, or tulips?

Mike Tyson comes from Brooklyn. And so do I.

In the big picture of America, I never had much going for me. And he had less.

I only learned, last year, that I can stop whatever violence starts with me. I only learned, last year, that love is infinitely more interesting, and more exciting, and more powerful than really winning or really losing a fight. I only learned, last year, that all war leads to death and that all love leads you away from death.

I am more than twice Mike Tyson's age. And I'm not stupid. Or slow. But I'm black. And I come from Brooklyn. And I grew up fighting. And I grew up and I got out of Brooklyn because I got pretty good at fighting. And winning. Or else, intimidating my would-be adversaries with my fists, my feet, and my mouth.

I never wanted to fight. I never wanted anybody to hit me. And I never wanted to hit anybody. But the bell would ring at the end of another dumb day in school and I'd head out with dread and a nervous sweat because I knew some jackass more or less my age and more or less my height would be waiting for me because she or he had nothing better to do than to wait for me and hope to kick my butt or tear up my books or break my pencils or pull hair out of my head.

This is the meaning of poverty: When you have nothing better to do than to hate somebody who, just exactly like yourself, has nothing better to do than to pick on you instead of trying to figure out how come there's nothing better to do: How come there's no gym, no swimming pool, no dirt track, no soccer field, no ice-skating rink, no bike, no bike path, no tennis courts, no language-arts workshop, no computer-science center, no band practice, no choir rehearsal, no music lessons, no basketball or baseball team? How come neither one of you has his or her own room in a house where you can hang out and dance and make out or get on the telephone or eat and drink up everything in the kitchen that can move? How come nobody on your block and nobody in your class has any of these things?

I'm black. Mike Tyson is black. And neither one of us was ever supposed to win anything more than a fight between the two of us.

And if you check out the mass media material on "us," and if you check out the emergency-room reports on "us," you might well believe we're losing the fight to be more than our enemies have decreed. Our enemies would deprive us of everything except each other: Hungry and furious and drug-addicted and rejected and ever convinced we can never be beautiful or right or true or different from the beggarly mon-

Tyson with Nelson Mandela and Don King

sters our enemies envision and insist upon. How should we then stand, black man and black woman, face to face?

Way back when I was born, Richard Wright had just published *Native Son* and, thereby, introduced white America to the monstrous product of its racist hatred. Richard Wright's Bigger Thomas did what he thought he had to do: He hideously murdered a white woman and he viciously murdered his black girlfriend in what he conceived as self-defense. He did not perceive any options to these psychopathic, horrifying deeds. I do not believe he, Bigger Thomas, had any other choices open to him. He was meant to die like the rat he, Bigger Thomas, cornered, and smashed to death, in his mother's beggarly clean space.

I never thought Bigger Thomas was okay. I never thought he should skate back into my, or anyone's community. But I did and I do think he is my brother. The choices available to us dehumanize. And any single one of us, black in this white country, we may be defeated, we may become dehumanized, by the monstrous hatred arrayed against us and our needy dreams.

Poverty does not beatify. Poverty does not teach generosity or allow for sucker attributes of tenderness and restraint. In white

America, hatred of blackfolks has imposed 360 degrees of poverty upon us.

And so I write this requiem for Mike Tyson; international celebrity, millionaire, former heavyweight boxing champion of the world, a big-time winner, a big-time loser, an African-American male in his twenties and, now, a convicted rapist.

Do I believe he is guilty of rape?

Yes I do.

And what would I propose as appropriate punishment?

Whatever will force him to fear the justice of exact retribution, and whatever will force him, for the rest of his damned life, to regret and to detest the fact that he defiled, he subjugated, and he wounded, somebody helpless to his power.

And do I therefore rejoice in the jury's finding?

I do not.

Well, would I like to see Mike Tyson a free man again?

He was never free.

And I do not excuse or condone or forget or forgive the crime of his violation of the young black woman he raped!

But did anybody ever tell Mike Tyson that you talk different to a girl? Where would he learn that?

Would he learn that from U.S. Senator Ted Kennedy?

Or from hotshot/scot-free movie director Roman Polanski?

Or from rap recording star Ice Cube?

Or from Ronald Reagan and the Grenada escapade?

Or from George Bush in Panama?

Or from George Bush and Colin Powell in the Persian Gulf?

Or from the military hero flyboys who returned from bombing the shit out of civilian cities in Iraq and then said, laughing and proud, on international TV: "All I need, now, is a woman"?

Or from the hundreds of thousands of American football fans?

Or from the millions of Americans who would, if they could, pay surrealistic amounts of money just to witness, up close, somebody like Mike Tyson beat the brains out of somebody else?

And which university could teach Mike Tyson about the difference between violence and love? Is there any citadel of higher education in the country that does not pay its football coach at least three times as much as its chancellor and six times as much as its professors and ten times as much as its social and psychological counselors?

In this America where Mike Tyson and I live together and bitterly, bitterly, apart, I say he became what he felt. He felt the stigmata of a prior hatred and intentional poverty. He was given the choice of violence or violence: The violence of defeat or the violence of victory.

Who would pay him what to rehabilitate inner-city housing or to refurbish a bridge?

Who would pay him what to study the facts of our collective history?

Who would pay him what to plant and nurture the trees of a forest?

And who will write and who will play the songs that tell a guy like Mike Tyson how to talk to a girl?

What was America willing to love about Mike Tyson? Or any black man? Or any man's man?

Tyson's neighborhood and my own have become the same no-win battleground. And he has fallen there. And I do not rejoice. I do not.

UNLIKE KENNEDY KIN, TYSON DIDN'T PRETEND

Sacramento Bee, March 21, 1993

by

Pete Dexter

I noticed in the papers last week that President Clinton had picked Ted Kennedy's sister to be the U.S. ambassador to Ireland.

While I have no real objection if the president wants to give one of the Kennedys meaningful employment—I imagine it's part of the overall plan to make the Clinton team look more like America—it is still impossible for me to read the name Jean Kennedy Smith without thinking of her son William Kennedy Smith, who is someplace out there right now pursuing a medical practice, and of Mike Tyson, who is doing six years in an Indiana prison for rape.

Looking back on it now, it seems to me that the thing which separates Tyson and William Kennedy Smith was not so much race or social advantage, but Tyson's blunt refusal to compromise himself before a system of justice which demands such a compromise from anyone, guilty or innocent, brought into its jurisdiction.

A system which relentlessly reflects fashionable social agendas of the time, and which jealously protects itself from anyone who would challenge its fundamental integrity. Which operates as if we were supposed to forget that it is run by lawyers. A system in which contempt of court is a crime.

UNLIKE KENNEDY KIN, TYSON DIDN'T PRETEND

Which rewards those who keep two sets of books.

Looking at it that way, you can understand how someone like William Kennedy Smith is walking around free while Mike Tyson is in prison.

Tyson, of course, was badly represented by his lawyers, who portrayed him so clearly as a sexual thug that Desiree Washington, the beauty pageant contestant who accused him of rape, should have known what he was up to when he called her at her hotel in the middle of the night and asked her out.

And while that is true, it is absolutely unfashionable in the current climate to suggest that a woman who accuses a man of rape may hold some of the responsibility for the event itself.

Even without a competent defense, however, the case against Tyson was riddled with reasonable doubt. The woman accepts a date in the middle of the night, goes to the hotel room of one of the richest and most famous men in the country and a few days later claims that she was raped.

No witnesses to the event, no conclusive physical evidence. Just her testimony against his and then, after the verdict, her tearful interview with Barbara Walters—someplace in which, it seems to me, she said she felt sorry for Tyson and was trying to help him come to grips with what he had done.

Well, as it happens, I am beginning to feel sorry for Tyson myself. I am sorry that witnesses who saw him and Ms. Washington being physically affectionate on the way into the hotel were not allowed to testify at his trial.

At least two members of the jury which convicted Mike Tyson have said that they would have voted the other way if they had been allowed to hear all the evidence.

I am sorry that Ms. Washington's testimony indicating she was not interested in monetary gain from her accusations didn't invalidate the verdict as subsequent investigation showed that at the time of this testimony she had hired a lawyer on a contingency basis to represent her in the matter.

I am sorry that the previous man Ms. Washington accused of rape— or who says she accused him of rape—did not find his way into the witness chair during Tyson's trial.

According to the man, Wayne Walker of Coventry, R.I., Ms. Washington made that accusation after the two had had consensual sex back in high school. He said that Ms. Washington was afraid that she was pregnant and that her father would find out that she was no longer virginal, and so she told him she had been raped.

Later, after her father had called Mr. Walker's home, she backed away from the charge, and her attorney now says that no such charge was ever made and that no sexual intercourse ever took place.

I think the jury should have heard these things as I think they speak to Desiree Washington's credibility and, by implication, to reasonable doubt.

And that is still the rule of law, even in cases of rape. The same principle of reasonable doubt was stretched as thin as a line of spit, after all, and still held William Kennedy Smith's weight.

Of course, he played the game in the courtroom, and walked. Before the jury, he became someone reasonable, a young man incapable of assaulting a woman—and for that lie he was given the benefit of the doubt.

Tyson was Tyson in front of his jury and was given six years. Whether he is a rapist I don't know, and at least some members of the jury which convicted him don't know either.

It's no revelation that as the courts follow the lawyers and the lawyers follow the politicians, our system of justice does not hold rewards for those who tell the truth.

THE EDUCATION OF MIKE TYSON

Esquire, March 1994

by

Pete Hamill

An artificial Christmas tree stands in a corner of the waiting room, with a bunched-up bedsheet at its base feigning snow. Unmatched pieces of cheap furniture some wicker, some plastic, are arranged awkwardly around the edges of the room. It could be the antiseptic lobby of a second-class motel except for the view through the picture windows behind the Christmas tree: two parallel steel-mesh fences topped with barbed wire and a slope of sour lawn rising toward blank walls and tan-brick buildings. The complex is called the Indiana Youth Center. But it's not a place where schoolkids play checkers or basketball on frigid afternoons. The barbed wire makes it clear that this is a jail.

So does the posted rule against bringing drugs or alcohol on visits; so does the order to place wallets and handbags in a locker in the far corner, along with all cash in excess of five dollars, any pens, notebooks, tape recorders, books, all hats and overcoats; and so does the stamping of your hand with invisible ink, the emptying of pockets into a plastic tray, the body search, the passage through a metal detector.

The rules of entrance obeyed, I walk down a long, wide ramp into the prison, pause at a sign forbidding weapons beyond this point, and wait for a steel-rimmed glass door to be opened. Up ahead there are other such doors, with guards and a few prisoners moving languidly along a corridor that is lit like an aquarium. The door in front of me pops open with a click. I turn right to a guard's booth, where I hand over my pass and am told to thrust my right hand into a hole in a wooden box. An ultraviolet light certifies the stamp. I am then instructed to go through the door to the left, into the visitors' lounge, and give the pass to the guard behind the high desk in the corner. I do what I am told and wait. In the lounge a dozen couples sit facing each other on thick plastic-covered chairs, maintaining space and privacy, drinking soda bought from machines, trying hard to be loose, glancing tensely at the clock, conscious of time. Behind them a wall of picture windows opens upon a vista of gray grass and blank, tan walls. The Indiana sky is the color of steel.

Then, suddenly, from another door, Mike Tyson appears. He smiles, gives me a hug, and says, "How are ya, buddy?"

Twenty-two months have passed since he vanished from the night-sides of cities, from the bubble of champagne and the musk of women, from the gyms where he prepared for his violent trade, from the arenas that roared when he came after an opponent in a ferocious rush, his eyes hooded, gleaming with bad intentions. Twenty-two months have passed since he was convicted of raping an eighteen-year-old beauty-pageant contestant who consented to leave her own Indianapolis hotel room at nearly 1:30 in the morning, who moved around the streets for a while with Tyson in his rented limousine, who then went to Tyson's suite in the Canterbury Hotel, where she sat on the bed with him, went to the bathroom and removed her panty shield, on the way passing the door that led to the corridor and the possibility of flight. Twenty-two months since the jury believed Desiree Washington lay helpless while Tyson had sex with her. Twenty-two months since the jury believed that it was perfectly normal for a rape victim to spend two more days taking part in the Miss Black America pageant of 1991. Twenty-two months since Michael Gerard Tyson, twenty-five-year-old child of Amboy Street, Brownsville, Brooklyn, was led away—refusing to express remorse for a crime he insists he didn't commit—deprived of his freedom, his ability to earn millions, his pride.

But if there is anger in him or a sense of humiliation, neither is visible on this gray morning. He is wearing jeans and a white T-shirt—with his prison number, 922335, hand-lettered over his heart—and to a visitor who first met him when he was sixteen, he looks taller somehow. In the TV-news clip that plays every time his name is mentioned, Tyson weighs about 250 pounds, swollen and suety in a tight-fitting suit as he smiles in an ironic way and holds up his cuffed hands on his way to a cell. Now, a few days before his second Christmas in prison, he is about 220, the belly as flat as a table, the arms as hard as stone. He looks capable of punching a hole in a prison wall.

"Yeah, I'm in good shape," he says, "but not boxing shape." He works out in the prison gym every day, a self-imposed regimen of calisthenics, weights, running. "No boxing," he says, the familiar whispery voice darkened by a hint of regret. "They don't allow boxing in prison in Indiana." He smiles, nodding his head. "That's the rules. Ya gotta obey the rules."

We walk over to the chairs, and Tyson sits with his back to the picture windows. His hair is cropped tight, and he's wearing a mustache and trimmed beard that emphasize the lean look. Then I notice the tattoos. On his left bicep, outlined in blue against Tyson's ocher-colored skin, is the bespectacled face of Arthur Ashe, and above it is the title of that splendid man's book *Days of Grace*. On his right bicep is a tattooed portrait of Mao Tse-tung, with the name MAO underneath it, in cartoony "Chinese" lettering. I tell Tyson that it's unlikely that any other of the planet's six billion inhabitants are adorned with *that* combination of tattoos. He laughs, the familiar gold-capped tooth gleaming. He rubs the tattoos fondly with his huge hands.

"I love reading about Mao," he says. "Especially about the Long March and what they went through. I mean, they came into a village one time and all the trees were white, and Mao wanted to know what happened, and they told him the people were so hungry they ate the bark right off the trees! What they went *through*. I mean, *that* was adversity. This . . ."

He waves a hand airily around the visiting room but never finishes the sentence; he certainly feels that the Indiana Youth Center can't be compared to the Long March. I don't have to ask him about Arthur Ashe. For weeks Tyson and I have been talking by telephone, and he has spoken several times about Ashe's book.

THE EDUCATION OF MIKE TYSON

"I never knew him," Tyson said one night. "I never liked him. He was a *tennis* player, know what I mean? And he looked like a black bourgeois, someone I couldn't have nothin' to do with. Just looking at him I said, '*Yaaagh*, he's *weak.*' That was my way of thinking back then." A pause. "But then Spike Lee sent me his book, and I started reading it, and in there I read this: 'AIDS isn't the heaviest burden I have had to bear . . . being black is the greatest burden I've had to bear. . . . Race has always been my biggest burden . . . Even now it continues to feel like an extra weight tied around me.' It was like *wham!* An extra *weight* tied around me! I mean, wow, that really *got* me, and I kept reading, excited on every page."

On the telephone, with the great metallic racket of prison in the background, or here in the visiting room of the Indiana Youth Center, Tyson makes it clear that he doesn't want to talk much about the past. He doesn't encourage sentimental evocations of the days when, as a raw teenager from a reform school, he learned his trade from the old trainer Cus D'Amato in the gym above the police station in Catskill, New York. He doesn't want to talk about his relationship with Don King, the flamboyant promoter whose slithery influence many blamed for Tyson's decline as a fighter and calamitous fall from grace. He is uncomfortable and embarrassed discussing his lost friends and squandered millions. He has no interest in retailing the details of the case, like another Lenny Bruce, endlessly rehashing what happened on July 19, 1991, in room 606 of the Canterbury Hotel or the astonishingly feeble defense offered by his high-priced lawyers or his chances for a new trial. He wants to talk about what he is doing now, and what he is doing is time.

History is filled with tales of men who used prison to educate themselves. Cervantes began *Don Quixote* in a Spanish prison, and Pancho Villa read that book, slowly and painfully, while caged in the Santiago Tlatelolco prison in Mexico City more than three hundred years later. In this dreadful century, thousands have discovered that nobody can imprison the mind. In the end, Solzhenitsyn triumphed over Stalin's gulags, Antonio Gramsci over Mussolini's jails, Malcolm X over the joints of Massachusetts. From Primo Levi to Václav Havel, books, the mind, the imagination, have offered consolation, insight, even hope to men cast into dungeons. I don't mean to compare Mike Tyson to such men or the Indiana Youth Center to the gulags; Tyson is not serving his six-year sentence for his ideas. But he understands the opportunity offered by doing time and has chosen to seize the day.

"Sometime in that first month here," he said one night, "I met an old con, and he pointed at all the guys playing ball or exercising, and he said to me, 'You see them guys? If that's all they do when they're in here, they'll go out and mess up and come right back.' He said to me, 'You want to make this worth something? Go to the library. Read books. Work your mind. Start with the Constitution.' And I knew he was right."

And so Tyson embarked on an astonishing campaign of exuberant and eclectic self-education. Early on he read George Jackson's prison classic, *Soledad Brother*, "and the guy knocked me out. It was like any good book: The guy sounded like he was talking directly to me. I could *hear* him, I can hear him *now*. He made me understand a lot about the way black men end up in prison, but he didn't feel *sorry* for himself. That's what I liked. I got so caught up with this guy, he became a part of my life."

Tyson has been reading black history too. He is fascinated by the revolution in Haiti in the early nineteenth century, "the only *really* successful slave revolt, because blacks took *power*." He can quote from John Quincy Adams's defense of the slaves who mutinied on the Spanish ship *Amistad* in 1839 off the coast of Cuba and sailed for fifty-five days all the way to New York. "They landed in Long Island," he says. "Imagine! Long *Island*."

The process of self-education did not begin smoothly. In his first weeks in jail, Tyson enrolled in a school program, then quickly dropped out. "You know, I'm out on the streets, I'm out there, or I'm training, or I'm in the bars, I'm chasing these women. Then I come to this place after not going to school since I was what? Sixteen? Seventeen? They hit me with this thing, they said, 'Bang! Do this, do this work. . . . ' It was like putting a preliminary fighter in with a world champion."

Dispirited, angry at the teachers and himself, he dropped out for a while. "Then I started very gradually studying on my own, preparing for these things. Then I took that literacy test—and blew it out of the water."

THE EDUCATION OF MIKE TYSON

He went back to classes, studying to take a high school equivalency examination, and met a visiting teacher from Indianapolis named Muhammad Siddeeq.

"He was just talking to the other kids one day and said, 'Does anybody need any help? If so, I'll help you in the school process.' And I said, 'Yeah, I need help.' So he showed me things, in a simple way. . . ."

One thing Tyson learned quickly was the use of percentages and decimals. "I never learned that before," he says, still excited. "It's a small thing, maybe, something I shoulda learned in grammar school. But you come from a scrambled family, you're running between the streets and school, missing days, fucking up, and you end up with these *holes*. One thing never connects to another, and you don't know why. You don't know what you didn't learn. Like percentages. I just never learned it, it was one of the holes. I mean, later on I knew what a percentage was, you know, from a $10 million purse, but I didn't know how to do it myself. That was always the job of *someone else*." He laughs. "One thing now, I can figure out how to leave a tip. There's restaurants out there where I should eat for free for a couple of years."

He isn't simply filling those gaping holes in his education that should have been bricked up in grammar school. He reads constantly, hungrily, voraciously. One day it could be a book on pigeons, which he raised with great knowledge and affection in the Victorian house where he lived with D'Amato and D'Amato's longtime companion, Camille Ewald, whom Tyson calls "my mother." But on other days he could be reading into the history of organized crime, thrilled to discover that the old Jewish gangsters of Murder Inc. hung out near Georgia and Livonia avenues in Brownsville, walking distance from his own childhood turf. He discovered that Al Capone was from Brooklyn and went west to Chicago. And there were black gangsters too.

He talks about Lucky Luciano, Meyer Lansky, Bugsy Siegel, Frank Costello—some of the Founding Fathers of the Mob—with the same intensity and passion he gave as a teenage fighter to Ray Robinson, Mickey Walker, and Roberto Duran. The old gangster he's most impressed by is the gambler Arnold Rothstein. "He was smart— Damon Runyon called him the Brain—and figured out everything without ever picking up a gun. He helped teach these younger guys, like Lansky and Luciano, you know, how to act, how to dress, how to behave. In *The Great Gatsby*—you know, by this guy F. Scott Fitzgerald?—the gambler called Meyer Wolfshiem, he's based on Arnold Rothstein. I mean, this guy was *big*."

In one way, of course, studying such histories is a consolation; in a country where the percentage of young black males in prisons is way out of proportion to their numbers in the general population, it must be a relief to learn that the Irish, Italians, and Jews once filled similar cells. But Tyson's study of organized crime is part of a larger project.

"I want to find out how things *really* work. Not everything is in the history books, you know." A pause. "Some of those guys didn't like blacks. They sold drugs to blacks. They poisoned black history. They didn't respect us as human beings. But most of them couldn't read and write. The first ones came to this country ignorant, out of school, making money. They didn't have any kind of morals. They wanted to be big shots and they wanted to be respected by decent people. They tried to be gentlemen, and that was their downfall. When you try to be more than what you really are you always get screwed up."

He emphasizes that gangsters are not heroes. "You can read about people without wanting to be like them," he says. "I can read about Hitler, for example, and not want to be like him, right? But you gotta *know* about him. You gotta know what you're talking about. You gotta know what *other* people are talking about before you can have any kind of intelligent discussion or argument."

So it isn't just gangsters or pigeons that are crowding Tyson's mind. He has been poring over Niccolò Machiavelli. "He wrote about the world we live in. The way it really is, without all the bullshit. Not just in *The Prince*, but in *The Art of War, Discourses*. . . . He saw how important it was to find out what someone's motivation was. 'What do they want?' he says. What do they *want*, man?"

And Voltaire. "I loved *Candide*. That was also about the world and how you start out one thing and end up another, 'cause the world don't let you do the right thing most of the time. And Voltaire himself, he was something, man. He wasn't *afraid*. They kept putting him in jail, and he kept writing the truth."

He has recently read *The Count of Monte Cristo* by Alexandre Dumas, aware that the grandmother of the French writer was a black woman from Haiti. "I identify with that book," he says. "With Edmond Dantès in the Château d'If. He was unjustly imprisoned, too. And he gets educated in prison by this Italian priest." He laughs out loud. "And he gets his *revenge* too. I understand that; I feel that. Don't get me wrong, I don't want revenge against any person. I don't mean that. I mean against fate, bad luck, whatever you want to call it."

He is familiar with the Hemingway myth that so exhilarated earlier generations of Americans: Hemingway the warrior, Hemingway the hard drinker, Hemingway the boxer. But he talks most passionately about Hemingway the *writer*. "He uses those short, hard words, just like hooks and uppercuts inside. You always know what he's saying, 'cause he says it very clearly. But a guy like Francis Bacon, hey, the sentences just go on and on and *on* . . ."

Obviously, Tyson is not reading literature for simple entertainment, as a diversion from the tedium of prison routine. He is making connections between books and writers, noting distinctions about style and ideas, measuring the content of books against his life as he knows it. But he is not taking a formal course in literature, so I asked him one night how he made the choices about what he reads.

"Sometimes it's just the books that come to me. People send them and I read them. But sometimes, most of the time, I'm looking. For example, I'm reading this thing about Hemingway and he says he doesn't ever want to fight ten rounds with Tolstoy. So I say, 'Hey, I better check out this guy Tolstoy!' I did, too. It was hard. I sat there with the dictionary beside me, looking up words. But I like him. I don't like his writing that much because it's so complicated, but I just like the guy's way of thinking."

Along with literature, Tyson has been reading biographies: Mao, Karl Marx, Genghis Khan, Hernán Cortés. In casual talk, he scatters references to Hannibal, Alexander the Great, Oliver Cromwell. "When you read about these individuals, regardless of whether they're good or bad, they contribute to us a different way of thinking. But no one can really label them good or bad. Who actually knows the definition of good or bad? Good and bad might have a different definition to me than it may have in *Webster's Dictionary*, than it may have to you."

He knows that for *his* life, the models in books might not always apply. But in all such books, he insists that he finds something of value.

"I was reading Maya Angelou," he said one evening, "and she said something that equates with me so much. People always say how great a writer she is, and people used to say to me, 'Mike, you're great, you could beat anybody, you don't even have to train.' But you know how hard it is for me to do that? To win in ninety-one seconds? Do you know what it takes away from me? And Maya Angelou said about herself it takes so much from me to write, takes a lot out of me. In order for me to do that, she says, to perform at that level, it takes everything. It takes my personality. It takes my creativity as an individual. It takes away my social life. It takes away *so much*. And when she said that, I said, 'Holy moley, this person understands me.' They don't understand why a person can go crazy, when you're totally normal and you're involved in a situation that takes all of your normal qualities away. It takes away all your sane qualities."

In prison Mike Tyson is discovering the many roads back to sanity.

One of those roads is called Islam. Tyson was raised a Catholic by his mother, Lorna, and during the upheaval in that time before he went to jail, he was baptized as a favor to Don King in a much-photographed ceremony presided over by Jesse Jackson. But water, prayer, and photographs didn't make him a born-again Christian. "That wasn't real," he says now. "As soon as I got baptized, I got one of the girls in the choir and went to a hotel room or my place or something."

Now he has embraced Islam. In a vague way, he'd known about Islam for years; you could not grow up in the era of Muhammad Ali and know nothing about it. "But I was avoiding it because people would press it on me. I always avoided what people pressed on me. They wanted me to do the right thing—and Islam, I believe, is the right thing—but all these people wanted me to do the right thing for the wrong reason."

In prison, through his teacher, Muhammad Siddeeq, Tyson started more slowly, reading on his own about the religion, asking questions. He insists that Siddeeq is not a newer version of Cus D'Amato. "He's just a good man," he says, "and a good teacher." Nor does Tyson sound like a man who is making a convenient choice as a means of surviving in jail. He admits that "there are guys who become Muslims in jail to feel *safe*—and give it up the day they hit the streets again." Tyson might do the same. But in repeated conversations, he sounded as if he'd found in Islam another means of filling some of those holes.

"I believe in Islam," he told me one night. "That's true. It's given me a great deal of understanding. And the Koran gives me insight into the world, and the belief of a man who believes that God has given him the right to speak his word, the prophet Muhammad, peace be unto him. I look at Islam from different perspectives, just as I look at everything else. I find it so beautiful because in Islam you have to tolerate *every* religion, you know what I mean? 'Cause everyone has different beliefs. Most so-called religious leaders are bullshit. Voltaire knew that, knew organized religion was a scam. Their object is power. They want power."

Tyson's skepticism about organized religion includes some of the sects and factions within Islam. He pledges his allegiance to none of them.

"One guy says, 'I believe in Islam, I live out of the Koran.' Well, I believe in *that* but *other* than that, please. . . . They got a sect here and a sect here. Unbelievable. I just don't understand that. How can *I* be a Muslim and *you* be a Muslim, but we have two different beliefs?"

Tyson thinks of Islam as not simply a religion but a kind of discipline. He says he prays five times a day. The Koran is a daily part of his reading (but obviously not the only reading he does). "And you know, I got a sailor's mouth," he laughed. "But I've cut down my cursing at least 50 percent." He clearly needs to believe in something larger than himself, but his choice of Islam is entwined with a revulsion against certain aspects of Christianity.

"If you're a Christian," he says, "and somebody's a Christian longer than you, they can dictate to you about your life. You know, *this* is what you should do, and if you don't do *this*, you're excommunicated. I just found that bizarre . . . in conflict with human qualities, you know what I mean? I couldn't understand why a person couldn't be a human and have problems and just be dealt with and helped. In Islam there's nobody who can put you in your place. They can let you know this is wrong, you need help on this. But the only one that can judge you is Allah."

I asked Tyson how he could reconcile his embrace of Islam with the fact that many of the slave traders were Muslims. The horrors of the Middle Passage often began with men who said they accepted Allah. Tyson answered in a cool way.

"Look, everyone in Arabia was a slave, know what I mean? They had white slaves, black slaves, Arab slaves, Muslim slaves. Everybody there was a slave. But the slave traders were contradicting Islam and the beliefs of Islam. The prophet Muhammad, he wasn't a slave trader or a slave. As a matter of fact, the Arabs were trying to kill him, to enslave him. People were people. But Europeans took slavery to a totally different level. Brutalized, submissive, abhorrent. But you can't condemn all the Jews or all the Romans because they crucified Christ, can you?"

Tyson emphasizes one thing: He's a neophyte in his understanding of Islam and has much to learn.

"Being a Muslim," Tyson says, "is probably not going to make me an angel in heaven, but it's going to make me a better person. In Islam we're not supposed to compete. Muslims only compete for righteousness. I know I'm probably at the back of the line. But I know I'll be a better person when I get out than I was when I came in."

For the moment, jail is the great reality of Tyson's life. Unless a court orders a new trial or overturns his conviction, he will remain in prison until the spring of 1995. The Indiana Youth Center is a medium-to-high-security facility and looks relatively tame compared with some of the others I've seen in New York and California. Boredom is the great enemy. "I get up and eat and go to class," he says, explaining that he doesn't eat in the prison dining room, because "the food is aaaccch," but goes to a commissary where he can buy packaged milk, cereals, and other food, paying from a drawing account called the Book. He works out in the gym every day, shadowboxing, doing push-ups, running laps to keep his legs strong and lithe. "There's nothing else to do," he says. "You gotta keep busy so you don't go crazy."

But it's still prison. For now it's the place where Mike Tyson is doing time, using all of his self-discipline to get through it alive.

"I'm never on nobody's bad side," he says. "Even though there's guys in here just don't like the way you walk, the way you look, or whatever, I just—I'm never on nobody's bad side. I don't like to be judgmental, because we're all in the same boat. I have to remember to be humble. But sometimes I get caught up with who I was at one time, and I must remind myself my circumstances have changed."

There are still a lot of hard cases on the premises, including Klansmen and members of the Aryan Brotherhood. Tyson laughs about their swastikas, shaved heads, white-power tattoos. "They talk back and forth," he said. "But they realize once they're in prison, no one gives a fuck about them."

More dangerous are people who seem to crack under the stress of doing time. "A couple of days ago, this guy who never bothered nobody just cracked a guy on the head with a lock in his sock," he said in an amazed tone. "And there are other guys—they'll do something disrespectful to some guy, and they'll walk around with their headphones on, acting like they didn't do anything, jamming, dancing, then, next thing you know—*ka-pow!*—they get clocked."

In the bad old days, Tyson might have empathized with such people; he is, after all, the man who as champion once socked an off-duty heavyweight named Mitch Green in Harlem at 4:00 in the morning. But in prison, he is at once part of the general population and detached from it because of his celebrity. "When I get out, I have a future," he says. "A lot of these guys don't." Sometimes he even volunteers for a form of solitary confinement ("to be alone, to focus, to meditate, to read, *to get some fucking sleep*"). But he also looks with compassion on his fellow prisoners.

"They send some guys to prison that don't necessarily have bad records," he says. "Instead of rehabilitating him, they *de*habilitate him by sending him to prison. Without him even being attacked or molested, just from what he witnesses, some things that are so taboo to his humanity. It could totally drive him insane."

Among the scarier aspects of prison these days is AIDS. "They are falling like flies in here," Tyson said. "And some of these guys keep boning each other over in the dorms." There are other people for whom prison is life itself. "There's one guy here who's been inside for thirty-one years. Not in *here* but in other prisons. There are other guys with so much time. . . . I watch them adapt. This is their home. You don't go in their door without knocking."

Tyson said that much of what he has seen is sad and comic at the same time.

"You see a guy, he's doing all the time in a lifetime, he's talking to a girl on a phone. I mean, he's doing *ninety years*. And what's he saying? 'Don't go out tonight, baby. Don't go out tonight, baby. Don't go out tonight, baby.' "

Tyson laughed in a sad, rueful way.

"Most guys that are in here, they got a lot of time, so they lose hope. They get caught up in the sideshows, like homosexuality, drugs, you know what I mean? It's very difficult for me to think about participating in the things these guys do. You talk to the guys, and to me they seem rather sane. But to see their conduct, some of them, they're in a totally insane frame of mind. The fact is, prison is like a slave plantation. We have no rights which the authorities respect. I wasn't a criminal when I got put in here. I didn't commit no crime. But we become the problem *out there*, because we're not aware. We become the problem because out there we're robbing, we're stealing, we're selling drugs, we're killing. I hear people talk about revolution. They mention Castro, Mao, Lenin, the Black Panthers. But how can you have a revolution when you have crime, when you have people selling drugs, you have people murdering? There's no collective ideas there."

I asked Tyson if the young prisoners from Indiana resembled the young men from his Brooklyn neighborhood. He said that many of them did. When he was champion, Tyson refused to offer himself as a role model; he certainly doesn't see himself as one now. But he does understand the Brownsvilles of America.

"At the age of ten or fifteen, you become very influenced by what you see," he said. "You see these guys looking good, with fly cars, nice girls on their arms. You think this is what you want to be. But any kind of proper success has to do with education, unless you're an athlete, and everyone's not going to be Michael Jordan or Muhammad Ali. You fall in bad company. You see drug dealers and gangsters with all their bullshit. You know *they* didn't go to school. So you don't fill the *holes*. You go after the wrong shit. The thing I've noticed in here, with the white kids and the black kids and the Latin kids and the Asian kids—the only thing they have in common is poverty."

I asked him if drugs were another common factor. Tyson himself was never a druggie in the conventional sense; his drugs were liquor and celebrity. He whispered, "Of course.

"Drugs and women," he said. "You know, we all run through the same complexities in life."

Among those many complexities in American life is racism.

"It's very difficult being black," he said one evening. "These reporters came to interview me from South Africa, and one of them asked me was I racist. And I said, 'Yes, I am a racist—to people who are racist toward me.' I never liked to believe that I'm a racist because of the way I was brought up, both from my mother and from Cus and Camille. But, you know what I mean, sometimes things are in the air and people say or do things detrimental or hurtful towards you. You strike back at them. That's what I meant in that interview. Not *all* white people. Shit, no. *Those* people. Those specific people. I just want to be treated the way I treat people."

Behind many of these feelings are jagged memories of that Brownsville childhood. "Too many guys, too many black people, men and women, *hate* themselves. They see the shit around them and they give up before they ever start. They get one or two little tastes of power—sticking a gun in somebody's face—and then it's over."

He was in jail when the riots erupted in Los Angeles, and he hated what he saw on CNN.

"It could have all been prevented if people believed in fairness and equality. But you have to understand: The things that people do and what they *should* do are totally different. We should live like every man is equal, every woman is equal. But how we *do* live is, You get yours, I get mine, fuck you." He talked about Rodney King. "Some guys in here, they heard Rodney King and they laughed. But what he said was powerful, man. Why *can't* we live together? Why the *fuck* can't we all live together?"

In jail Mike Tyson is engaged in an admirable attempt to find out who he is, to discover and shape the man who exists behind the surface of fame and notoriety. There is no Cus to explain the world, to tell him what to do. In the end, there's only himself. And because he is in prison, this is no easy process.

"You have good days, and you have bad days, but you just think to yourself, *This isn't the end*. You say, 'I was kind of wild out there; maybe I was heading for something more drastic.' Which is all a part of playing head games so you won't get insane."

Like anyone in prison, Tyson misses life on the outside. He misses certain people, and in most of our talks he circles back to Cus D'Amato. "A lot of things Cus told me, they are happening now," he says. "But at that time, I didn't keep them in mind, because I was just a kid. Cus tried to store everything in my mind so fast. He didn't think that he was gonna be around. He tried to pack everything in at one moment, you know what I mean? I'm trying to be a fighter, I'm trying to have some fun on the side, and I'm just running crazy. Now I think about him all the time. Like, damn! Cus told me that. And God! He told me this too. And, oh! He told me that.

"He was always saying to me, before I was anything: 'What are you gonna do? Look how you talk to me *now*,' he said. 'Look how you act. How you gonna act when you're a *big-time fighter*? You're just gonna dump me.' I said, 'I'm not gonna do that, Cus. I'm not gonna do it.' And I didn't." He laughs. "I used to say, 'Cus, I'll sell my soul to be a great fighter.' And he said, 'Be careful what you wish for, 'cause you might get it.'

"I miss him still. I miss him. I think about him. No, I don't dream about him; I don't dream much in this place. But I miss Cus. I still take care of him, make sure nothing bad happens, 'cause I promised Cus before he died to take care of Camille. I was young, I was, like, eighteen, and I said, 'I can't fight if you're not around, Cus.' And he said, 'You better fight, 'cause if you don't fight, I'm gonna come back and haunt you.' "

The ghost of Cus D'Amato doesn't haunt Tyson; if anything, the old manager instilled in the young man a respect for knowledge and a demand for discipline that are only now being fully developed. "Cus had flaws, like any man," Tyson says. "But he was right most of the time. One thing I remember most clearly that he said: 'Your brain is a muscle like any other; if you don't use it, it gets soft and flabby.' "

Other things do haunt Tyson. One of them is that fatal trip to Indianapolis. "I had a dick problem," he admits. "I didn't even want to go to Indianapolis. But I went. I'm in town with the best girl [rapper B Angie B] that everybody wants. And I had to get this—why'd I have to do that, huh, man? Why'd I have to do that? I had a girl *with* me. Why'd I have to make that call? Why'd I have to let her come to my room?"

He has his regrets too, and says that he is trying hard to acquire some measure of humility, leaning on the Koran.

"Remember, when I accomplished all that I did, I was just a kid," he says quietly. "I was just a kid doing all that crazy stuff. I wanted to be like the old-time fighters, like Harry Greb or Mickey Walker, who would drink *and* fight. But a lot of the things I did I'm so embarrassed about," he says. "It was very wrong and disrespectful for me to dehumanize my opponents by saying the things I said. If you could quote me, say that anything I ever said to any fighters that *they* remember—like making Tyrell Biggs cry like a girl, like putting a guy's nose into his brain, like making Razor Ruddock my girlfriend—I'm deeply sorry. I will appreciate their forgiveness."

He isn't just embarrassed by the words he said to fighters. "I have girls that wrote to me and said they met me in a club," he says. "And I said something crazy to them. And I *know* I said that, you know, 'cause that was my style. And I say, wow, what was going through my *mind* to say that? I don't dwell on it too much. But I just think: *What the* hell *was I thinking?* To say this to another human being?"

Tyson tries to live in the present tense of jail, containing his longing for freedom through a sustained act of will. But when I pressed him one evening, he admitted that he does yearn for certain aspects of the outside world.

"I miss the very simple things," he says. "I miss a woman sexually. But more important, I miss the pleasure of being in a woman's presence. To speak to a woman in private and discuss things. Not just Oh! Oh! Oh! More subtle than that. I just want to be able to have privacy, where no one can say, 'Time, Tyson! Let's go!' You miss being with people. I miss flying my birds. They're not gonna know me, I'm not gonna know them, 'cause there're so many new ones now 'cause of the babies. I miss being able to hang out. Talk to Camille. Laugh. I miss long drives. Sometimes I used to just get in the car and drive to Washington. I miss that a lot. I miss, sometimes, going to Brooklyn in the middle of the night, pulling up in front of the projects and one of my friends will be there, shooting baskets. I'll get out of the car, and we'll talk there, like from 4:00 in the morning until 9:00 or 10:00. People are going to work, and we're just talking." A pause. "I miss that."

He insists that he doesn't miss what he calls the craziness. "It was all unreal. Want to go to Paris? Want to fly to Russia? Sure. Why not? Let me have two of those and three of them and five of those. Nobody knows what it's like—fame, millions—unless they went through it. It was unreal, unreal. I had a thousand women, the best champagne, the fanciest hotels, the fanciest cars, the greatest meals—and it got me here."

He does have some specific plans for the future. "I want to visit all the great cities, I want to see the great *libraries*," he says. "One of the few things I did that impressed me was going to Paris that time and visiting the Louvre. I was *devastated* by that place, man. I want to see all of that, everywhere."

Yes, he said, he will box again. He will be twenty-eight when he returns, the same age as Ali when he made his comeback and certainly younger than George Foreman when he made his. He asks repeatedly about active fighters and how they looked in their latest bouts, because he only sees brief clips on CNN. "I'm a fighter," he says. "That's what I do. I was born to do that."

He wants to make money; nobody knows how much Tyson has left, not even Tyson, but his return to boxing could be the most lucrative campaign in the history of sport. "I want to have money for a family," he says. "In the end, that's how you can decide what kind of man I was. Not by how many guys I knocked out. But by the way I took care of my kids, how I made sure they went to college, that they had good lives and never wanted for nothing. And what I taught them. About the world. About character."

Tyson would even like to try college himself. "I'd like to go to a black college that's not well-known," he says, "to study and learn. But also to have some kind of exhibitions, too, fights to benefit the college. I don't have to fight benefits for a church or a mosque. But the black colleges, *that* I want to do. . . ."

In the end, of course, all education is self-education, and Tyson is clearly deep into the process. The faculty of Tyson's university includes Cus D'Amato and Alexandre Dumas, Machiavelli and the prophet Muhammad, Dutch Schultz and Ernest Hemingway, and dozens of others. Part of the curriculum includes what some academics call life experience. There are millions of college graduates who don't know what Tyson knows. About writers and thinkers. About life itself.

"A lot of people get the misconception that by being free that you're *free*," he says. "That's not necessarily true. There's people on the outside who are more in prison than I'll ever be in here." He chuckles. "You know, it's human to fall. But it's a crime to stay down and not get up after you fall. You must get up."

In the visitor's lounge at the Indiana Youth Center, he smiles when a woman offers to buy him a soda. "Sorry, thank you, but I don't drink soda." He looks at his hands. Twenty-two months earlier, he'd come to this elaborate cage like a man knocked down. When he started school, he got to one knee. Now he's standing up.

"I know this," he says. "When I get out, I'm gonna be in charge of my own life. I used to leave it to others. I'd say, 'Hey, I'm the boss.' But then I'd leave it to people, to Cus, to Don King, whatever. But that's what you do when you're a kid. You can't do that when you're a man."

I utter some banality about the dangers that might still confront him on the outside, how powerful the pull of the ghetto spirit might be when the bad guys from the neighborhood come calling on him again.

"Well, that's no problem anymore," he says and laughs. "They're all dead."

He turns and glances at the picture window. Fat white snowflakes are now falling from the steel-colored sky, out there in the world of highways, car washes, diners, and motels. Another prisoner's name is called, and a black man rises and touches his woman's face. Time is running out.

"Sometimes I get so frustrated in here, I just want to cry," says the fighter who once described himself as the baddest man on the planet. "But I don't. I can't. Because years from now, when this is long behind me, I want to know I went through it like a man. Not to impress anyone else. But to know it *myself*, know what I mean?"

A departing visitor nods, recognizing Tyson, and he nods back, a look granted like an autograph. He turns to me again, his hands kneading each other, his right leg bouncing like a timepiece.

"When you die, nothing matters but the dash," Tyson says abruptly. "On your tombstone, it says 1933-2025, or something like that. The only thing that matters is that dash. That dash is your life. How you live is your life. And were you happy with the way you lived it."

A guard calls Tyson's name now. Time is up. Tyson rises slowly. He tells me to send his best to friends in New York. He promises to stay in touch. We embrace awkwardly. He looks as if he wants to freeze the moment, freeze time itself. Then he turns and nods politely to the guard and flashes a final goodbye grin to his visitor.

"Take care," number 922335 says, and returns to the world of rules, to sleep another night where the snow never falls.

TYSON VS. SIMPSON

The New Republic, April 17, 1995

by

Robert Wright

According to one poll, 68 percent of American blacks think O. J. Simpson is innocent, and 61 percent of whites think he's guilty. Presumably this gap looks about equally mystifying from either side. Speaking from the white side, at any rate, I can attest to having wondered at the suspicion so many blacks harbor toward the courts and police. But I've cut down on my wondering since Mike Tyson got out of jail. His case reminded me why blacks often think the deck is stacked against them: because it is.

When Tyson was convicted three years ago, almost all opinion leaders were delighted. Liberals hailed the case as a landmark in date-rape jurisprudence. ("A KNOCKOUT OF A VERDICT" was the imaginative title of a *Washington Post* column.) Conservatives were less vocally supportive, but they certainly didn't leap to defend a man aptly characterized by one beauty-pageant contestant as a "serial buttocks fondler." Black protesters who had crowded around the Indianapolis courthouse with "FREE MIKE TYSON" signs were dismissed as sadly deluded. But the protesters were right. Tyson was wrongly convicted. He may well have raped Desiree Washington—indeed, he *probably* raped her—but he definitely wasn't guilty beyond a reasonable doubt.

TYSON VS. SIMPSON

Tyson and Washington agree that she willingly went up to his hotel room around 2 a.m. He says she consented to sex, and she says she didn't. The limousine driver who drove her away afterwards said she seemed dazed and upset, exclaiming "Who does he think he is?" That's certainly the way she might have behaved after rape; it's also the way she might have behaved if, after intercourse, she learned that his sexual interest didn't signify anything more. And Tyson is not one to mince words. (Witnesses said Washington expressed gold-digging interest in Tyson.)

The main other evidence against Tyson were two small vaginal abrasions found twenty-six hours after the incident, when Washington first reported it. An expert testified that consensual sex only rarely produces such abrasions. Then again, consensual sex only rarely involves a 108 pound woman and Mike Tyson (225).

Washington had some weak spots in her story (though fewer than Tyson). She said she never envisioned sex, yet right before the sex she went into Tyson's bathroom and removed a sanitary pad. (She would have replaced it, she testified, but her purse was in the bedroom.) She said she didn't permit Tyson to touch her before going to his room, yet observers said they saw the couple necking in the limousine and holding hands upon leaving it. But the judge nixed these witnesses, who had surfaced only after the trial began. (Stuart Taylor of the *American Lawyer* noted that this and other ratings gave Tyson a compelling case for appeal, which was then denied by 2-to-1 vote.)

Now, in Florida a few months earlier, William Kennedy Smith, a well-born white man, had been tried for date rape and acquitted. Smith's guilt is more likely than Tyson's, three women recalled being sexually assaulted by him in similar circumstances. But this time the judge excluded mainly the damning evidence—their testimony. Meanwhile, the jury was alienated by an inept prosecutor, awed by Kennedy potentates and won over by Smith, who is a police and innocuous-looking white guy. Tyson, by contrast comes off as middle America's nightmare a crude, violent, sexually aggressive black male—threat to home, wife, daughter. Significantly, the Tyson jury was at first split evenly by gender, with men wanting conviction and women acquittal.

There were two ways for liberals to react to the Tyson verdict. One was to compare it with the Smith verdict and decry racial or class injustice. The other was to applaud it as a victory for feminism—gratifying proof, after the frustrating Smith trial, that date rape needn't be tolerated. The trouble with the second reaction is that it jettisons a core part of liberalism—a principled refusal to imprison people just because they *probably* committed a crime and the mob is clamoring for law and order. Feminism won this miniature struggle for liberalism's soul, a fact crystallized by an editorial in *The Nation* that glibly celebrated Tyson's conviction. (The alternative would have been to confront the painful fact that date rape, by its nature, rarely admits to proof in American courts.)

All told, blacks had cause to feel doubly betrayed—by the Tyson verdict, but also by liberals. To be sure, one double betrayal is hardly enough to explain the paranoia now seen among some blacks (such as tales that AIDS is government sponsored genocide.) Still, that not a single white op-ed columnist seems to have noted the manifest credibility of black doubts about the high-profile Tyson verdict suggests that tons of valid black grievances may have accumulated over the years without the rest of us noticing. (It took Rodney King to show me what many already knew about the LAPD.) It's hardly shocking that so many blacks reflexively side with Simpson.

Which isn't to say their sympathy is well placed. Assuming reports about the coming DNA evidence are correct, it alone will establish with around 99.9999 percent confidence that Simpson killed his ex-wife. Another contrast with Tyson is that Simpson isn't judicially handicapped by his race. He has a mostly black jury and, besides, is a country-club black, a glad-handing celebrity whom white jurors don't find threatening. Indeed, for practical purposes Simpson is an upper-class white defendant; his pricey lawyers tediously ensure that the standards of proof are higher for him than for the countless poorer blacks (and whites) who get convicted on flimsier evidence; he is the symbolic equivalent of William Kennedy Smith, proof of systemic discrimination by class—which de facto, means discrimination by race. That's why black outrage at a Simpson conviction would be misplaced.

But equally misplaced would be middle-class white-outrage over an acquittal. Pundits are already predicting "volcanic" white indignation about the courts' failure to protect law-abiding Americans. But in truth, convictions against garden-variety criminals are usually a cinch, notwithstanding those well-worn anti-ACLU anecdotes. If courts are failing the cause of law and order, it's largely because they're overloaded. And one reason for the overload is slow-motion trials for well-to-do people like Simpson. *That's* an appropriate source of middle-American outrage, whatever the Simpson verdict.

The most legitimately dispiriting thing about an acquittal would be the spectacle of a mostly black jury failing to condemn a plainly guilty black man—more grim testament to the widening gulf between white and black America. I'm actually predicting conviction (unlike most lawyers polled); I don't think race relations are *quite* that bad. But if they are, it's no wonder.

TYSON TESTS HIS DRAWING POWER

The Sunday Times, August 13 1995

by

Hugh McIlvanney

When Peter McNeeley is labelled 'The Irish Hurricane' it is proof that reality, which is never an assertive presence in Las Vegas, has been run right out of town. There is an acid irony in the publicity men's nonsense since McNeeley has been cheaply hired to be blown away.

If the 26-year-old from Boston stays in front of Mike Tyson for more than a minute or two in the ring at the MGM Grand Hotel on Saturday night, he will become an embarrassing blemish on an occasion that is meant to be about as competitive as a ticker-tape parade. What is planned is not a fight but an elaborate festival of rehabilitation, complete with an assembly line of celebrities and the theatrical effects of a rock concert—a spectacular relaunching of a fighting career that once seethed with excitement and money but must now recover from the pulverising impact of a rape conviction and the prison sentence it brought. Already the money is pouring back but if it is to swell into the predicted flood, Tyson must re-enter the public imagination on Saturday as the dramatic destroyer of old.

That is why McNeeley's credentials have been thoroughly vetted to ensure that the essence of his contribution to the party will be brevity.

TYSON TESTS HIS DRAWING POWER

During less than four years as a professional, he has won 36 of 37 fights, with 30 stoppages, and has not allowed any of his last dozen engagements to go beyond the second round. However, when names are attached to those statistics, a truer perspective emerges: Lopez McGee, Wayne Perdue, Quinton Hardy, and so on, a list of characters who could not embody obscurity more convincingly if they were called John Doe Hurricane? A zephyr would have flattened that lot.

All but seven of McNeeley's fights have taken place in his native Massachusetts, so it is not surprising that first-hand witnesses of his work are hard to find. But the evidence of a few brief film clips is sufficient to confirm that his attacking method has slightly less subtlety than a bayonet charge. 'Controlled fury, technical brawling' is his own description of his approach to the job. Such eagerness to rush into the cannon's mouth may enliven the seconds after the opening bell but, unless Tyson's artillery has been severely rusted by his three years in jail (and more than four out of the ring), the rashness should bring early destruction.

The real test here is not of Tyson's fighting capacities but of his post-prison earning power, particularly through pay-per-view television. That medium is opening up new horizons of plunder for professional boxing. Increasingly condemned as an anachronism too primitive to be tolerated in civilised society, the fight business is nevertheless approaching the millennium with a swaggering demonstration that its commercial vigour is undiminished. It is the dinosaur that adapted, effortlessly modifying its rich traditions of larcenous ingenuity to suit the electronic age.

No one is ready to dismiss out of hand the claims of Don King and his promotional associates that Tyson-McNeeley will break all records for sales of a boxing event on pay-per-view. The best return hitherto was achieved when Evander Holyfield beat George Foreman in Atlantic City in 1991, attracting 1.36 million armchair customers at an average cost of rather more than $35 to produce a gross take of $48.9 million. In talking confidently of pulling in 1.5 million buyers this time, King is reassured by the fact that the number of sets that can be reached by his signal is substantially greater than was the case four years ago.

Apparently reasonable estimates say the pool of potential customers across America, what the jargon of the trade calls 'the universe of addressable systems', may have grown by nearly 50 per cent since 1991, to around 24 million. It is a figure that obviously makes the 1.5 million sales target more attainable and, with the average price of connection for next weekend's show boosted close to $45, a gross of almost $60 million may not be outrageously optimistic. Even if the regional cable operators who do the connecting get the 50 per cent of that booty they regard as their due—rather than the 30 per cent originally proposed by Showtime Event Television, the company responsible for transmission—there should be unanimous satisfaction.

How much Tyson personally will gain from all this is a mystery the shrewdest outsiders are unable to penetrate. The series of deals he and his two managers, John Horne and Rory Holloway, have negotiated with King, Showtime and the MGM Grand is the subject of much speculation but, apart from the fact that the hotel has him contracted for six fights, no solid information has been released. It has been postulated, perhaps wildly, that when signing-up fees and other fancy inducements go into the pot, completion of Saturday's assignment will leave him $35 million ahead of the game. There are certainly immense fortunes to come, especially if the 17,000 spectators who are expected to fill the Grand Garden at the MGM, and the millions around the world who will watch a telecast, live or delayed, are thrilled by what they see.

If the star's wages are secret, the bit-player's are common knowledge. McNeeley is being paid $700,000 for the fight and nothing for training expenses, a deprivation that has obliged him to settle for one sparring partner. In spite of the modesty of his purse, he has been publicising the promotion with gusto, which sometimes makes him sound like a man using a loud hailer to attract a crowd to his own funeral. 'I am going to wrap Mike Tyson in a cocoon of horror,' he declared at a press conference in Los Angeles last week, treating us to a New England accent complicated by a nasal problem which will eventually require surgery. In his seat a few feet away, Tyson smiled broadly, as if contemplating operating procedures of a cruder kind. Asked if he would use McNeeley for an extended workout or go for a quick win, he smiled again at the naïvety of the question. 'I'll do my thing,' he said. 'You know what I do.'

Well, we know what he did at his best, which was deliver punches

TYSON TESTS HIS DRAWING POWER

Tyson vs. Hurricane McNeeley

of frightening power in swift, calculated combinations while moving his head and shoulders in rolling, weaving patterns that made him deceptively elusive to opponents brave enough to counter-attack. But before his imprisonment he showed alarming signs of having lost his fire and his discipline (not only in Tokyo, when James 'Buster' Douglas inflicted the one defeat of his 42-fight career, but in two subsequent meetings with Donovan 'Razor' Ruddock). He became ponderous, almost static, abandoning the sequences of blows he had thrown in a blur for laboured attempts to load up for single, murderous shots. Inevitably, there was a suspicion that the extraordinary precocity which saw him claim a world title as a boy-ogre of 20, and made him undisputed champion nine months later, might carry the penalty of premature burn-out for a rather squat body blatantly abused by his rampaging social life.

As he comes back at the age of 29, he has the good fortune to find a heavyweight division devoid of truly outstanding performers, one bearing no resemblance to the concentration of threatening excellence that greeted Muhammad Ali when he returned following the three-and-a-half-year exile imposed for his refusal to be drafted into the US armed forces. But if Tyson were to exhibit the weaknesses manifest when he was last seen as a fighter, even today's leading heavy-weights might be more than he could handle.

Eddie Futch, who turned 84 the other day but is in no danger of losing the title of the wisest man in boxing, has no doubt about the central question Tyson must answer. 'He must prove that the root of his effectiveness is still there, and that means his quickness,' Futch said. 'What made him so effective was the speed with which he delivered his power. He had the quickest delivery of any hard puncher since Joe Louis. There have been harder hitters, Earnie Shavers and Sonny Liston to name two. What set him apart was his speed. We must wait and see if he is still capable of the same lightning-fast delivery.'

Here it must be said that, on the limited evidence of his appearance in shirt and tie at the LA press conference, he looks well enough to make his assertions of physical and mental rejuvenation believable. His face is planed to leanness behind thin lines of moustache and beard and it has a glow of fitness that had deserted it by 1991. Under the clothes, his body gave an impression of hardness and of a bulk in astonishing contrast to the sense of diminution conveyed when he left jail. A carefully devised diet and programme of conditioning are credited with the rapid build-up of muscle. It must be quite a regimen.

Presumably his conversion to Islam has helped to rid his life of its tendency towards destructive chaos. Jay Bright, who was in Tyson's corner for seven fights before the fateful court case in Indiana and has just been appointed principal trainer for the comeback, said on Thursday: 'When Mike started to get his priorities wrong, letting people drag him here and drag him there, we had to track him down to get him to work. Now he is waiting with his bags packed, ready to go to the gym, getting us there early.' Once in the gym, according to Bright, he has been so brutal with a succession of sparring partners that many have fled to nurse their wounds.

The psychological blows Tyson has taken lately seem to have left something deeper than bruising, perhaps incipient paranoia. He talks darkly of forearming himself against betrayal and it is significant that Bright, Horne and Holloway are all friends from happier years in the home of the late Cus D'Amato, his guardian and boxing guru. Bright's lack of experience at his present job, and his habit of invoking the ghost of D'Amato in a manner more appropriate to a medium than a cornerman, raises questions about his ability to be an authoritative mentor. But he should be under no strain on Saturday.

Peter McNeeley's father, Tom, was knocked down ten times when he challenged for Floyd Patterson's world heavyweight title in 1961. The son's execution should be quicker and cleaner.

MIKE'S BRILLIANT CAREER

Transition 71, Fall, 1996

by

Gerald Early

The poor boy changes clothes and puts on after-shave to compensate for his ordinary shoes.—*Paul Simon*

I sincerely believe that only men can develop boys into men.—*Jawanza Kunjufu*

Mike Tyson. Our future.—*Don King*

When Don King started wooing Mike Tyson in the summer of 1988, the heavyweight champ was close to disaster: though he kept winning fights, he was boxing's most visible and spectacular casualty. Tyson's psychological unraveling was nightly fare on the TV news: Robin Givens, the minor actress he'd married earlier that year, was appearing on tabloids and television talk shows accusing him of spousal abuse; Ruth Roper, her impossibly domineering mother, was egging the media on in an effort to create a scandal. Tyson, who was taking lithium for a misdiagnosed manic-depressive condition, was making regular headlines with ever more bizarre explosions of temper: smashing up the furniture in his house, totaling his expensive cars. But perhaps the most disorienting blow dealt to him was the death of Jim Jacobs, Tyson's longtime and deeply trusted manager, from leukemia-a condition which Jacobs had kept hidden from him. Tyson was crushed, and desperately alone.

MIKE'S BRILLIANT CAREER

Enter Don King, the prince of boxing predators. That Tyson's personal life was in utter chaos, that a prominent black man was playing out the drama of his nervous breakdown before the entire fascinated American public, suited King just fine. The wily promoter invited the champ to his mansion in Orwell, Ohio, and proceeded to work his way into the boxer's trust by cementing a racial solidarity between the two men. Tyson's contract—which made Bill Cayton, Jacobs's partner, Tyson's sole manager in the event of Jacobs's death—had been signed by the champ without knowledge of Jacobs's terminal illness. King made a point of telling Tyson that Jacobs and Cayton were Jews, and that the Jews were trying to take over boxing. It was a shrewd device, exacerbating what King recognized as the fighter's core insecurity: everyone is against me, so I can trust no one. Tyson did not necessarily trust King; he doesn't appear to like him much, even now. But he had no one else to turn to, no family or friends of any use to him. The comfort of race, however flimsy and unconvincing, was the only refuge left.

Before Tyson left Ohio, King gave him a book that—whether he read it or not—in some ways serves as a key to the life and times of Mike Tyson: Jawanza Kunjufu's *Countering the Conspiracy to Destroy Black Boys*. King keeps more than a dozen copies of the book in his home, for the purpose of winning over reluctant black fighters. *Countering the Conspiracy to Destroy Black Boys* is a very short and easy-to-read piece of racial paranoia—a poorly reasoned, wretchedly researched, badly written book that is enormously popular in Afrocentric circles and among the black reading public generally. (At this writing it has gone through 24 printings.) It argues in almost laughably reductive Freudian terms that whites fear people of color because they (whites) lack color, and so want to rule and destroy them: women have penis envy, whites have melanin envy. Racism is thus a form of hysteria which is perfectly immune to remedy, a kind of genetic disorder.

If *Countering the Conspiracy to Destroy Black Boy* is a preposterous book when considered as an intellectual enterprise, it is less preposterous when considered as an emotional appeal. It is just the sort of book many people take seriously as "truth-telling," not because it proves itself through argument and evidence to be true but because its readers wish it to be so; as the saying goes, for those who like this sort of thing, this is the sort of thing they like. If Tyson read the book, he would have discovered a portrait of himself-the maladjusted ghetto youth, seasoned by the streets, living by a macho code of honor, confused and misguided after a fatherless childhood. Of course, he had also been spoiled and petted, made into a psychotic brat, and the loving attention that Kunjufu's book bestows on black men is not likely to discredit the concept of spoiling black men—only to suggest that they be spoiled differently, in a more "African" way. Nor is it likely to end the idea that men are special and more important than women. Black men are, after all, "our future," as Afrocentric speakers constantly remind their audiences.

King gives the book to his black fighters not to calm or cure their insecurities, but to worsen them. His encounter with King clearly made Tyson become even more fixated on his status as a man, and more self-conscious of the fact that his masculinity was a conundrum to be unpuzzled. He was surely, now, more self-conscious about the fact that his father figures, before King, were white men: Jacobs and Cayton, and his beloved trainer Cus D'Amato. (The major mother figure in his life, D'Amato's common-law wife, Camille Ewald, was also white.) The man who discovered Tyson, Bobby Stewart, and his first two trainers under D'Amato, Kevin Rooney and Teddy Atlas, were white. Tyson had to face the symbolic truth that he was the creation of white men.

When he was growing up in a very tough section of Brooklyn, from 1966 until about 1979, he was teased by the other boys for his lisp, his high-pitched voice, his "fucking eyeglasses," and his weight. Children always ridicule the odd, the helpless, the unfortunate; ghetto children are particularly vicious in this regard. (These rituals of intolerance are, perversely, self-protective: there might be a great many more murders among the poor if not for this technique of bearing one's life by being told how worthless it is.) Mike Tyson comes from an obese family; he weighed over 200 pounds at puberty. He was so big, in fact, that when Cus D'Amato, the man who taught him to fight and who would become his legal guardian, first saw him, he could not believe the boy's age. To be an overweight boy in a poor neighborhood with glasses and a lisp is to be taunted as a weakling, unless one can talk-or fight. On the streets Tyson had been known as "sissy boy." The brand of machismo he created with fury and deliberation was a sissy boy's revenge.

MIKE'S BRILLIANT CAREER

Like other black heavyweight champions-Joe Louis, Sonny Liston, and George Foreman come to mind-Tyson was a moody and skittish, seemingly slow-witted boy, all of which made it difficult to succeed in school. Those who are docile and articulate, or at least glib, and can fit in the desks have a better shot at making it through that pressurized labyrinth of conformity and obedience training. (Louis, Liston, and Foreman could not handle the discipline of schooling either, although they were formidably disciplined men in other realms.) Although a failure at school, Tyson was a success as a fighter on the streets of Brooklyn. He was born to be a fighter in much the way someone with perfect pitch is born to be a musician.

He fought so well that the boys left off taunting him and started to respect him, even fear him; José Torres reports in his biography *Fire and Fear* that once the ten-year-old Tyson discovered that he could easily beat up older boys, he enjoyed fighting, "kicking people's asses." In a world where most people are paralyzed by the futility of any kind of normal civic action—of any kind ofaction, period—Tyson acted decisively, if recklessly and destructively. His reputation proved to be a useful protection for his family, which encouraged his mother and sister to treat him as someone special: in the jungle, it is good to live with the lion.

"If you only knew," Mike Tyson told Torres (himself a former light-heavyweight champion and Cus D'Amato pupil), "I was a spoiled brat. . . . I think it's funny when people talk about me having a hard life." If Mike Tyson was indulged, it was because his pathological behavior made him the perfect denizen of his pathological world: as with some of the great boxers of the past, a life in the ghetto had given him an obsession with forms of honor and contest, with the imposition of will and the ruthless battering down of opposition. The stealing, lying, and violence that eventually led to his institutionalization were similar to the antisocial behavior of Italian fighters like Jake LaMotta and Rocky Graziano, whose boyhood and adolescent lives Tyson's greatly resembles. Had it not been for their fighting skills, the very combination of derring-do, cynicism, and barbarity that guaranteed their survival in the short term would have killed them all as young men. Instead they were channeled into the entertainment industry largely intact.

And yet, in examining the trajectory of his career, his profound insecurity is obvious. There is no sure thing in the ghetto; to rule there is a tenuous proposition. Surely Tyson was aware that his most admired qualities were inherently self-destructive, that he was in some sense both invincible and doomed, supremely powerful and relentlessly, irresistibly sliding toward an early grave. Cus D'Amato was right in his unending philosophizing about fear, for that is what kept Tyson alive—his monumental fear, his fundamental insecurity, and his belief that he could overcome it by winning a place in the mythology of professional boxing.

Tyson has a great consciousness of the history of his sport, its grand masculine pantheon. He has attempted to embrace this history, to acquire both the joy and the anxiety of influence offered by a set of ideal fathers. He is, in short, restlessly searching for what every great artist needs: a tradition. One of Tyson's biographers, Montieth Illingworth, describes the various fables of Tyson's manhood as "Cus and the Kid:' "Iron Mike:' and "The Public Enemy," to which one might add "The Regenerate Muslim."

The myth of Cus and the Kid was the longest lived. "Cus and the Kid" was invented by Jacobs and Cayton during the early days of Tyson's fighting career, a way to sell him as an amateur fighter despite the fact that in the ring he was mostly an intimidator, a knock-out artist-traits deplored at the amateur level, where scoring points, proper form, and fundamental skill development are doggedly inculcated and highly prized. Here was the sappy story of the black street orphan taken in by a crotchety but good-hearted white boxing trainer, whose only wish was to live long enough to see the kid become a champion. The truth value of this myth remains highly suspect; D'Amato was loved by literary types because he loved to hear himself talk, which made him much like a literary type, but whether he was a great boxing mind is debatable. Certainly Tyson would have become champion had he been instructed by almost any of the first-rate boxing teachers: Emanuel Steward, the late Ray Arcel, Eddie Futch, Lou Duva, or a score of others. D'Amato had no special knowledge of or insight into Tyson's ability. (The two champions D'Amato had trained before he discovered Tyson-Floyd Patterson and José Torres-were not particularly notable fighters, certainly not great ones.)

In fact, D'Amato indulged his star pupil. He never tried to help

Tyson with his problems, his emotional hang-ups and ghetto insecurities, because these were, to D'Amato's mind, at least, the psychological stuffings that made Tyson a good fighter. D'Amato did not care whether Tyson did well in school, or even if he went. He did not care about Tyson's attitudes toward women and sex, which already in his teenage years suggested a tendency toward violence. Tyson knew, too, that D'Amato took an interest in him only because he was a successful fighter. Tyson was often a recalcitrant student. He would disappear from D'Amato's training school for extended periods and was frequently bored by his coach's pontifications, spitting and cursing at him more than once.

Still, despite its manifold flaws, their fictive father-son relationship provided an irresistible formula for a rising boxing star. The sentimentality of racial paternalism is a narcotic of which we Americans, apparently, can never get enough. "Cus and the Kid" was an integrationist riff on the age-old myth of the coach-athlete friendship, that vision of transgenerational male bonding that remains the most celebrated teaching relationship in our culture. "Win one for Cus!" —corny, but effective. The myth presented Tyson to the white public as something more than your typical black fighter, as something more than an escapee from the nearest ghetto. It was an attempt to reinvent Tyson as the new Joe Louis, a black kid worthy to be champion because some whites vouched not only for his ability but for his character. Tyson was from the ghetto, the myth went, but he was not a thug like Liston, or a misanthrope like the young Foreman. If D'Amato, Jacobs, and Kevin Rooney could all love Tyson, why not the whites who watched him fight? Tyson's youth helped; he was under twenty-one when he won his first professional championship. He was also coming up in the wake of Larry Holmes, a very skilled, very capable, but not very popular champion. "Larry Holmes's personality left a lot to be desired:' King said recently, and accurately.

Once Tyson became a professional fighter, "Iron Mike" was born. This was Tyson as the austere warrior: coming into the ring crouching and weaving like Jack Dempsey, throwing punches like Henry Armstrong, swaggering like John L. Sullivan, eyeing his prey as scientifically as Joe Gans. His purity of purpose was almost religious. The Iron Mike myth was meant to place Tyson in boxing history by having him self-consciously refer to other great fighters, and to give him a mythic stature that could make him worthy of being compared to the greatest fighters of the past. Tyson named his first son D'Amato Kilrain Tyson after D'Amato and Jake Kilrain, John L. Sullivan's opponent in the last bareknuckle heavyweight championship bout in America— an arcane, but telling, reference. It was never the intention of D'Amato, Jacobs, and Cayton to make Tyson merely a champion, but to have the public recognize him as the greatest heavyweight fighter ever, the heir to a legendary patrimony.

Tyson has had two distinct, if somewhat contradictory, uses for the racialized history of professional boxing. His identification and expropriation of the great white fighters made him a mainstream figure, depoliticizing his masculinity by making him someone who identified with whites, and so someone with whom whites could, on some level, identify. He brought them into the ring with him by wrapping himself in the mantle of great white fighters of the past. But, as Don King knew, Tyson's early self-immersion in the minutiae of boxing history could prove a liability among his own youthful black fans. Identifying with black fighters of the past-or, more precisely, with the street life that produced them-promised to repoliticize Tyson's masculinity and stave off the charges of racial inauthenticity. The "Public Enemy" myth cooked up by Don King was Tyson's most convincing role, if only because it fit so neatly into the roles scripted for young and physically powerful black men in the American mind.

Tyson as "Public Enemy" identified with the black fighters of the past, casting himself as a sort of political and social rebel: the hip-hop bad boy from Brooklyn who could get respect. Like Jack Johnson, the first black man to hold the heavyweight tide (1908-15), Tyson has endured a scandalous trial and served time in prison. Johnson, who had numerous white wives and lovers, so infuriated the white public (and the authorities) with his sexual adventures that he was eventually convicted for transporting a woman across state fines for purposes of sexual intercourse under the terms of the 1910 Mann Act-a reform measure meant to stern the tide of poor-girl prostitution-and sentenced to a year and a day in federal prison. Johnson spent several years in forced exile, during which time he lost the tide; he then returned to the United States and served his prison term. Like Muhammad Ali, Tyson has endured a three-and-a-half-year break in the prime of his career. Tyson is also ambivalent about the monumental figure of Joe Louis, a black fighter adored by black and white alike, and something of a national hero; like Ali, Tyson, driven by the peculiarities of youthful black honor, wants to be the national hero and the national devil simultaneously.

The "Public Enemy" myth played to black prejudices, as well as white ones. Part of what politicizes Tyson's manhood is simply the fact that he is the champion of a sport that dramatizes male expendability, in an age when the concern with male expendability is, among blacks, almost an obsession. Many blacks believe that "the white power system" is out to destroy Tyson, as it is out to destroy all black men. In this line of reasoning, the most effective weapon in the destruction of the black man is the upwardly mobile black woman who, identifying with whites, tries to emasculate the black man by erasing his blackness. Tyson's disastrous string of relationships dovetails beautifully with this theory. His marriage to Robin Givens (a Sarah Lawrence graduate) lasted all of eight months, during which time she was clearly embarrassed by, and disgusted with, his friends, his taste, his background, and his profession. ("She thinks she's white:' Tyson once complained to his homies.) Desiree Washington, the woman who accused him of the rape for which he was convicted in 1992, was a college student and church school teacher, as well as a beauty contestant. His current girlfriend, Monica Turner—the mother of his second child—has been variously described as a pre-med student and a full-fledged pediatrician. Whichever, she is clearly far more educated than Tyson.

Tyson is obviously attracted to middle-class, educated black women, the very women who would not have given him a second look had he not been a successful boxer. Still, Tyson is their unwilling victim, as far as many of his fans are concerned. Most people in the black community, at least most men, feel Desiree Washington was out to get his money, a conviction which ignores strong evidence to the contrary. If she were only a gold digger, why did she turn down a multimillion-dollar settlement offer from Don King-a bribe, in effect, to drop the criminal charges? Why would she risk being cross-examined on the witness stand-risk being exposed as a liar-if the rape never happened? She could have skipped the criminal trial altogether and gone after Tyson in civil court, where a favorable judgment would have been much easier to obtain.

Tyson's defense at the rape trial made him appear out of control. He seemed less and less like a romantic hero and more and more like a pathetic and unbalanced bully. Tyson's lawyers argued, in effect, that he was a sex maniac, and that any woman interested in him would have known this, or should have. The stories of Tyson's marathon sex-capades, many of which are recorded in Torres's biography (a book which angered Tyson deeply, although he did not refute its charges), did little to help his image. One such story of Tyson reaching climax with twenty-five prostitutes in one night, reeked of particularly desperate braggadocio. (The ironic thing, of course, about this sort of "prowess," which turns sex into the equivalent of a cutting contest or a sparring session, is the terrible sense of inadequacy it masks.) Nor was Tyson helped by his boast, also reported in Torres's book, that the best punch he ever threw was against Robin Givens, when she bounced off of every wall in the room. He seemed depraved.

Tyson is now The Regenerate Muslim, a transformation that took place while he was in prison. Tyson had a Christian conversion when he first joined Don King in 1988, which was either insincere or did not take: after being baptized, he promptly went back to his former debaucheries. This time, things seem to be different. Tyson has politicized his prison experience in much the way Malcolm X did. Indeed, Malcolm seems the paradigm for Tyson: the Muslim conversion, the extraordinary amount of reading, the redemption of his manhood through religion and politics-a black baptism, meant to wash away the years with the whites. But there is also an echo of Muhammad Ali in Tyson's insistence that he was an innocent sent to prison, that the white system tried to break him but could not, in the end.

With his imprisonment and conversion, Tyson may be in a position to enjoy the sort of masculine influence Sugar Ray Robinson exerted on his generation four decades ago. Robinson, the great middleweight champion, was the epitome of cool, the single greatest influence on jazz trumpeter Miles Davis—who made cool an art form of precision, economy of expression, and taste. Robinson, who owned a popular nightclub in Harlem and was a gifted dancer (he made a living at it for two years during his first "retirement" from the ring), is considered the greatest fighter of all time. His conked hair and stylish clothes, his smooth, polished, but deadly ring style, and his gracious composure made him, except for Martin Luther King, the most popular black man of the 1950s. Robinson was the first and only boxer who ever gave the impression of being sophisticated, a cosmopolite-and yet he was unmistakably a black man, perfectly at ease with himself and his blackness. Robinson never needed to reach for the brass ring of respectability, nor did he seemed fueled by class resentment. As a result, he made black manhood and boxing into something like a pure aesthetic. Robinson's cool was too apathetic to be appealing to a young lack man in that age, but it was this political detachment that ultimately gave Robinson's demeanor its power and its endurance: Robinson's was a black manhood that transcended the need of political contingency or context. He had nothing to prove by being black. He was, therefore, a figure akin to someone like Duke Ellington, a race man whose pride was not dependent on reminding the world at every opportunity that he was a Negro. In the late 1960s, Muhammad Ali thought of himself as the reinvention and revision of Robinson, a heavyweight and a politically engaged black man.

Tyson thinks of himself as a further reinvention of this black masculine cool, the latest in a great masculine tradition, a revision of Muhammad Ali. Like Ali, Tyson is a Muslim and a politically changed black man. But unlike Ali, he does not try to turn his fights into political theater. And while Ali tended to bring out the best in his opponents, Tyson paralyzes his opposition. His challengers can invariably point to their bouts with Tyson as their worst fights. In most cases, they are hardly competitive. But the characteristic which most dramatically sets Tyson off from Ali is his total lack of any sense of humor: like Huckleberry Finn, another archetype of American innocence, Tyson takes himself seriously.

Though Tyson craves stability, a final resting place in the pantheon, does he fully understand the complexity of the tradition (and the tragedy) that characterizes this intersection of attitude and history? Joe Louis, whose most important fight was his 1938 rematch against German heavyweight and former champion Max Schmeling-a fight freighted with large political implications-became an American icon. He died a pauper in Las Vegas, old, sick, and consumed with paranoia. Sonny Liston, whose most important fights were his degrading losses to Muhammad Ali in 1964 and 1965, was a national villain, a convict and mobster who died grotesquely, a needle hanging out of his arm, in 1970. George Foreman was at first an Olympic ero, then a villain, then, in his return to the ring, an avuncular comedian. Even the vaunted Robinson died from Alzheimer's disease, aggravated by the punishment he took from over two hundred professional fights.

Tyson, only thirty years old, has already gone through more avatars than any of these men, and he is likely to go through still more. Today, tattoos of Arthur Ashe and Mao Tse-tung-an odd couple, if ever there was one-line his biceps. The two images are meant to symbolize both his newfound self-control and his revision of black cool: Arthur Ashe, as Tyson admits, was not a man he would have liked personally, but he admires Ashe's literacy, his ability to negotiate the white world, his politics. Mao Tse-tung represents strength and authority, a kind of ideological commitment to the power of transformation itself. Tyson has encased himself with images that represent what is, for him, masculine heroism; the bruiser has scarred himself with men who have qualities that he would have wished for in his own father, but who better serve him not as father figures but rather as icons of mythic liberation and mythic discipline. Mao, the father of a totalitarian nation, and Ashe, the only major black figure in a white-dominated sport: Tyson seeks, through these figures, the piety of manhood.

What Tyson lacks, and what both Robinson and Ali had, is an opponent worthy of him, against whom he can dramatize his manhood. Tyson was beaten only once, by a journeyman fighter who will probably not fight him again; there are no longer fighters capable of challenging him. He has dominated the ring even more thoroughly than Joe Louis did during his reign. Without a ring nemesis, Tyson cannot really evangelize his fights, nor can he give them any greater purpose than to enrich himself and those legions who bet on him.

Tyson is not the sum of his myths; he is the remainder. Myth tries to invest lived experience with greater meanings, but despite the stories that have proliferated around him, Tyson's life can never point to anything larger than itself, his own self-serving actions, his own madness, his own befuddlement and consternation before the revelation of his limitations. Tyson's tragedy, finally, is his solipsism: his biggest drama was and continues to be with himself, for the salvation of himself alone.

NOTHING IS FOREVER

from *Dark Trade*, 1996

by

Donald McRae

J ay Bright was regarded by most boxing connoisseurs as the personification of a bad joke. He was an overweight and bearded white guy in his early thirties who, according to the sceptics, used to make quiche with Camille Ewald while Mike Tyson and the other boys boxed in Cus D'Amato's home in the Catskills. Jay, they said, knew little about boxing. To them he was just Tyson's latest bucket-carrier. He was merely another 'yes-man' who wore a white towel around his chunky neck to differentiate him from the other Team Tyson sweeties lining up to kiss the pouting posterior of the boxer they also called Mighty Mike.

Cus had taken Jay in when he was an unhappy and plainly fat teenager. Bright remained a walking-talking D'Amato doll who would transcribe the 'Testimony According to Cus' more promptly than any bible-puncher could reach for his hottest hellfire quote. The boxing critics, especially the inner-circle from New York, had much fun in ridiculing 'the dullness of Bright', a man they could never imagine having the necessary steel to stand up to Iron Mike even if, as they doubted, he could spot the holes in a rusted reputation.

In his previous fight, his second since his release from Indiana,

NOTHING IS FOREVER

Tyson had looked terrible. Although he'd knocked out Buster Mathis in the third round, in December, he had missed his portly opponent so many times that it appeared as if he had lost all sense of the timing which had once been as natural to him as breathing. Tyson's claims that his repeated fresh-air swings were purposeful, that he was merely trying to 'lullaby' Mathis with the whistling of his windy misses, were greeted with scorn. If Tyson had a decent trainer, the boxing writers sneered, he would have been made to confront the full extent of his woeful decline. They said a cunning old craftsman like George Benton or Angelo Dundee would force him to relearn the basics he had neglected so wantonly—ever since the first Bruno fight in 1989 which marked the début of Jay Bright as a junior under Tyson's former trainer, Richie Giachetti. The boxing commentators would have been happiest if Tyson had hooked up again with the abrasive Kevin Rooney who had coached him during his great early years when he unified the various heavyweight titles. Rooney himself, knowing both Tyson and Bright better than most, laughed bitterly when asked to assess the qualities which Jay brought to the corner. 'None,' Rooney snorted. 'He's got nothing—unless you count quiche-making as a useful quality in boxing.'

Teddy Atlas, another renowned trainer who had once lived with D'Amato and Tyson, was equally mocking of Bright. 'It's like wearing plastic thongs under an Armani suit. It's ridiculous—a multi-million-dollar fighter surrounded by a menagerie of frauds.'

As we drove through Las Vegas, with the sun sliding in gently through the open windows, Jay Bright spoke methodically about Tyson's improvement under his tutelage. The words were articulate but I thought more of the hurt which lay beneath them.

'Mike is very sharp,' Bright repeated as we side-stepped downtown and took the highway back towards the Strip. 'For the first two fights, against McNeeley and Mathis, we were just working on the big things, the most crude basics of boxing. After three and a half years away he had forgotten what being punched felt like. We also had to get him used to throwing punches again. Now we've been able to pay attention to some of the finer details. Timing. Combinations. Movement. The small things which make the difference between a good fighter and a great fighter. Those things are coming back. I didn't want Mike to think that these things would be there automatically. Cus taught us that human physiology and human nature is such that frustration builds if expectations are not met. So we're taking it slowly—like Cus would have wanted. Cus always told us that boxing is something you learn, or in Mike's current case, re-learn, through repetition. The more he repeats the training, the more he repeats the process of fighting, the more fluid and automatic it will become. We're just following the template of Cus D'Amato.'

It sounded as if Jay Bright carried the ghost of Cus inside his head; but I was more interested in the man beyond Cus, in the Jay who had to hear himself being vilified. He did not look like another Panama Lewis. I could not imagine Jay Bright yelling 'crackhouse whores' back at his critics. He looked a more sensitive soul.

But Jay did not miss a beat. 'I don't get hurt because Cus taught me to be a professional. He taught me not to allow anything to distract me. He told us, me and Mike, about the kind of envy and greed which manifests itself in boxing. I have not forgotten his voice, his words. They still guide me, like they guide Mike.'

'So even when Kevin Rooney rips you to shreds, you don't feel anything?'

'Look,' he said as he stroked his silvery beard, 'a lot of these people have their own agendas. There are trainers and writers out there who wish they were as close to Mike as I am. They covet my position— either for themselves or for their allies. We're talking about boxing. The schemes and the plots are endless. They will do their best to destroy me but they can only do so on the basis of speculation. They have no concept of the improvement I monitor in Mike Tyson. They have no idea of how I'm training him at the moment. When we won't allow them to see him in the gym, naturally we're going to take heat. I'm smiling through the heat.'

'And what about those who might say you're too nice a guy, a "yes-man" in their words, to tell Mike he looks shit?'

'A lot of people, unfortunately, think a boxing corner should be reminiscent of a bad Hollywood movie. Y'know, they expect the trainer to be slapping his guy in the face, the blood flying, shouting, "I'm gonna cut you if you don't shape up, Muggsy!" I'm sorry, it just isn't like that. If you watch film of Cus in the corner with Floyd Patterson he was calm

and collected. Cus taught me that the trainer is there for inspiration
and instruction. I will be forceful if I think it's necessary but I won't just
do it for the sake of drama. Y'see, Mike and me are together because of
the Cus D'Amato link—but also because of the Jay Bright link.'

There was a long pause as Jay gathered breath. I could feel his passion.

'It's not like I'm some nobody out of Cus's past who has just come
back from Nicaragua. I've known Mike since he was thirteen. Me and
Mike were raised by Cus. We have the same roots. We've been friends
for a long time. But once we're inside that gym the friendship stays on
the outside. If I was just a boot-licker like they say, I wouldn't be
helping Mike. You have to give him the honest, concrete truth. If he
looks horrible he must be told he looks horrible. If he looks a million
dollars he must be told that truth. Mike trusts me. He's receptive to the
fact that I'm not going to lie to him, that I'm not going to say something saccharine just to make it sound good to his ears.

'So I tell Mike his biggest problem in the ring. He wants to live up
to his image as a destroyer too much. He craves that mystique that
Mike Tyson will go out and vaporise every opponent who crosses his
path. He sometimes likes to think that a punch from him can annihi-
late a man. When you go out with that in mind you don't throw combinations. You go looking for the one big bomb. And the opponent has
time to spot it because it is so pronounced a punch. But Mike has so
much more than just power—he has speed, elusiveness, co-ordination
and ferocity. But, most of all, he has such a strong mind—it's that
determined mind which is his greatest asset.'

We had reached the bowels of the MGM Grand garage. The gloom
of the underground made me voice another of my doubts. 'But Jay,' I
said, 'from the outside, his mind seems clouded . . . '

'Why do you say that?'

'He was in a good mood this afternoon,' I admitted.

'Sure he was—he trained well.'

'But there's darkness around him. He sounds like the most troubled
man in boxing.'

We circled the carpark as Jay Bright thought of an appropriate
answer.

'Mike is my friend,' he eventually said.

'I know—but he doesn't talk often of friendship, of happiness.'

'Mike, basically, is a very private man. A very, very private individual. An extremely private person. And you know, when he was still young, like me, he lost his best friend. He lost Cus D'Amato. We talk about Cus a lot. A lot. I miss him every day. So does Mike. I still live in Cus's house. Me and Camille. She's ninety-one years old. She's happy me and Mike are together. But, still, we miss Cus. He was our mentor, our teacher, our best friend and we lost him. Maybe we're still recovering. Maybe Mike's still grieving . . . '

There were many loud and ostentatious members of the Tyson entourage. But when it came to bombast there was only one leader. His name was Steve Fitch or, as he preferred to be hailed, 'The Crocodile'. A short and beefy black man dressed in combat fatigues, a bandanna and sunglasses, Crocodile liked to walk around the MGM Grand and shout.

'Guerilla warfare!' he would holler excitedly. 'Eight days to wake-up! It's time for guerilla warfare!' It was a chant of which he never tired. Occasionally, for the sake of starting a new cycle, Crocodile would break in with a harshly melodic rendition of 'London Bridge is burning down, burning down . . . ' as if Bruno was the bridge and Tyson the great fire of 1996.

Tyson looked askance at his cheerleader as his hands were bandaged in the MGM's white media tent. He did not seem to be in the mood for guerilla warfare, let alone the constant pop of flashbulbs as a pack of photographers crowded in on him. 'Here Mike!' they bellowed. Tyson looked elsewhere instead. 'This way Mike!' they pleaded as Tyson, rather, stared that way.

In the end they decided to zoom in on Crocodile's wide open mouth yelling out his prophecy. Tyson didn't care—as long as they left him alone.

Eventually he had to do what they wanted. He climbed into the makeshift ring and allowed them to pull on his gloves and headgear. Mike Tyson, the bonneted baby again, seemingly oblivious to the squeaky cries of his toy Crocodile.

'Guerilla warfare!' echoed around the tent. A hundred reporters watched Tyson trundle through the motions like a man wading in a vat of treacle. He held and shambled and held again as Jose Ribalta clutched onto him.

I leaned against a metal barrier alongside John Horne as, over the ropes, Jay Bright called mildly, 'Snap it, Mike, go with your instincts.'

Knowing how bad Tyson looked, Horne leaned down and whispered in my ear. 'You know how Mike hates doing these sessions. It don't mean nothing. He just doesn't want to be here. He can't think why he should spar for the benefit of the press.'

Ten minutes later Bright called a merciful halt. As Tyson rushed away to his waiting Range Rover without a word being said, the new trainer addressed the cynical banks of watching pressmen. 'He had an off-day. We all have them . . . '

'Shit,' John Horne muttered, unhappy at such public acknowledgement of Tyson's mediocre performance. I knew then that Jay Bright would have some excuses to make when next he was behind a closed door with the Team Tyson management. 'Let's get out of here,' Horne said to me. 'I'll meet you round the back.'

Horne wore an expensive yellow short-sleeve pullover to match the canary colour of his gleaming Ferrari.

'Yeah,' he smiled, when I commented on his colour co-ordination as, a few minutes later, the Ferrari purred into a slot just outside Don King's trailer in the MGM's private carpark. 'They go well together,' he said with the casual tone of a man who might have bought the car just to duplicate the shade of his jersey. 'Could I get you a drink, a Coke or something?' Horne asked. He was being far friendlier than I had expected. He was portrayed most often as the 'venomous' and 'viper-tongued' Horne. But, with me, he was cautious but cordial. He looked like a man who was open to being questioned.

I had long been interested in John Horne. He had first appeared in reports of Tyson's life soon after the boxer's first co-manager, Jim Jacobs, died in 1989. Tyson was particularly vulnerable, having lost D'Amato and Jacobs while caught up in battle with Robin Givens. The traditional version of Horne's emergence rested on the belief that he was a stooge, one of Don King's 'boys' who had been planted to steal Tyson away from Bill Cayton. He had known Mike in upstate New York and, being young and black, he was seen as being the exact opposite of the patriarchal Cayton. In all the Iron Mike biographies and Tyson features, Horne was painted as a crude homeboy on King's payroll, the guy who did the early spadework for big Don to move in later and sow his 'it's all a white conspiracy to destroy young black boys' denunciation of Cayton and HBO.

I had never been able to square the depictions of Horne as being merely a dupe of Don whenever I saw the intelligence in his lean and handsome face. Horne exuded an instinctive sharpness at odds with media sketches of him as just another fool in the expanded Tyson asylum of gangbangers, homies and assorted crazies. There was an aloof arrogance about him, a cutting vitriol in most of his dealings with the white media. And yet he had a certain sophistication, élan even, which suggested that there was something beyond the coarse caricatures of him as a snake-like hustler.

'My enemies,' Horne smiled as he took off his shades, 'always have to throw in their petty jibes that I'm just Don King's boy. They do this to satisfy themselves. Don never had a real relationship with Mike until I came along. But they prefer to cast doubt on me, to see me as a pawn in some big bad plan. I tell you, man, in this society, when you are a young black man you have to work twice as hard to become successful. And when you do reach the top they hate it if you do not seek out their approval. They hate it if, as a young black man, you keep to yourself and your own people who were with you from the start. They hate it if you do not covert their chatshows or their magazine covers. The flipside to you struggling in the ghetto, the image of you sitting at the wheel of something big and powerful, is not one which sits comfortably with their agenda. And yet I truly believe that as soon as a black person starts looking for acceptance from white America he will never be at peace with himself—because they will never give that acceptance to him.

'The whole situation with Mike Tyson is a perfect illustration. Their Mike Tyson story is not about truth. It's all about Mike Tyson conforming to their preconceived notions. They expect him to act in a certain way, they expect him to do certain things. And they will print it whether it's right or wrong. If he does not follow the path they have laid out, he'd better watch out. They're gonna get him.'

Horne leaned in towards me. He was pleased to be talking, to see how closely I was listening.

'Mike Tyson is one of a tiny handful of young black men who have found a way out. Look at the trouble he has encountered. Look at the troubles of rappers like Tupac Shakur and Snoop Doggy Dog. Let me tell you what happens. You'll understand this, being attuned to South Africa. This society, America, creates all these illegitimate black kids who know that, as they grow up, maybe one in a hundred thousand of them will have the opportunity to make something out of their lives. Now, white America's kids will buy the records made by Tupac and Snoop, they'll pay to watch Mike Tyson fight. But there is no enduring love or concern for young black people because there should be a million Tupac Shakurs, a million Snoop Doggy Dogs. They just need the chance. Without that, what hope can they live on?

'But the people in power in this country do not support the likes of Tupac or Snoop—despite their popularity. They castigate them for being negative, for focusing on the violence and prejudice of this society, for telling stories about ghetto life. But before they became famous they were just ignored. They were just part of the voiceless black underclass. It's okay for millions of black kids to live this dangerous ghetto life, to be limited, to be jailed, to be murdered. Yet as soon as they start writing about it, as soon as they start rapping about it, making a living out of it, creating something out of their pain and suffering, then they are damned. Where's the fairness in that?'

'Do you think Tupac and Snoop, and Mike for that matter, glamorise violence?'

'No. They show it how it is. That does not mean they condone ghetto-life. Let me give you an example. Before Mike Tyson became a fighter and found something he could excel at, something which could offer him an exit, he was in juvenile homes for mugging and stealing and everything else. Yet as soon as Mike found something to focus on, as soon as Mike found someone who would care about him, as soon as Mike saw a way to make a living, he stopped the old life. There's not been a day since when Mike Tyson has mugged anyone or stolen anything. If he was a natural-born thief he would keep at it. He has not. But people who are born that way, whether black or white, always find a way to keep on stealing at a higher level.'

'Many have accused Don King of stealing from fighters like Mike,' I interjected.

'I dispute that. I love Don King. I love him for his values and for what he has created. Don King is the best promoter in the world. He is more involved in his promotions than anyone else. He engenders more atmosphere. Even without Mike Tyson he has proved that he's the best at selling boxing. He creates more fights and generates more money for more fighters than anyone. Mike knows that; that's why we work with Don.'

'How did you and Mike start working together?' I wondered.

'We knew each other as young men. I was from Albany and Mike was in Catskills with Cus. But we went in different directions. Mike was into boxing. I love entertainment. I headed out west, to LA. I started doing stand-up comedy and some movie work. I was in *Harlem Nights* and *Coming to America*. Eddie Murphy is a good friend of mine. Now round about this time Mike was more and more in Vegas. He was in the midst of his marital troubles and strife with Cayton. He did not have anyone to trust. But he knew me in California. So he started coming over. I could tell he really liked being with me. He talked persistently about his troubles. He confided in me. We were friends but he knew I was very business-orientated. Slowly, it evolved. I was doing a lot of Mike's business even before I officially came on board. But Don and I took over when we got him out of his contract with Cayton.

'Now the situation obviously changed when Mike went to jail. There was a lot of jive as to who Mike was gonna work with on the outside. But we were cool. By April '94, almost a year before Mike was released, he asked me and Rory to become his co-managers. He's known Rory from his youngest days and so Rory is a rock for him to lean on. We're a team—it's a family affair.'

I knew that Horne was more likely to make the key financial and promotional decisions in liaison with King.

'Well,' he nodded artfully, 'I've always seen myself as a leader, as a positive thinker. There's no glamour for me in being a gangbanger. I can be sitting in a room and all my friends can be smoking this or that. It doesn't faze me. I have my own path to follow. If anything, I'll just say, "How can you do that?" It goes back to my parents. I was fortunate to have very loving parents. Sadly, a lot of black Americans don't have that support. Look at Mike's hardship. I was so lucky to have both my parents, Nettie and Odell. They're still together after forty-six years, having raised a large family. I was the seventh child of nine. But they gave me the love and the confidence I needed to do well. I still feel their influence in decisions I take for the benefit of Team Tyson.'

NOTHING IS FOREVER

'How much say did you have in the decision to keep Tyson off the interview treadmill?'

'I must say that I'm the one who had the most input into that policy. It helped that Mike's not mad about being interviewed, but I felt it was the right tack. The bulk of the American media, especially the writers from New York, have their own warped perspective on Mike Tyson. They're so biased and hateful. I knew they would twist anything he said. So I was determined that they should be given no access to him. Then, just as he came out of prison, I saw how crazy the situation had become. People were desperate to get a chunk of him. I knew that Mike could not meet their demands. What was most important was Mike being given the chance to restore some order in his life. He had to look after himself both as a human being and as a fighter. He had to regain focus. I knew that all the interviews would just harp on about jail. He had to concentrate instead on his future, on the things he truly loves which, you know, are his family and boxing.

'Now, a week tomorrow, on Saturday, 16 March, he has the opportunity to rebuild his identity as he believes in it. When he beats Frank Bruno he will, for the first time in six years, be able to call himself the WBC heavyweight champion of the world. That will be part one in his return to greatness. I know he will then go on to reclaim the WBA and IBF titles. He will again be the undisputed champion. That will bring him fulfilment. Y'see, I know exactly who and what Mike Tyson is— more than the media. He's an exceptional man. Once he got himself together—mentally, physically and professionally—the world media would be even more hungry for him. The demand would be even greater.'

'His silence, in other words, enhances his allure?' I said, tempted to call him Greta Garbo in drag.

'Exactly!' John Horne enthused. 'Supply and demand. But, beyond that, his boxing is what is important. What brings all this attention on Mike Tyson, besides the hoopla, is his fighting in the ring. He's simply a ferocious fighter. That is the source of his fame. He's fighting for the heavyweight championship of the world again. That's what people love. It's not what the media think. People want to see him fight rather than hear him talk about gossip. The gossip is fine sometimes, it's natural to be curious about a man like Mike Tyson—but, listen, we're talking about a man's life here. His life is no joke. He's deadly serious.'

'And what about your life, John,' I said, 'say in five years time, once you've made all that money with Mike?'

'I love being able to make people laugh,' he said earnestly. 'I'd love to be a stand-up comic again.'

'Are you a funny guy?'

John Horne laughed out loud and hammered his knee in delight. 'Yeah, man, I think I'm a funny guy. I've heard I've been pretty good as a stand-up!'

I thought about asking Horne if he had any Tyson jokes to tell but I was still angling for my next Mighty Mike interview. I laughed along and asked him about the movies instead.

'Oh yeah!' he exclaimed. 'Even at this point I would love to be producing films. Did I tell you about Eddie Murphy? Right! You should meet Eddie. He knows Mike. But I figure the movies will still be there when we're through with boxing.'

'What about Mike, though?' I said. 'Where do you think he sees himself five years down the line?'

John Horne shifted in his chair. He knew what I was thinking. While it looked like he was a happy man with his future inked out in glossy detail, Mike Tyson's own horizon was smudged.

'Mike is the kind of guy . . . ' Horne said as he eyed my tape-recorder carefully. He began again, considering the best words to use. 'It's very difficult for Mike to talk about his life five years from now. I'll be honest with you. There are days when Mike just does not believe he is still going to be here five years from now. He's not sure how much time is left for him. He does not know what life might throw at him next.'

'Does Mike feel doomed?'

'No, not necessarily. Perhaps it's better if I say that, rather than making any long-term plans, Mike takes one day at a time. But I don't want you to misunderstand me. Mike Tyson loves life. He loves being alive so much that he does not want to be disappointed. Mike just feels it more than you or I might. Mike, I think, lives a little closer to the shadows than the rest of us. Maybe he's more honest than any of us in the end, knowing as he does that nothing is forever.'

'But, in the meantime, he knows he'll get paid $30,000,000 for fighting again next Saturday. It must be confusing, having all this wealth and fame after prison.'

'Mike is a very giving person. He just doesn't like to tell the whole world how much he uses his money to help other people. I would like to publicise his charity work more but Mike does not want the fuss.'

'But the overwhelming bulk of that thirty million will be shared by Mike, Don and yourself,' I suggested.

Horne had moved onto a higher plane. He replied in bizarre fashion. 'To God,' he said, 'no one is more important than anyone else. It is just the way that society is constructed on an economical basis. But I truly believe that most people with economic power have been put there by God because, generally, they are the ones with the capability of spreading that wealth.'

I must have stared in surprise at Horne's theory for he added, 'Well, I know some slip through the net and refuse to help others—but myself and everybody else I've been around lately are people who are committed to having a positive impact on other people's lives. Most of the people I grew up with and all my family are good people, very good people, but I honestly believe that I am the one most equipped to take wealth and share it around. I can help them the most. Do you understand?'

'Er, I think so,' I stumbled, before flashing my most winning grin. 'Do you think you might be able to help me too, John?'

John Horne leaned back in his chair and smiled broadly. 'Yeah, I just might. I checked up on you . . . '

'You did?'

'Sure. I've looked into your dealings with Mike and some other fighters. We're happy. Mike's happy to talk to you. I'm happy he talks to you. So, yeah, you're the one guy we're gonna go with in Vegas this time. Mike ain't talking to anyone else. We've decided to go with you. I'm gonna get you and Mike together. You got a deal with us, man.'

We agreed to meet four days later, on the Tuesday before Tyson stepped into the ring to challenge Bruno. Horne and Rory Holloway were due then to meet the media in the MGM press tent and, once that onerous chore had been completed, we would drive out to see Tyson. Despite finding a way into Tyson's hermetic camp I was still edgy about the outcome. It would not be a done deal until I had Mighty Mike across the table from me, knowing that he had no way out until he agreed to read out and discuss his latest book list.

I was intrigued, too, by the prospect of talking to Holloway—the less refined partner of the managerial duo. Holloway did not have either the candy or viperous tongue of Horne but he had known Tyson longer than almost anyone else. If there were still secrets to be discovered about Tyson there was as good a chance as any that Holloway would be in on them.

A few days before I met Horne, Holloway had spoken to the British press pack outside Golden Gloves. After ridiculing Bruno's prospects, Holloway said, softly, 'People make the mistake of thinking Mike no longer has the fire inside him. They are wrong. Mike is much more humble and far less vocal but he is still vicious deep inside . . . he's been knocking out two sparring partners a day. We came here with fourteen and we've only got three left. They've been leaving camp in the middle of the night without their pay-cheques. Some of 'em have been hit so hard they think that Tyson has a personal vendetta against them.'

If Jay Bright could unravel a little of the mysterious hold Cus D'Amato exerted on Tyson, and if Horne uncovered a measure of his fighter's fatalism, I felt sure Holloway would be able to tell me more about the disturbing intensity of Iron Mike. There was a chill to those words—'he is still vicious deep inside'—which suggested that Holloway had seen something in the post-prison Tyson which went beyond rhetoric.

But, along with two hundred others, I waited hopelessly for Horne and Holloway that Tuesday morning—with nothing to entertain us beyond the increasingly frenzied pitching of Don King conducting five-minute live interview bolts with radio and television stations around America. With a seemingly impossible gusto and zing, King sat in the centre of the ring and sold his promotion to listeners in New York and Los Angeles and to viewers in Detroit and Miami. His torrential stream of consciousness was overwhelming.

'Frank Bruno has changed tremendously,' he gushed. 'Bruno is no longer the reticent young man. He is still a very distinguished, classy guy, a quintessential Englishman of royal stature. But now the fellow is becoming somewhat loquacious. He dares to say with Churchill's fortitude—remember we will fight them on the beaches, we will fight them in the breeches, we will fight them in the trenches—that he will knock Mike Tyson into my lap.

'Now Tyson used to be the guy who would say "I'm gonna knock your nose back into your brain, I got bad intentions!" But now Mike Tyson is a family man. He just had a little girl, y'know, Rayna by name, a beauty by nature. So Mike has quietened down. So what we have here at the MGM Grand is the startling sight of two fighters turning each other round. One's become more loquacious, the other less loquacious. An', man, I just love it. I think the contrast makes for a helluva fight, one which you just cannot afford to miss! So call your pay-per-view cable operator NOW! DO IT, BABIES! SIGN UP!'

King then stepped up his polemic as he examined each boxer's particular allure. 'Frank Bruno is the Scarlet Pimpernel. You seek him there, you seek him here, you seek him everywhere but no one can find that darned Scarlet Pimpernel. But he will show up on Saturday night. Y'see, Frank is not only practising boxing, he is also practising the magic of Siegfried & Roy, selling the illusion that he can knock Tyson right into my lap. But, hey, this is Las Vegas, fantasy-land, and we're all travelling the Yellow Brick Road. Bruno is the champion. He is so popular in Britain, man, that when he beat Oliver McCall to win the title they had a procession through London-town on a day they called VB Day, "VB" meaning "Victory for Bruno"! There was a crescendo at Trafalgar Square before 100,000 merry Englishmen. Yessireee, even the pigeons were paying homage to him, floating around, making a crown of pigeon-glory round his head. Those pigeons gave Frank Bruno British pride, they had him walking in clouds. You can see it. This is a confident man, an extraordinary man. Frank Bruno is just ripped—you should see this guy's body, baby!

'And yet, and yet . . . ' Don paused to briefly mop his fevered brow, 'Frank Bruno does not have that boy Winston in his corner. So we will have to send him back with a lot of politeness, love, understanding and fraternity because Mike Tyson is determined to regain his title which he rightfully describes as belonging to him. Tyson will demonstrate his savage talents and show the world he is truly the baddest man on the planet. He will become the world's first billionaire athlete. The

Tyson vs. WBC Heavywieght Champion Frank Bruno, 1996

smackeroonies will just keep rolling in for him. This is a man who will make more in a night than Michael Jordan gets paid in a year. That is the hard cash scale of this man mountain. But Mike Tyson has become a much more mature human being. He's found God and I think he's gonna be a tremendous asset to society. He's a gem. I love the man. But Tyson in the ring is gonna be evil and hostile. Bruno will have to give way to such a malevolent force. Iron Mike will not yield. He is fulfilling a prophecy laid down in holy writ. I met an old Chinese Martial Arts guru and he says, "Ah-So, Ah-So! Mr Tyson! He has double-joint power! He is guru of boxing! Ah-So! Ah-So!" Double-joint fisticuffs will be declared on Bruno. It's gonna be war! It's gonna be sensational! You cannot be left snoozing like Rip van Winkle. Call your operator NOW! HURRY! HURRY!'

King had a right to be happy. Not only had he regained control of boxing and the heavyweight division, but he had stayed out of jail. Four months before, in mid-November, he'd been on the verge of being found guilty of fraudulently claiming $350,000 from Lloyds of London—a charge which had hung over his shocked head of hair for more than two years. If convicted, King knew that he could face up to forty-five years in a federal prison and be fined $2.25 million on nine counts of insurance wire fraud. Desperate Don insisted on his innocence but the evidence was piled high against him.

Yet, in the end, as if to prove that he could still work miracles, King escaped when Judge Lawrence McKenna lamely declared a mis-trial after describing jurors as 'hopelessly trapped' in their efforts to reach a decision. The normal procedure would have seen the judge order the jury back in again to debate the verdict further. They had apparently spent little more than five hours in serious discussion of the six-week long trial.

'We thought he would send us back in with more information,' said Michelle Lieber, one of the jurors. Yet McKenna was compromised by the fact that he'd already dismissed all four alternate jurors even though he knew that one of the black women sitting in judgement of King had a firm commitment to fly to South Africa on 17 November whether a decision had been reached or not. On that exact day, as they announced their deadlock, with only a slight majority voting that King should be found guilty, McKenna said, 'I'm very reluctant to permit an eleven-member jury as this is a very close case. I don't want to do this any more than you do—but I have to declare a mis-trial.'

Both the FBI and Lloyds professed outrage at Dashing Don's getaway and vowed to seek 'a prompt retrial'. But Don King smiled hugely. He was still free to bark 'Only in America!'

In Las Vegas, King, in a manner of speaking, thanked his 'lucky stars and stripes and the family that is America!' He turned briefly away from 'those contesting gladiators, Mr. Bruno and Mr. Tyson', to reveal his renewed humility. 'My liberty prevails because of my fellow Americans. The day I allow my ego to possess my humanity to such an extent that I say, "It is all I and not we," then my star will cascade to earth precipitously and there will be no more Don King. But, fear not, viewers, that shall not happen. I am a promoter of the people, by the people and for the people. My whole thing is people! My magic lies in my people ties!'

My own ties to Team Tyson, however, seemed to have lost their lustre. John Horne and Rory Holloway refused to leave their guerilla warfare bunker to meet the press that day. Like Tyson himself, they had gone into hiding, finding renewed power in seclusion. The Mighty Mike interview seemed to be slipping away, lost in his desire to be alone. Surrounded by the roar of Dangerous Don, I could not blame him.

• • •

The night before the fight. My room was quiet. I pulled back the curtain on Las Vegas. Mike Tyson still rotated on the MGM's monstrous metal cube. He gave me that same death-head stare, his clouded eyes revealing nothing.

By then I knew that, like everyone else, I would have to wait a while longer for Tyson. He'd appeared with Horne and Holloway at an obligatory press conference on the Wednesday at the same MGM theatre staging Michael Crawford in EFX's virtual reality extravaganza. Yet Tyson had no time for fantasy. He was even more loath to part with words.

I had snuck a way into the front-row seat—which still left me twenty feet away from the two-tiered table seating forty-eight fight participants. Tyson kept his head down, looking at no one, while Horne nodded and smiled at me. I smiled back, resigned at last to the enforced silence between us. He lifted his right shoulder in a gesture of apology and held an imaginary phone to his ear. Perhaps we would yet talk—later.

After enduring seventy-five minutes of rumbustious blather from King, Tyson was coerced into taking a turn at the mic. While Rory Holloway appeared alongside him in burgundy morning-dress and trilby and John Horne dazzled in a white suit, Tyson had chosen a starker look. His black leather jacket and jeans were topped by a brown baseball cap which read 'Live Hard'. Tyson was at his most forbidding and monosyllabic in his sixteen-second delivery.

'I'm just happy to be here,' he said dourly. 'I'm in great shape. I'm fit. I'm ferocious and I'm looking forward to a good fight and to being victorious and champion of the world. That's all I have to say. I'm ready to get it on.'

Jay Larkin, the executive director of Showtime, was bemused. 'I've seen more levity at a funeral,' he said on the podium. 'If I was making this kind of money I'd be grinning from ear to ear.'

Tyson made no effort to link his ears with a smile. His scowl deepened. He did not need to be told that he should feel happy. He nodded faintly when he was hailed from the floor by a young black woman who praised him for the $50,000 donation he had made that day to the Martin Luther King Youth Center in Las Vegas. When asked to comment on his contribution, Tyson resisted. 'These are just projects I involve myself in,' he said blankly. 'It doesn't make me a nice guy . . . everything is more of a burden now, more responsibilities. I don't know if I should use the word "burden". But I'm just not a happy type of guy . . . I try to do my best but I always fall short of the mark.'

He had only a few more questions to endure for it seemed as if even the media realised the futility of forcing Tyson to speak. I remembered some of his earlier words. 'I'm very excited,' he had murmured of baby Rayna. 'Her mother is beautiful, but [Rayna] is so beautiful and gorgeous that she makes her mother look like a yard dog.' Tyson brooded down on us as if he knew he could still fight like a yard dog himself.

Surprisingly, he spoke again. 'I'm competitive, that's the way I am. I'm ferocious that way. It's just been bred into me. I've been conditioned to fight since I was twelve years old. It's all I know.'

After the obligatory stare-down with Bruno, Tyson was gone. He was ushered away by Horne, Holloway, the Crocodile and rest of the coterie, bar Jay Bright who was still in trouble for criticising Tyson in public. A flurry of journalists and TV crews tried to break through the security and clamber on stage. I was relieved to know that my own hustling was over. Tyson pulled free from the rest to walk ahead, alone again. My urgency to meet with him had always been built on an eroding pretence. I could no longer sustain the belief that an hour in his company would solve either the mournful contradictions of his character or the enigmas of my fascination with him.

There were times when Tyson had become more than a person to me. His violence in the ring and his discontent on the outside had tapped into something darker in my own life. With Alison I was happier than I had ever been; and yet Tyson reminded me of sadness and pain in the past, of all I had left and lost in South Africa, of the moments which, much as I parried the thought, I knew would return again in new form. They would come again, for different reasons than before, but still they would come. There would have to be some sorrow and loss in the years ahead.

Tyson, meanwhile, lived and fought with the fury of knowing that 'nothing is forever', as if it was hard for him to find any lasting joy in the present. Even his gorgeous daughter made her beautiful mother look like a yard dog.

I felt sorry not only for Monica Turner, Tyson's mysterious girlfriend, but for the fighter himself. There were distressing streaks of hurt in so much of what Tyson said. No wonder he preferred to shut his mouth.

But Tyson, as an icon, as some more personal symbol for me, was not solely a barometer of heartache. As the illuminated steel head spun slowly on its emerald MGM dais, I could picture his face softening above the little boy as he scribbled his name over a boxing image. Outside the Golden Gloves gym he had been patient and gentle with the tiny collector, looking up at me with that brief smile he sometimes used. It was then that Tyson rekindled my memories of Soweto, when I had come face to face, heart to heart, with the self-proclaimed township hardcases, the militant boys, the 'comrades' who had been through detention and would do so again before apartheid was over. They were the guys I used to shiver to meet, wondering what they would make of a soft white teacher, no older than them, from the rolling suburbs.

But, ultimately, they were exceptionally good to me, opening up and telling me jokes and stories to which I could respond—despite a relationship built on the ironies of our difference. They stopped being 'comrades', clandestine soldiers, and became friends instead. They offered proof to me, in the early '80s, that as troubled a country as it was, South Africa could still be a place like no other, a fantastic amalgam of colour and emotion, of tumult and hope. We were buddies, and it almost broke my heart to leave them. Who in England would talk to me about boxing like they had done, who would be as activated by the emergence of the young Tyson as those township believers, those Soweto schemers, those Diepkloof dreamers?

Well, I did find other people in London. I found Alison. Yet I could not forget the eloquent bruiser who, instead of handing in essays about *Tess of the D'Urbevilles*, took it upon himself to write me poems about Muhammad Ali. I still have those boxing poems of his, of Gibson Khumalo's, with their hand-written words drifting off the page in praise of 'Bra Ali's' dancing feet. And I recall almost weeping when, a few years later, he wrote to me in London. Gibson was not long out of prison. After his 'problems', Gibson said, he was 'relatively well'. He was nearly fine again. He was going to be okay. He felt good enough to pick up a newspaper. He had even managed to read an article. It was a piece about Mike Tyson, ruling the ring in 1988, and the words had made Gibson think of the schooling he had never finished, of the poems he had once written in class.

'Hey, bra,' he wrote to me, 'I thought of you when I read again. This Tyson. Do you like him too? I'm sure. I find him most interesting. Boy! I composed a poem. After so long, can you believe? This is what I write today:

Iron Mike
Iron Mike
Fists forged
Full of fire
And fury
With skin as dark as mine
From a heart as black as mine
As savage as mine
As sad as mine
From here to there
New York to Soweto
It's a hell of a way
Will he ever know my name?
Will he ever know my name?
I think not
I think not
Iron Mike
Iron Mike.
Please correct any spelling.'

My Soweto days had gone forever but Tyson helped me to remember. The fiercest men were not always the hardest. 'Comrades' and boxers, fighters and soldier-boys, Toney and Tyson, my friends from home, sometimes they blurred into one and the same, into people I knew. Even Tyson. At last, no longer begging my way towards an interview, I could think of him not just as the Baddest Man or Iron Mike or Mighty Mike. He was another man. A man on his own, alone with thoughts and feelings. But, still, not a head or an icon; just a man.

I worked through much of that night, transcribing my tapes of James Toney, Eddie Mustafa Muhammad, Jay Bright, John Horne and Don King—men who all laid claim to some corner of Tyson's heart even if they secretly knew that, in the end, he preferred to be on his own. As I listened and wrote down their words I would sometimes look out at the shimmering neon below and then back to Tyson's turning head. It was John Horne's voice which struck me the most as it resounded through the tiny headphones.

'Mike is the kind of guy . . . ' he started and stopped and started again. 'Mike, I think, lives a little closer to the shadows than the rest of us. Maybe he's more honest than any of us in the end, knowing, as he does, that nothing is forever . . . '

15 MARCH 1996

There was a less poetic strain to the songs sung about Mike Tyson by Frank Bruno's supporters—although the bemused Americans seemed to find them quaint. 'Ain't this swell?' and 'They got some rhythm, all right' were a couple of comments I overheard late on Saturday afternoon as I struggled through the crowds of British fight fans and American visitors to Vegas. It made for a startling collision of cultures as, outside the MGM's Mexican Coyote Café, boozy banks of Union Jack-draped lads pumped out their raucous terrace chants to beaming white Nevada families and glitzy African-American lovers out for a night with Mighty Mike. Perhaps because they could not fully decipher the Essex lilt embedded into the words, the Americans loved the sound of men singing together. After a dozen years on the North Bank, hearing Arsenal ditties, my ear was more attuned to the message. At first there was the pleasantly familiar adaptation of Saturday afternoon crooning: *There's only one Frankie Bruno, Only one Frankie Bruno, Walking Along, Singing a Song, Walking Along in a Winter Wonderland.'*

But, as the beer began to lend an edge of gravel to the voices, another British football melody was given a whirl and a slight change of text: *'Tyson is a rapist, Tyson is a rapist, La la la, La la la, Tyson is a rapist, Tyson is a rapist, La la la, La la la!'*

'What are they saying now?' one black woman dressed in a spangly dress turned to ask her heavily jewelled Mr T lookalike.

'Beats me, baby,' he muttered, 'but it sounds kinda pretty.'

NOTHING IS FOREVER

There had been less of a misunderstanding two nights previously, on the Thursday evening, when Tyson and Bruno stepped on the scales. While some of the British fans did not quite get the street-slangy joke embossed into Tyson's 'Phat Farm' jacket, they clearly decoded the sign given to them by his cheerleader. The Crocodile yelled 'Guerilla warfare, two days to wake-up time, guerilla warfare!' and then, pointing to Frank Bruno's wife, Laura, drew a finger across his throat. 'Hey baby,' he shouted to Laura, 'your man is gonna get hurt by my man!'

Standing with her two daughters and a whole gang of friends from Brentwood a few feet in front of me, Laura reacted with fury. 'Fuck off!' she screamed at Crocodile. 'You can fuck right off!'

Her indignation was picked up by the English boys in the balcony. 'You fat bastard, you fat bastard,' they harmonised as Laura turned to give them the thumbs-up, her face glowing with excitement.

They resumed their chronic paean to masturbation when Tyson stripped down to his gleaming white underpants to weigh-in at 220 pounds. A sea of fists jerked in the air at Tyson, the barracking Brits feeling safe to mock and heckle at a distance. Bruno was the one who would do their fighting. He cut an imposing and confident figure as his 247 pounds of chiselled muscle were clenched for the sake of both the scales and the cameras. He held up a single finger and pulled his face into a grimacing mask of defiance. He did not look like a man who might fear Mike Tyson. He was the heavyweight champion of the world.

Tyson let slip a smirk as he glanced up at the title-holder. Frank Bruno had owned the WBC belt for six months. But Tyson knew. Nothing lasts forever. There had been so much uncertainty around Tyson, and so little to laud against McNeeley and Mathis, that his return to the ring was questioned by many. A solid body of boxing opinion predicted that he would be tested by Bruno. I felt my own doubt drain away as the two fighters took their time-worn walk to the ring.

Tyson looked oddly serene in his eagerness to climb through the ropes. His movements were fluid, his face calm. He did not have any need to sneer or gesture for he had reached his spiritual home, the 'dark hearth' of which Mark Kram had written. He wore a black towel over his head.

Bruno, in contrast, was dressed in a red, white and blue satin dressing-gown which I imagined Laura had helped choose for him. His own face was smeared in thick patterns of Vaseline. But not even those whitened stains could hide the misgiving which tumbled through him. The long wait must have been unbearable, for it seemed as if all kinds of terrible visions had been let loose in his mind. He looked confused and apprehensive. He was about to fight Mike Tyson. It was hard to imagine the full extent of feeling which had taken hold of him, making him mark the sign of the cross every few steps. His constant genuflecting was a more moving emblem of a certain rout than the repeated hand across the throat slash favoured inside the ring by the dubious Crocodile.

Ringside was electric. Don King's hair stood to attention in tribute both to the American anthem and the sheer charge of the crowd. There must have been at least forty people between the ropes before, eventually, they were cut down to three after the referee's shriek: 'This is for the championship of the world. Any questions, Mr. Bruno? Mr. Tyson? Let's Get It On!' Mills Lane stood between the two boxers, alone at last in their opposing corners. His arm dropped as the bell sounded. The noise from sixteen thousand people was frightening, but exhilarating.

Tyson was quick and elusive, like the Mike of old, from his chilling youth. He moved inside and hit Bruno with one, two, three hard punches. Bruno forgot his ramrod jab and grabbed Tyson by the head, trying to delay the certain damage by holding him in a vice-like grip. Tyson broke away. Bruno missed again. Tyson hammered home a combination of blows. Bruno snatched his neck and tried to grapple. When he did manage to land a left hook to the body, Mighty Mike simply walked through the heavy punch to detonate a right against Bruno's swelling head. Tyson's malice was controlled and even graceful for a heavyweight. Bruno was fretful and cumbersome, fouling Tyson incessantly in a failed attempt to disrupt the accelerating tempo of his attack.

By the end of the first, there was a deep red groove above Bruno's left eye. Even his most resolute followers were not blind. They could tell. Although they unleashed their 'Broooo-no, Broooo-no, Broooo-no!' cry, it sounded like the lowing of cattle being led to the slaughterhouse. The second round was an equally bitter experience for Bruno. Even his persistent holding was interrupted—first by Tyson who used the weight of a meaty forearm to push him back and then by Lane who deducted a point.

But there was never going to be any need to resort to the scorecards and, in the next, fifty seconds into the third, Tyson ended the fight with characteristic brutality. He was, as Rory Holloway had promised, 'still vicious deep inside'. Bruno turned southpaw, leading with his right hand. Tyson ducked under the clumsy guard to bang a right to the body and a left to the chin. As Bruno said later, Tyson was on him 'like a harbour shark', throwing punches so fast and furious, so icily accurate, that they left the bigger man sprawling against the ropes. Hooks and uppercuts fired from Tyson, shooting up the powerful expanse of his body to hit Bruno with sickening impact. Tyson had discovered himself in boxing once more. He was the champion of the world again.

Mills Lane sank down to lift the guard from Bruno's mouth before his arms encircled him in a conciliatory hug. Tyson turned away with his arms spread wide as if to say 'see, I told you'. He fell onto his knees and kissed the sky-blue canvas. He was alone for maybe two seconds before they climbed into the ring to lift him high.

Crocodile was screaming, the back of his jacket rippling with the words printed out in deference to Tyson: 'Liked By Few, Hated By Most, Feared By All!'

Even in his triumphant moments of pitiless violence, those words did not reveal the full story of Mike Tyson—either as a boxer or a man. I looked away from the howling entourage and followed Tyson with my eyes. He walked alone, pushing his way through the ring, heading for Frank Bruno slumped on his stool. Laura held her husband but she made room for Tyson to stretch out and embrace Bruno. I could see him talking to Bruno, whispering compassion into his ear, trying to break the stricken champion's fall. He had words then. He wanted to speak. Tyson stayed low, cradling Bruno, rising only to stroke him on the head with his open glove. He looked lost in his own world, Tyson, gently stroking the head of a man he had just beaten. They would call him 'The Baddest Man' again; but, then, he was just a man, trying to comfort another.

WHY HOLYFIELD WAS NOT AFRAID OF TYSON

The New York Times, November 11, 1996

by

Dave Anderson

LAS VEGAS, Nev.—It was as if Evander Holyfield were an evangelist missionary beating up a tribal executioner, a teacher's pet battering the schoolyard bully, a friendly sheriff gunning down the notorious gunslinger.

Quite simply, Holyfield not only wasn't afraid of Mike Tyson, he was tougher and stronger. And with his 11th-round knockout on Saturday night, he's now the World Boxing Association heavyweight champion.

Holyfield wasn't afraid because he had been in the ring with Tyson before, in 1984 when both were Golden Gloves champions. Holyfield was a light heavyweight then, but the day they sparred, they were so vicious, trainers jumped in the ring to separate them before the three-minute round ended. Tyson, then 18, already had the image of an assassin. But Holyfield didn't freeze into an ice sculpture and then melt as so many Tyson opponents would.

Their professional careers were on a collision course in 1990. Tyson was the champion, but Buster Douglas, who also wasn't afraid, dethroned him in Tokyo. Holyfield then dethroned Douglas, but to justify the title, he knew he needed to fight Tyson.

WHY HOLYFIELD WAS NOT AFRAID OF TYSON

Tyson vs. Holyfield, 1996

"Make the match," he told Lou Duva, his co-trainer. "I know Mike. I'll beat him."

Tyson's damaged ribs canceled their 1991 bout and his subsequent three-year prison term, along with Holyfield's three losses (two to Riddick Bowe, one to Michael Moorer) cast doubt on its revival. When Holyfield struggled to beat Bobby Czyz, he appeared to be just another statue to be shattered in Tyson's comeback.

But this was no statue. In the MGM Grand, where "The Wizard of Oz" is part of the film heritage, the 34-year-old Holyfield turned the brute known as Iron Mike into the Tin Man.

"You got to fight him to get his respect, then box him," Holyfield said two months ago. "You got to box him to get him in a corner, then fight him. He's probably going to hit me, and I'll drop, but if I hit him, he'll drop too. He's not the type of person to get up a lot. Most punchers aren't accustomed to taking punches."

And because Holyfield wasn't afraid to punch, Tyson was literally out on his feet.

By the time Holyfield arrived in the post-fight interview tent, Tyson was already on the dais, patting the lumps on his face and forehead with a towel. Whenever they were together on other recent occasions, Tyson had glared and snarled at him, but now, as Holyfield walked behind him, Tyson turned and smiled. "I just want to shake your hand, man," Tyson said.

Tyson would acknowledge not remembering being knocked on the seat of his black satin trunks in the sixth round by Holyfield's left hook, not remembering being battered in the final seconds of the 10th, not remembering the referee, Mitch Halpern, rescuing him after 37 seconds of the 11th.

"I was tired. He just kept fighting. I got caught in some exchanges. In the last round, I didn't know where I was at," Tyson was saying now on the dais. Then he smiled and offered his right hand to Holyfield, sitting nearby. "Thank you very much. I have the greatest respect for you."

The late Cus D'Amato taught him that boxing wasn't so much a clash of power and strategy as it was of wills. And because Holyfield hadn't been afraid of Tyson, he was able to impose his will while breaking Tyson's will.

"I don't think about being hit," Holyfield said. "I'm trying to hit him."

The 34-year-old Holyfield also thanked his belief in God's will.

"I prayed in training," he said. "I prayed in the ring. I prayed when I was fighting."

Holyfield is now a symbol for the power of prayer and the power of heart—he needed clearance by the Mayo Clinic before the Nevada Athletic Commission would license him. Most of Tyson's other opponents were too busy cowering to punch. Of Tyson's 47 fights, he had 30 knockouts within three rounds, including 20 in the first round.

But in Tyson's fifth fight since his release from prison, he wasn't in there with Peter McNeeley, who disappeared in 89 seconds, or Bruce Seldon, who vanished in 109 seconds. He wasn't in there with Buster Mathis Jr. or Frank Bruno, who wilted in the third.

In those four farces, Tyson fought a total of 18 minutes 20 seconds. In the seventh round Saturday night he had been in the ring longer than that. Instinctively, he continued to punch, but, just as he wearied in the late rounds against Douglas, he didn't display the mental stamina needed to survive a grueling brawl.

If Tyson's corner men, especially the trainer Jay Bright, told Tyson how to adjust to Holyfield, it wasn't apparent. "You can't have three or four guys talking to the fighter," Kevin Rooney said. "Only one guy should be talking."

WHY HOLYFIELD WAS NOT AFRAID OF TYSON

During Tyson's early years en route to being the youngest heavy-weight champion in history at age 20 in 1986, Rooney was that one guy. He recently was awarded $4.4 million by a Federal jury in his breach of contract litigation against Tyson, who has appealed the verdict. Tyson would be better off rehiring him.

"I would've told Tyson to jab, jab," Rooney said from his Catskill, N.Y., home where he had watched the bout on television. "Tyson's used to guys falling down. When Holyfield didn't fall down, Tyson gave up. And all that bragging before the fight. You don't do that. Once you start bragging, you're hiding something.

Tyson was not only hiding the rust from his prison term but also hiding behind the bravado of every schoolyard bully.

"You can intimidate Tyson. He hit Holyfield a couple good shots, but Holyfield fired back."

Duva said: "When Evander hit him back, Tyson couldn't believe it. Tyson can punch, but he can't fight."

Duva glowed. In addition to his share of Holyfield's $11 million purse, he said the Duva family had won $230,000 on Holyfield in the Las Vegas sports books. "We got $10,000 down at 16 to 1," Duva said, "and $5,000 down at 14 to 1."

Having exorcised Tyson's ghost, Evander Holyfield should retire now. He even indicated he'll think about it. But he's a fighter, so look for a rematch in March or June. Even Don King wants a rematch. When Tyson was dethroned by Douglas, King, who suddenly was out, whined about a long count when Douglas was down.

But this time King has the promotional rights, so he's already touting and shouting.

"Now the real fight starts," Duva said. "The fight to cut up the millions."

TYSON'S STORY COULD HAVE MORE CHAPTERS

The New York Times, November 17, 1996

by

Robert Lipsyte

M ike Tyson's life has become the rap opera of our time, grit and juice, as much a window on race and celebrity as the trials of O. J. Simpson or Muhammad Ali's journey from ridicule to beatification. Don't count out Tyson quite yet; if he doesn't find a way to self-destruct in the next few weeks, he may yet find a way to reinvent himself. That he has survived this long is more of an upset than Evander Holyfield's technical knockout.

He makes people crazy. Some of Tyson's most fervent early white boosters crowed the loudest at his defeat in Las Vegas eight days ago. They imagined that good had triumphed over evil, that the lesson might inspire the Kurds and homeless women. They felt betrayed by Tyson, at the least manipulated by him, and they were right. But even opera is never quite that simple.

Like Simpson and Ali, Tyson was discovered by white men who set about to exploit amazing athletic talent; at the time, there were no blacks with, as Ali put it, "the complexions and the connections to give me good directions." Jim Brown tried to put together a black-run sports combine in the 60's but was stymied.

TYSON'S STORY COULD HAVE MORE CHAPTERS

Simpson, the first great black athletic cross-over star, pioneered the junior college/four-year-college, National Football League, Hollywood/TV route. Handsome and politically nonthreatening, he could have dressed up crowd scenes for life. That he thought he was an honorary white, or at least beyond race, was a powerful force in his psyche.

Ali dumped the Louisville millionaires who originally sponsored him and turned over his affairs to a son of the leader of the Nation of Islam, a black separatist group that frightened both liberals and reactionaries in the 60's. Let us never forget that it was Ali who brought Don King into the boxing tent, and supported his use of the race card to squelch criticism.

Tyson, who is 30, was raised in Brooklyn, by his own account poor and ugly, a bully, a truant and a mugger, in that pre-Magic-Michael-Denzel-Spike-Tupac-Clarence Thomas time when Simpson and Ali were the major role models.

The romance that so many writers, including this one, found in his story began when he was quarried out of a juvenile facility, trained and then adopted by a legendary boxing master, Cus D'Amato, whose companion, Camille Ewald, became Tyson's mother figure. D'Amato and his business partner and disciple, Jimmy Jacobs, groomed Tyson to become heavyweight champion of the world. The conceit of the romance is that D'Amato and Jacobs did not have time to also groom Tyson to be a complete and moral man. There is a strain of racism in that conceit, and it overlooks an upbringing in which Tyson was allowed the arrogance and entitlements of a future star.

It also excuses the reflexive criticism of his present co-managers, John Horne and Rory Holloway, friends from high school who have been characterized as the Beavis and Butthead of boxing, and as King's stooges. But who else has been willing to create a comfort zone for Tyson, to insulate him from the world, hang with him, suffer his moods and whims?

Tyson survived a Dickensian childhood, punk crime, the reformatory, the deaths of D'Amato and Jacobs, and a humiliating marriage to the actress Robin Givens that included one of the heavyweight championship's lowest moments, a TV interview in which a seemingly medicated Tyson was jabbed into corners by Givens and Barbara Walters. He survived that, as well as street fights, car wrecks and assault charges that seemed like cries of help from a soul out of control. And then three years in jail for rape.

And he came out to fight again.

For those who love Mike Tyson—and there are more than you might think—his abandonments, humiliations, betrayals, persecutions and prosecutions are theirs writ larger, their rap opera, too. He gives them heart because he has not quit, he has not stopped boxing, and he has remained true to his posture: he has not begged forgiveness, turned to crack, committed suicide, or dumped his old friends.

Holyfield is a thoughtful and decent man with family values—he has fathered six children by four women, and recently got married, for the second time, to a doctor he met at a prayer meeting of the evangelist who healed the suspected "hole" in his heart. I hope this doesn't sound too sarcastic, because I did root for Holyfield to win.

But not because I hate Tyson or think he is unworthy to be champion. I am a romantic, too, and laid over current snapshots are my memories of the charming, quick, brimming youngsters that O. J., Ali and Mike once were. All have changed over the years, in complex ways. I hope Tyson changes some more.

Tyson has survived this long, under far harsher circumstances than Simpson or Ali faced, because he can adapt. With some luck and good advice, he may have successful rematches with life as well as with Holyfield, be a champion again, and be remembered as a man who took some very hard shots, stood up to them, learned from them and taught us something about hanging tough.

THE MIKE MYTH

New York, June 23-30, 1997

by

John Lombardi

Feeding the seals" is Don King's ungenerous description of the press conferences he presides over whenever it's time to hype another Mike Tyson heavyweight-title fight. The feeling is mutual. When Tyson, as is his custom, failed to show up on time for February's packed news conference announcing his rematch with Evander Holyfield (who'd stopped him on a TKO in a huge upset last November), a grizzled sportswriter loudly explained to the main "print" table in the Tower Room of the Equitable Building on Seventh Avenue, "He's downstairs, stealing some hubcaps." Mike Katz of the *Daily News* made his feelings even plainer: "Holyfield-Tyson II—The Fix!" he proclaimed.

The reference was to the fact that the first Holyfield-Tyson fight grossed more than $100 million—boffo movie-box-office money— and Tyson had been a 10-to-1 betting favorite, expected to knock Holyfield out in one or two rounds. The rematch, on June 28 at the MGM Grand in Las Vegas, has the fighters at virtually even money and is perceived as a turning point for Tyson—another loss could conceivably end his career. But since both boxers are among the biggest pay-per-view draws in sports history (Holyfield's personal career earnings are estimated at close to $200 million: Tyson's at $300 million-plus), a Tyson win would virtually guarantee a third fight. And since this one is expected to be the highest-grossing pay-per-view sports or entertainment event ever, earning between $175 million and $200 million in worldwide cable sales for Viacom's Showtime Event Television and Don King Productions, the projected box-office drop on the next one is mind-boggling. King's minions are already seeding the "possible triple-crown event" buzz with rumors of a $300 million "electronic" gate for Tyson-Holyfield III. Those are Jim Carrey and Steven Spielberg numbers.

Of course, the "fix" remarks and racist cracks never quite make it into anyone's column. The enmity between the King-Tyson camp and the New York sports press is old and corrosive but fairly sophisticated by now, dating back to 1988, when Don, according to the conventional wisdom, "stole" Mike away from promoter Bill Cayton, the money man behind Tyson's original discoverer and trainer, Cus D'Amato, and his first manager, Jimmy Jacobs (both of whom have gone to their rewards). D'Amato, a saintly eccentric, had found Mike upstate at the Tryon School for Boys when he was only 14 and serving an indeterminate term for mugging old ladies in Brownsville. Cus then channeled the kid's mesomorphic rage into the one sport where "acting out" pays off handsomely.

Out of such roughage came the media's "Cus and the Kid" myth, a John Badham-style fairy tale scripted by sportswriters from an outline by Jacobs and Cayton—who were nothing if not image-savvy. According to the story's architects, Mike's life under D'Amato's tutelage, in a bucolic country house in Catskill, overlooking the winding Hudson, was on the level of, say, Rudy Giuliani's in his dad's wholesome postwar nest in Brooklyn. It was only when bad Don King, the sho'nuff numbers boss of Cleveland's Tenth Ward, seduced Tyson after Cus's death that Mike began to go wrong—spending lavishly, partying with "ho's," and reawakening a kind of Mr. Hyde who'd slumbered peacefully within him during the good years. And, the pundits implied, it was Don's rotten influence that started Mike down the path that finally led in 1992 to an Indiana rape conviction and three-year sentence: "King destroyed Mike as a fighter and human being," rumbled Katz of the *News*, righteously quoting Cayton (who could hardly be objective, having just lost the biggest-money fighter in boxing to Don). "King . . . contributed to the diminishment of Tyson's talent and character," screamed Jack Newfield in the New York *Post* (Newfield's own ties to Cayton can fairly be described as "social"). "Tyson, this nightmare in a suit," chimed Mark Kriegel, then at the *Post*. "Psycho-pup!" barked Robert Lipsyte, the normally mild sports essayist of the New York *Times*.

This is blind pack journalism, King and Tyson's obvious flaws notwithstanding. By buying into the standard Saint Cus story line, these writers ignore the fact that Tyson was frequently in trouble in Catskill under Cus and had been running away to Albany and Brooklyn for years to indulge his gangster fantasies. By the time he let King manage and promote him, he was older and richer and more jaded than he'd been when D'Amato pulled him out of reform school. His resulting troubles—as he'll tell anyone—"were of my own making." In the end Tyson chose King over Cayton and the white press not because he had been hustled by King but because, as fellow felons, they were two against the world. They also cracked each other up.

Which is not to say that Tyson is happy with King. While Mike was serving time in the Indiana slammer, Newfield and Katz broke a number of stories detailing alleged illegal debits to Tyson's accounts by Don—$750,000 for professional "upkeep" of King's former offices; a $2 million deduction from Tyson's purse for a 1991 Razor Ruddock fight; and questionable payments to Don's wife and daughter out of Mike's end on virtually every fight.

But Tyson seems less exercised by such perceived fiscal irregularities than he was by King's failure to get him out of prison early or to make certain fights happen (he badly wanted to box Riddick Bowe, a neighbor and rival from Bedford-Stuyvesant, now retired, and Lennox Lewis, a "pretty boy" from England who had "dissed" him and "needs a lesson") and by King's vulgar huckstering. More than once, Mike has told Don before reporters to "shut up while I'm talking," and at the Tower Room press conference, he interrupted King's Shakespearean soliloquy on St. Ides Malt Liquor, the corporate sponsor of Holyfield-Tyson II, to announce that (as a Muslim) "I don't drink. . . . I don't sponsor liquor. I don't believe in it, and I'm not sponsoring St. Ides. . . . You don't hear me on the radio rapping about it like Snoop Doggy Dogg. . . ."

THE MIKE MYTH

Tyson's personal code of honor, it would seem, allows him to let King manipulate his finances occasionally, as long as Don makes it up later. It's a form of mental bookkeeping incomprehensible to those who've always had money, or who possess conventional corporate sensibilities, like Seth Abraham (president of HBO Sports and a deadly King enemy since Don pulled Mike out of his HBO contract in 1990 and signed him with Sumner Redstone's competing Showtime network) or like syndicated columnist Mike Lupica; or NBC sports commentator Bob Costas, two media stars who've assumed the burden of "cleaning up boxing," turning it into a healthy, family-oriented game like baseball, and who periodically weigh in on the evils of Mike and Don.

In response, Tyson has dug himself deeper into his persona, surrounding himself with a Tonton Macoute-style crew who only hurt his public image: John Horne and Rory Holloway of Albany, two old running buddies who are nominally his "managers" but whose real role seems to involve throwing up a color-coordinated, homburg-hatted wall of defense against the hated media ("We're suppress agents," Horne told me): "Crocodile," a loudmouthed street guy who acts as a private cheerleader—a darker version of Muhammad Ali's man, the late Bundini Brown; Richie Giachetti, Mike's current trainer and a former bad-debt collector whom King picked up in Cleveland; "Death Threat," a short gentleman who once advised me to stop interviewing Don's son Carl . . .

By continuing to employ such "real" people, Tyson may think he's being true to his roots, not "going corporate," as fellow boxers Sugar Ray Leonard and George Foreman did; not shilling for "the man," as even Ali and Michael Jordan do, with their d-Con roach spray and sneaker commercials. Tyson's surliness at press conferences and refusal to hustle St. Ides are the last vestiges of a street code that cohered in Brownsville in the early eighties. He's a pure puncher, like Jack Dempsey and Sonny Liston were, trapped in a Website culture that gapes at but doesn't really credit what it is he does for a living: He hurts guys.

Tyson is 31 now; he quietly married his longtime girlfriend Monica Turner, a Georgetown doctor, recently; he's losing interest in training, and if his performance in Holyfield I was any evidence, in boxing alto-

gether; he's postponed seven major fights, three of them since coming out of jail two years ago.

King, too, is scaling back, giving up a number of his fighters, diversifying his interests, and bracing for yet another federal insurance-fraud case in September. King will be 67 soon after the trial starts, and whether Tyson wins or loses on June 28, his era is about to end. It's just corporate boxing now. Which isn't the same thing as saying the sport has been cleaned up.

DEFENDING TYSON

PDXS, July 9, 1997

by

Katherine Dunn

This goes to the press before the Nevada Athletic Commission disciplinary decision in the case of Iron Mike Tyson biting the ears of Evander Holyfield. As of this writing we don't know whether Tyson will be fined 3 million bucks and suspended for a year, or pounded for thirty million and a life time suspension. (The Nevada Commission subsequently fined Tyson 3 million dollars—the highest money penalty in sports history—and revoked his license for a year.) No matter what the commission decides, the verdict is already shrieking from the headlines and TV sets of America. TYSON BAD! The cover of *Sports Illustrated* magazine blasts "MADMAN!" in huge type. The tag is "A crazed Mike Tyson disgraces himself and his sport." Columnist Dave Anderson of the *New York Times* describes Tyson as a "mad pit bull." The adjectives are flying thick and nasty—"dirty, disgusting, repellant, bestial, loathsome, vile, animalistic, vampiristic, deranged, maniacal, cannibalistic, murderous, cowardly . . ." Bill Clinton was horrified. John Sununu and Geraldine Ferraro held a Crossfire debate on "Tyson Bite" which degenerated into a "Ban Boxing" rally. The press could scarcely be more enflamed if the guy had reached up Holyfield's rectum and ripped out his heart in front of the TV cameras. The conviction of Tim McVeigh didn't trigger this kind of venom. In fact, we haven't seen this much hysteria since the first O. J. verdict. "Bad" black men drive the press batty.

Tyson is being treated more viciously by the press and the public than any boxer in history—with the possible exceptions of Muhammad Ali in his anti-war, anti-white years, and Jack Johnson, who pissed off all the white folks by beating white fighters and marrying white women.

Other fighters have fouled as badly as Tyson in recent memory and have been dealt with very differently. Heavyweight Andrew Golota repeatedly hit Riddick Bowe with blatant low blows in two, back-to-back bouts. In each bout Golota was actually winning when he fouled. He was disqualified and lost, but he was not suspended or fined. In fact, Bowe's entourage was punished for the post-fight riot in Madison Square Garden. Roy Jones lost his title on a D.Q. for hitting Montell Griffith in the head while he was on his knees. Terry Norris lost his world title twice on D.Q.s for hitting Luis Santana when he was down. Neither Norris nor Jones were penalized further. Ray Mercer offered Jesse Ferguson a hundred thousand dollar bribe in mid-fight to take a dive in their 1993 bout. Mercer was never punished beyond losing the match. If Mike Tyson were burnt at the stake tomorrow, every sports reporter in America would apparently stand up and cheer.

But there is another way to look at the Tyson Bite affair. Try this. The bites were against the rules and should be penalized, but they were understandable and even justified. The sanctified Holyfield was fighting dirty. The ref was doing nothing to stop it. Tyson had to defend himself. The tradition in boxing is, if you're being fouled, foul in return.

MOUNTAINS OF MISINFORMATION

Much of the commentary assumes that Tyson often commits fouls and the bites are merely an extreme version of his usual unsportsmanlike tactics. Yet, despite being hyped as a monster throughout his career, Tyson is not a particularly dirty fighter. He rarely throws low blows even though he's shorter than most of his opponents. He hits on the break or after the bell occasionally, and he can wield a potent shoulder and elbow. Sometimes he clinches too much. This pattern is mediocre in the dirty boxing spectrum. Only the bites were extraordinary.

No one but Mike Tyson himself knows what was going on in his head that night, and his public apology explicitly said that he "snapped" as a result of the severity of the cut over his right eye which came from Holyfield's head butt in the second round. Immediately after the bout he said Holyfield was butting repeatedly and he had to retaliate to prevent further damage.

Tyson's version of events has been ignored, discounted as lies. *Sports Illustrated* described the bites as "completely unprovoked," and that is the prevailing view.

Two basic theories of motivation have been adopted by the critics. Both theories depend on the idea that Holyfield was completely dominating Tyson. 1) The Thug Impulse theory says Tyson is a brutal, animalistic thug and he behaved like a thug/brute under stress. The bites were impulsive results of rage at his inability to bully Holyfield. 2) The Premeditated Escape theory says Tyson deliberately set out to get himself disqualified to avoid the humiliation of losing to Holyfield again. This is Holyfields' own opinion, as expressed immediately after the bout. It has been augmented by the fact that before the bout trainer Teddy Atlas predicted a third round disqualification. Atlas was at a TV fight party at reporter Jack Newfield's place in New York and word of his prescience spread rapidly. Asked afterwards how he knew, Atlas replied, "I know his character." Let it be noted that Atlas, for all his excellent abilities, has a deep personal rift with Tyson.

Having watched a videotape of the three rounds of the fight several times in slow motion, I think Tyson was telling the simple truth. Holyfield was headbutting repeatedly and intentionally. The ref, Mills Lane, was doing nothing to prevent it. Tyson retaliated for furious revenge and to convince Holyfield to stop the tactic.

This is what I saw:

Holyfield came out from the opening bell with a rough-house strategy including consistent fouls—throwing low blows, holding and hitting, wrestling and shoving, and above all using his head as a third fist. Toward the end of the first round the referee warned him about wrestling. "You know better!" Lane told Holyfield. The ref warned Holy for one low blow in the third round but ignored the rest. I counted three.

Taller than Tyson by at least three inches, Holy bent and crouched constantly to swing his head against Tyson's, and he frequently made contact. Tyson, having been cut and concussed by head butts in his first bout with Holyfield, was dipping and ducking throughout trying to avoid that cranial battering ram. Halfway through the second round Holy got the desired result. A headbutt produced a large, copiously bleeding cut beneath Tyson's right eyebrow. A training cut in the same spot had caused the bout to be postponed from its original date in May. My view, based on the videotape, is that the butt was deliberate. The ref called the headbutt "unintentional." No points were docked from Holyfield. The cut was perfectly located to drain into Tyson's eye, obscuring his vision. The possibility loomed that the ref would soon have to stop the fight because Tyson could not see to defend himself.

Holyfield won both the first and second round on the judges cards. Tyson's use of the jab from outside—reportedly a strategy devised by his new trainer, Rich Giachetti—was not working against the longer armed Holy. But these were not lop-sided, humiliating rounds. Tyson held his ground and was still in the fight.

Between rounds, the plastic surgeon, Ira Truckee, who was serving as Tyson's cut man managed to stop the bleeding, but a flicked feather would make the cut spill open again.

THE MOUTHPIECE MYTHS

Much has been made of Tyson coming out of his corner for the third round without his mouthpiece. Referee Mills Lane noticed it immediately and sent him back for it. Trainer Richie Giachetti was standing on the ring apron with the mouthpiece in his hand and slipped it in. The critics like to claim this as a sign that the bites were premeditated, that Tyson intended to come out without his mouthpiece so he could bite freely.

This doesn't make sense. The fighter doesn't control the mouthpiece between rounds, the corner man does. These PPV shows have microphones and cameras in the corners so there should be clear evidence if Tyson refused the mouthpiece. Certainly he and Giachetti could have cooked up a scheme days in advance—"when I tip you the wink, don't give me the mouthpiece . . ." But it's a big gamble to bet you can get in a bite before your unprotected jaw gets shattered by one of the best heavyweights in the world. And any competent referee will catch you before the first punch is thrown, as Mills Lane did. Nah. Far more likely

Mills Lane penalizes Tyson

that Rich Giachetti was rattled and forgot it. In every other case where a boxer comes out without his mouthpiece, the corner man goofed.

Once his mouthpiece was in, Tyson attacked in his old fast hooking fashion, looking for openings for a massive right hand. Holy covered to weather the storm and struggled to stay in the game, and get inside again with his head. A Tyson right to the body followed by a crunching left to the chin had Holy hurt and buckling when, in the split second before the first bite, Holy slammed the right side of his head against the cut on Tyson's eye. This placed Holy's ear just below Tyson's mouth and the video-tape clearly shows Tyson reacting to the pain of the butt and then instantly chomping on that ear.

Holyfield claimed, after the bout, that Tyson spit his mouthpiece out first and then bit. That is the scenario used by all the critics to prove calculated premeditation. In fact, the video clearly shows Tyson's mouthpiece was still in place when he bit. This style of mouthpiece bonds with the upper teeth and allows the lower jaw to open. Only after Holyfield pulled away from him did Tyson bend over and spit the mouthpiece out, along with the chunk of Holy's right ear. The black mouthpiece and its trajectory are apparent on the video tape. Mills Lane, stepping in, bends immediately to retrieve the mouthpiece.

Holyfield swirls stamping in pain, then turns his back and walks away. Tyson rushes and pushes at his back with both gloves. Holyfield bounces against the ropes.

Then there's a break in the action. Mills Lane first declares Tyson disqualified for biting, then changes his mind when the Nevada Commission doctor, Flip Homansky, says Holyfield can continue. Lane deducts two points from Tyson, one for the bite, one for the shove.

The fight resumes, Tyson has Holyfield hurt again, Holyfield's head swings into his face again and Tyson bites again. The left ear this time. His mouthpiece is still in. They continue fighting to the bell. Tyson walks to his corner with the mouthpiece in his mouth.

Tyson dominated this round on the judges score cards but the docked points eliminate the gain. Between rounds Mills Lane stops the fight, disqualifying Tyson for the second bite.

Tyson had turned the momentum of the fight and had Holyfield in trouble when the first bite occurred. If there had been a fourth round, Holyfield might have been stopped. Claiming that Tyson was looking for a D.Q. escape from humiliation doesn't compute.

Maybe Tyson didn't believe the ref would stop a mega-million dollar fight on the grounds of the fouls he committed, two bites and a shove. The cut made him vulnerable. He said he had to retaliate to protect himself. He couldn't butt in return because he would have been the more damaged party. Low blows weren't really an option—he's not adept at throwing them and his style doesn't lend itself to them. We think the bites were impulsive self-defense. Biting is against the rules. He shouldn't have done it. But obviously he couldn't rely on Mills Lane to prevent Holyfield from butting.

THE NEUTRAL REFEREE

Tyson's idiot handlers, John Horne and Rory Holloway, made a monumental mistake before the fight when they objected to the assigned referee, Mitch Halpern, and allowed Mills Lane, the former District Attorney, now Washoe County District Judge, to fill in. (Mills Lane has since retired from the ring and after failing with a "People's Court" style TV show, has become a boxing promoter.) Lane has reportedly been a friend of Holyfield's for years. According to Holy's trainer, Tommy Brooks, "The night Holyfield lost to Riddick Bowe, Mills Lane cried tears." Lane has also been quoted long before this bout, saying that Tyson is a vicious criminal who should never be allowed to box. It's not surprising that Lane failed to notice the sustained strategy of fouls that the Holy one was using.

The blindness of the ringside commentators and the hundreds of reporters in the arena is more disappointing. They bought all the years of hype from both sides. Holyfield, the Christian Warrior, is good and everything he does is saintly. One irate fan told us, "It's not so much the bite as who he bit!" Tyson, the street thug, is bad. They've been wanting to punish him for a long time. Apparently there is nothing on the planet more terrifying and evil than a bad black man.

THE SPIN DOCTORS

Tyson faced a press conference alone the Monday after the fight and read a complete apology. He said he was wrong to bite. He said he would accept without contest whatever punishment the Commission handed out. He asked not to be suspended for life. He didn't blame Holyfield or Mills Lane or anyone else. He took total responsibility for his actions. Many reporters dismissed the apology claiming it was "spin doctors" at work. No. "Spin" is when you try to pin the rap on somebody else. "But is he sincere?" they keep asking. Please. Obviously Tyson is deeply sorry. Nobody goes looking for this kind of shit storm. Did anybody ask if Bill Clinton was "sincere" when he apologized to the victims of the Tuskeegee Experiment?

HINKY ON BITES

Biting is against the rules but rules don't exist unless there is some common inclination to act the opposite way. Biting is far from "abnormal" behavior, and this is not the first time fang met flesh in a boxing ring.

A favorite tale of Portland fight manager Mike "Motormouth" Morton involves his instructions to Andy "The Scapoose Express" Kendall the night before Kendall fought Dick Tiger in Madison Square Garden back in the 1960's. "Andy," Morton advised, "When the bell rings for the first round go out and hit him hard in the balls. The ref will take a point away. When the bell rings for the second round, rush out and bite him hard on the ear. The ref will take

After the disqualification

another point away. So you've lost two rounds, but you've got eight more rounds to work and your opponent is damaged." Kendall failed to follow this canny strategy and lost a ten round decision to the master technician, Tiger.

Others have not been so persnickety. Heavyweight Andrew Golota bit Samson Po'hua on national TV two years ago and it raised a few eyebrows but not a ruckus. In fact Golota went on to win the bout with a fifth round TKO. Bobby Czyz declares he has been bitten. Jimmy Ellis has confessed to biting. No suspensions or fines resulted. Evander "Holy" Holyfield himself has admitted biting "Jakey" Winters while Winters was beating him in an amateur match when he was 17. Winters says Holy drew blood. Holy points out that he bit the shoulder, not the ears, but amateur helmets cover the ears so there's no virtue in that.

Naming no names, we've seen boxer bites even in the Pacific Northwest. One dangerous ex-middleweight of our acquaintance reminisces fondly on the psychological terrorism of a well timed bite, and boasts of following up by blowing his nose on the wound. Boxing is not ping-pong.

Bites also occur in other sports. High school and college wrestlers have been known to take a nip. Tree Rollins bit Danny Ainge, and the

NBA fined Rollins $5,000 and suspended him for two games. Not exactly the thirty million dollars and lifetime exile that many demand for Tyson.

Fight folk and experienced fans know all this but still, reflexively, declare themselves "shocked and appalled" in the face of the usual screams to ban the always maligned sport. No one calls for basketball to be banned when Dennis Rodman headbutts a referee or kicks a photographer. There is no roar to abolish the Catholic Church when priests molest choir boys. But boxing is different. And Mike Tyson is America's bogey man.

BIG MONEY, BIG FALLOUT FOR TYSON

The New York Times, May 24, 1998

by

Barry Meier and Timothy W. Smith

Early last February, Mike Tyson, staggering from an unpaid $12 million tax bill and suspended from the sport that had provided him with riches, left his Las Vegas estate desperate for cash and for a divorce from his longtime promoter, Don King.

In recent years, the former heavyweight champion had spent millions buying mansions and collector cars. But Tyson believed King's financial misdealings, rather than his own spending, was the real reason for his straits. Just days before, Tyson and King had engaged in a shouting-and-shoving match outside a Los Angeles hotel.

On that February morning, Tyson met with Arthur Goldberg, the president of the Hilton Hotels' gambling division, to propose a maverick maneuver to raise cash quickly. For an advance of $10 million to $15 million, Goldberg said Tyson told him he would break with King and, upon his reinstatement to boxing, hold his next five fights at the Las Vegas, Nev., casino of Goldberg's company.

"He said he wasn't happy with the way Don had financially treated him over the last couple of years," Goldberg said.

BIG MONEY, BIG FALLOUT FOR TYSON

A stunned Goldberg declined the boxer's offer. But soon Tyson made another move: He filed suit against King, accusing the promoter and his two managers of having bilked him of more than $100 million in earnings over the years.

To many, it is no surprise that Tyson and King, who had raked in some $200 million in purses since 1988, are in a slugfest over the object of their mutual affections: money. Tyson, a talented, violent fighting engine and the sport's top draw, spent his money with epic immodesty. And King had forged a reputation as a brilliant, manipulative businessman who, many have claimed, exploited any number of boxers and deals he touched.

Neither man agreed to be interviewed for this article. But what emerges from dozens of interviews with people involved with Tyson and King is a tale of extraordinary financial recklessness by Tyson.

And, if Tyson's charges are true, the story of how King may finally have been undone over, of all things, the marketing rights to a Tyson action doll. The events also illuminate the curious world of boxing, where friendships can be for sale and vast amounts of money change hands in only the most loosely monitored of deals.

King, on trial in Manhattan on Federal insurance fraud charges, denies any wrongdoing with respect to Tyson. And Tyson, waiting out his suspension for biting Evander Holyfield's ear during a fight last summer, has allied himself with yet another set of handlers, this time a band of Hollywood promoters and lawyers, including one, Jeff Wald, who has managed the comedian Roseanne, and another, Irving Azoff, who managed the Eagles, a rock band. The two men once promoted two fights involving George Foreman, the former heavyweight champion.

Still, in a measure of boxing's inexhaustible intrigue, there are many people who confidently predict that, despite all the litigation, King and Tyson will one day wind up together again.

"Tyson suing King is like the Devil suing Satan," Foreman said. "Can you imagine that?"

Tyson, who first won a heavyweight title in 1986, has made few public comments about his break with King. But when Tyson filed suit last February he said, in an interview, that people were not taken advantage of "because they are stupid, but because they trust one another."

King initially sought an interview with *The New York Times*, but then declined, citing his Federal trial. However, in a statement, he said: "What saddens me the most is the way Mike Tyson is being manipulated by certain people who have their own agendas. Mike knows the truth. He knows that I treated him fairly."

BUILDING CONTRACTS ON TOP OF CONTRACTS

In a lawsuit filed this spring in Federal court in New York, Tyson claimed that King and his company, Don King Productions, defrauded him when he, among other things, negotiated two gigantic contracts in 1995. For instance, under a deal with the Showtime Networks, a cable television company, Tyson received purses of up to $30 million a fight for 10 bouts over a three-year period.

A copy of that contract indicates it was signed by Tyson on March 20, 1995, five days before his release from an Indiana prison where he had served three years for rape. One of the lawsuit's charges is that King, in signing a contract with Showtime for Tyson's fights, used that relationship to negotiate another $42 million in fights for other boxers without sharing any of the proceeds with Tyson.

The boxer's lawsuit also claims that King charged him for millions of dollars in expenses, like renovations to King's home and offices, and put members of King's family on the boxer's payroll at inflated salaries.

"It would appear that there was some widespread looting of Mike Tyson's money by Don King Productions," said Dale Kinsella, one of Tyson's lawyers in Los Angeles. "The sums of money that were diverted to Don King Productions were completely disproportionate to what any boxing promoter would have asked for. The sums are just astronomically ridiculous."

Tyson's most recent managers, his onetime friends John Horne and Rory Holloway, have also been sued. For years, Horne, a failed stand-up comic, and Holloway, who met Tyson when both were teenagers, had worked as his aides, cheering section and party companions.

But four years ago, Tyson appointed both men, neither of whom had ever negotiated a contract, to serve as his managers. Tyson has now charged in a separate lawsuit filed in California that Horne and Holloway had failed to protect his interests in dealings with King because the men were paid puppets of the promoter.

Holloway did not respond to messages left for for him seeking comment. But Horne said that neither he nor Holloway had any improper dealings with King and had always acted in Tyson's best interests. "No one has performed and achieved for a client what we have under the most negative conditions," he said.

King is no stranger to legal trouble. He is currently being retried on Federal charges that he defrauded an insurer by submitting false claims in connection with a canceled fight involving Julio Cesar Chavez. His 1995 trial on the same charges ended in a hung jury. Moreover, a long line of boxers—Tim Witherspoon, Tony Tubbs, Larry Holmes—have claimed in court papers or in interviews that King cheated or misrepresented them.

Last year, Terry Norris, the former superwelterweight champion, sued both King and his former manager, Joseph Sayatovich, in New York, charging that his manager had negotiated a cheaper deal for a fight contract with King because Sayatovich had received a $200,000 interest-free loan from the promoter.

Court documents show that the loan, which King could have recalled at any time, was secured by Sayatovich's home. Sayatovich did not dispute receiving the loan, but he insisted that Norris knew about it.

QUESTIONS ABOUT GAINING INFLUENCE

Tyson has long been portrayed as a lethal fighting machine who, unable to control his appetites and anger, could be easily manipulated by others. Early in his career, Tyson's impulses were often policed by his first trainer, Cus D'Amato. But in King, who took over Tyson's career in 1988, the boxer found a charismatic figure who, according to people close to Tyson, not only indulged his tastes for spending and nightlife, but also fed his insecurities by insisting that his previous managers, who were white, had exploited him because of race.

"By going with King, Mike was able to do anything he wanted," said Teddy Atlas, who helped train Tyson in the 1980's. "He was able to thumb his nose at certain people. Maybe that's why he didn't look at things a little closer."

But others say that King may have tried to buy the influence of those close to the boxer from the start.

Joseph Maffia, a former accountant with Don King Productions and a key Government witness in its current criminal case, said he recalled writing at least one company check for $5,000 to Horne in 1988, well before Tyson first signed with King.

Maffia, who split from King in 1991, said the check was recorded as a consulting fee, but he said he believed the money was paid to Horne in order to have him help persuade Tyson to join with King.

Horne denied that claim and said he did not recall receiving such a payment. A spokesman for King said the promoter's accountants have not been able to find the check, if it exists.

Tyson, anyway, appears to have had early warnings about King's dealings. As part of a 1992 lawsuit filed by Tyson against his former manager, Bill Cayton, Maffia submitted sworn affidavits stating that King had effectively siphoned millions from Tyson in the early 1990's by charging him for expenses owed by King. Those charges, which are repeated verbatim in Tyson's current lawsuit, also maintain that King had paid extravagant salaries to family members for menial jobs.

For several years, one of King's daughters received $52,000 annually for being president of the Mike Tyson fan club. And King also charged Tyson hundreds of thousands of dollars for rent and renovations to a variety of corporate and personal residences operated by the promoter, Maffia's affidavits stated.

While King disputed the affidavits, Tyson did nothing more than suggest that the accountant stay out of his business, Maffia said.

"I guess his attitude was that I'm making $20 million and if Don was skimming some off the top, so what, everyone was comfortable," Maffia said.

The lawsuit also questions the role of Horne and Holloway, the boxer's managers. In theory, they, as managers, should have worked together with King to get the best deals for Tyson. But a manager must also be prepared to confront a promoter to make sure his fighter maximizes earnings.

Under the terms of their contract, King received 30 percent of Tyson's earnings, with Horne and Holloway each getting 10 percent. But Tyson's lawsuit charges that King was able to steal additional funds from the boxer because he purchased the loyalties of Horne and Holloway by enriching them through deals, at Tyson's expense.

At minimum, many in the boxing world say, the pair were ill

equipped for the new roles. "To call them naive is an upgrade," said one sports industry executive who has dealt with both Horne and Holloway.

It was in August 1994 that Tyson, while still imprisoned, appointed Horne and Holloway as managers. Horne insisted he and Holloway worked to strike the best terms for the boxer and talked to numerous promoters before deciding that King would continue to handle Tyson's fights after his prison release.

"When we signed as managers, Don King didn't know a thing about it until it was completed," Horne said.

That suggestion is disputed by others, including a man who was Tyson's religious adviser. After Tyson had converted to Islam in prison, many people suspected he might hire a Muslim promoter. But Muhammad Siddeeq, the religious adviser, said King had cut a deal with Horne and Holloway before the boxer appointed them his managers.

Siddeeq said that in June 1994 he met with King, Horne and Holloway in an Indianapolis hotel suite and was offered a job as part of a group that would guide the boxer's career after his release.

"They said they had met and that it was a unanimous decision that they wanted me to be a part of Team Tyson," he said, adding that King gave him about $800 at the meeting.

Siddeeq said he accepted the offer. A spokesman for King denied he had offered Siddeeq a job. But a few days after the Indianapolis meeting, court documents filed with Tyson's lawsuit indicate, the boxer signed an exclusive contract with King.

Siddeeq said his promised job evaporated soon after Tyson got out of prison in March 1995.

Both Siddeeq and Butch Lewis, a boxing promoter, say they believe Horne was always improperly in league with King.

"I don't have to be a genius who works for the Kennedy Center to know that John is Don's man," Lewis said. "John was part of Don King Productions. He would sit in on meetings with Don when I was negotiating contracts with my fighters with Don."

AN ACCOUNTING REVEALS TROUBLE

Tyson's lawsuit could resolve whether King shortchanged the boxer. But clearly Tyson used his part of the $120 million in purses he earned after prison on some wild spending. During one spree in 1995, Tyson reportedly purchased 10 BMW's, four Rolls Royces, several Bentleys and a $3 million Las Vegas home into which he poured another $8 million. The spending could be financed as the $30 million paydays kept coming. But his suspension last year ended the paydays and helped set in motion Tyson's break with King.

Those close to Tyson have said that the boxer used his time away from the ring last year to review his finances. "He has been taking stock," said Michael Steele, the fighter's brother-in-law.

One major problem was the Internal Revenue Service. Last spring, Tyson did not have the cash to pay his 1996 Federal taxes. And by the fall, that bill had grown, with interest and penalties, to $12 million, said two people who have reviewed his finances. King and Tyson scrambled to raise funds to pay off the debt.

King, for example, approached Showtime executives seeking an advance of $5 million to $10 million on the unpaid portion of Tyson's contract with the cable company, said two sports industry executives. That effort failed, but the promoter then signed a $3.5 million deal with the World Wrestling Federation for Tyson to promote and appear at a March 1998 match.

As 1997 came to a close, Tyson and King were still a team. But then, in late January, Tyson and Craig Jones, a friend and aide of the boxer, flew to Los Angeles looking to get into the music business. And within days, the decadelong relationship between Tyson and King shattered.

Tyson went to California to meet with Jeff Wald, the Hollywood talent manager who had known King and the fighter over the years, even defending the promoter against a critical television documentary.

Initially, Wald said, he and Tyson talked only about the boxer's music plans and the manager recommended that the boxer contact his friend in the record business, Irving Azoff. But their conversation eventually shifted to the boxer's finances.

Wald said Tyson was upset about his W.W.F. contract because a wrestling executive, Shane McMahon, had told him that King had demanded $300,000 for the rights to the boxer's likeness. However, in an interview, McMahon said Tyson was not concerned about the $300,000, which he said was paid to King for his help in promoting the boxer's appearance at the March match.

But McMahon did say that he told Tyson that the fighter could be making a financial killing if he were to market an action figure doll as many professional wrestlers had. McMahon said it was then that Tyson realized he would have to go through King to get those deals because the promoter had secured the rights to his likeness.

"I said, 'Mike, you are the hottest property in sports,' " McMahon said. "The next thing I knew, he started to sever his relationship with Don."

Wald said Tyson's anger at King was further fueled when Wald asked the boxer to produce his financial records, which were kept in Horne's Los Angeles office. "I told him they were not financial statements, they were ridiculous," Wald said. "Just numbers typed on pieces of paper."

At Wald's urging, Tyson contacted John G. Branca, a Hollywood entertainment lawyer with ties to Wald and Azoff. Branca said he reviewed Tyson's contracts and told him they were grossly unfair. Tyson called up Horne to complain, according to Wald. But Horne swore at Tyson, telling the boxer that he had caused his own financial problems by biting Holyfield's ear. A spokesman for King said Wald called King in late January and urged the promoter to fire Horne and Holloway and hire Wald and Azoff as replacements—something Wald denied. Soon after, King arrived in Los Angeles and got in a shoving-and-shouting match with Tyson outside the Bel Air Hotel, where the fighter was staying.

The flare-up reignited later in Wald's office, where King accused Wald, Azoff and Branca of trying to steal Tyson. Lawsuits were threatened. Wald said King asked that Tyson not take any legal action against him or his managers until his criminal case was over. In return, King said he would release Tyson from his contract after the trial, said Wald. But Wald said King balked when asked to do it in writing.

It is not clear whether Tyson's claims will ever go to trial. And it is uncertain whether Tyson will stick with his new advisers, who have been trying to cash in on their moment of opportunity. For example, Wald recently tried to sell publishers on the idea of a Tyson autobiography.

Tyson has since paid down his tax bill to $7 million. Soon, millions more should roll in if Nevada boxing regulators, as expected, reinstate his license. Tyson, despite all his problems, remains the sport's biggest draw. The question that remains is who will share the bounty with him.

GOOD MIKE, BAD MIKE AND THE ANTI-MIKE

The New York Times, January 24, 1999

by

Robert Lipsyte

With Mike gone, only the Anti-Mike can save us.

This is about our two Mikes, Jordan the Good Mike and Tyson the Bad Mike. You might also call them the Cool Mike and the Hot Mike, the Plastic Mike and the Iron Mike, the Angel Mike who is applauded for skipping out on us and the Devil Mike who can't even get credit for a clean knockout.

Consider Jordan's Second Leaving. It is still being treated as an arrival, the next stage in his celebrityhood, instead of what it is, a great performer's loss of interest in entertaining us. This rejection of the audience is being spun as a wonderful opportunity for the National Basketball Association to redefine itself—yet again and become richer; are we supposed to infer that Mike planned it this way, saving the valley and then moving on, like Shane? It's a clever scenario to help sell books and magazines, and to support his many sponsors, understandably concerned that Mike playing golf, taking his kids to school, and doing the dozens with his old frat brothers will not have the commercial appeal of Mike above the rim.

If you think that Mike will live forever, remember the role Johnny

Carson played in the national culture (he was the Michael Jordan of late-night TV) and the enormous coverage of his retirement and his replacements. How often have you thought of Carson since? And he had a clothing line, too.

Meanwhile, Tyson's latest comeback has been treated with a puzzling contempt.

Were the sports-talkers disappointed that he hadn't driven Francois Botha's nose bone into his brain? Or bitten it off? Tyson is that rare athlete who didn't completely lose his legs in prison and who has come back from deserved punishment and humiliation. He showed poise and professionalism in the Botha fight. He was losing for four rounds, but never lost his composure, even as the White Buffalo taunted him, fouled him, made Tyson look as clumsy as he was. But Tyson waited for his time, then threw the punch that won. Had any other fighter—any athlete—displayed such control, it would have been lauded as a victory of character.

Was there wishful thinking among commentators that Tyson, who is clearly not yet bored with us, was coming apart, rather than back? As with Jordan, investors are not likely to drop him until he is commercially wrung out.

This Mike and Anti-Mike business is not new. Post MagicBird, when the N.B.A./Nike combine bought into Air Jordan, everything Mike did was golden. Anti-Mike was a gold mine, too, but a guilty pleasure brought to us by Don King (the Anti-David Stern?) and Las Vegas casinos. Mike was beloved by the suits, Anti-Mike by an 80's hip-hop generation. When Mike came to life mainly in big games, it was proof that he was willing to empty out body and soul for us. Had that been Anti-Mike, he would have been accused of coasting on a regular basis. When Jordan gambled between playoff games, it was evidence of his fierce need for constant competition. Tyson would have been suspended or at least censured, to protect the perceived integrity of the spread.

If Jordan had appeared on a Barbara Walters broadcast, heavily medicated, or crashed cars into trees, he would have gained sympathy as a courageous example of an emotionally troubled man struggling for stability instead of a pathetic, henpecked sicko. If Jordan had come back from years in prison and then from months of a recent banishment with his physical skills diminished, he would have been extolled for making up in finesse what he had lost in muscle. Which is, of course, how Mike was treated when he returned from his baseball sabbatical. Anti-Mike is being dismissed as being finished.

The high concept of Good Mike and Bad Mike is as much business decision as moral judgment, and both Mikes have been happy enough over the years to model their assigned roles, Jordan gracious and diplomatic in public, Tyson snarly and unrepentant. Each knew his constituency, Jordan with the haves, those who identified with the members of the board, Tyson with the have-nots, those who identified with the members of the band. For those who "feared being left behind," according to Nelson George's rewarding 1998 book, "Hip Hop America," the "fierce, reckless fury" of Tyson's "rapid rise from thug to champion" offered hope.

George wrote: "The challenge Tyson, and his generation's particular brand of pride, faces is whether he has the staying power to thrive in a highly uncertain future."

We will find out soon enough. I'm rooting for the Anti-Mike, who has always seemed more real to me than Mike, less calculating, closer to the edge. Tyson talks money, but is about passion, fear, disgrace,

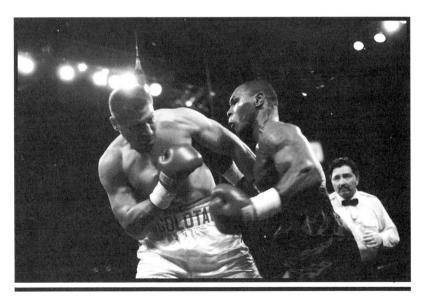

Tyson vs. Golota

redemption. Jordan talks about the love of the game, but everything he has ever done has been for money.

The Anti-Mike is back and could save us by turning the sports century around before it's too late, before the jock-industrial complex convinces us that the only way to truly win is to control market share.

TYSON'S UNHOLY FASCINATION

The Voice, February 15, 1999

by

Tony Sewell

I N A CHANGING world there are still a number of all-White male bastions which will take more than a French Revolution to over-throw.

The sports desks on most newspapers spring to mind and, in particular, boxing journalists. Strange, this, in a sport that for most of this century has been dominated by Black men.

The recent condemning of Mike Tyson by most of these writers after his jail sentence is just hypocritical.

These were the same writers who waxed lyrical about Tyson as the greatest athlete on earth and gushed orgasmically at the power of his punches.

Now, like scorned lovers, they rail against him, trying to consign him to the dustbin of boxing history.

PUNISHMENT

Why didn't these same adoring boxing writers condemn the judge for giving Tyson a custodial sentence?

It was obvious to the world that the man's road rage was linked to deep psychological problems that needed treatment.

TYSON'S UNHOLY FASCINATION

The judge should have offered Tyson two options: spend six months at a rehabilitation clinic or go down for a year.

This is not a soft sentence because, had Tyson been Elizabeth Taylor, Paul Gascoigne or Paul Merson, we would have all been sympathetic to the idea of the need for care and treatment—not punishment.

The reality is that Tyson is a Black man who is expected to perform as gladiator, clown or buffoon. If he does not meet any of these expectations then he's considered to be a wild animal that needs to be locked away.

We should never condone Tyson's actions but on the other hand, he has been a great source of enjoyment for middle-aged hacks who can only envy his strength.

This love/hate response to Tyson tells us more about the sexual confusion of White men than it does about the problems of Iron Mike.

OBSESSION

If we look at the work of boxing writers down the years, behind the obsession with Black boxers is a form of sexual envy.

We see it in the work of Norman Mailer.

In 1963 American writer Norman Podhoretz wrote in his essay, "My Negro Problem and Ours."

"Just as in childhood I envied Negroes for what seemed to me their superior masculinity, so I envy them today for what seems to be their superior physical grace and beauty.

"I have come to value physical grace very highly and I am now capable of aching with all my being when I watch a Negro couple on the dance floor, or a Negro boxing or playing basket-ball.

"They are on the kind of terms with their own bodies that I should like to be on with mine and for the precious quality they seem blessed to me."

Tyson was the great symbol of the White man's obsession with the Black body.

However, like in all perverted, exploitative relationships, they only wanted him on certain terms—as the gladiator or as a lost, sad boy with a high-pitched voice.

Tyson was thus available for them to use and "abuse" according to their desires.

However, they were also ready to turn and make him their prey when he went "savage" or "native."

It reminded me of a mixed gay couple I heard about.

Every time the Black man in the relationship slept around, the boyfriend would not only get jealous but would call him an "animal" or an "oversexed beast."

DAMNED

These journalists are no better; they want to bed Tyson, but only on their terms.

The media is no longer interested in understanding Tyson. Instead, he is damned.

And so Tyson's bitter, generally accurate observations about the way he has been used—quotes which once might have been fought over, analysed, debated to a ridiculous degree—are tossed idly into columns as further tiresome evidence of his self-indulgence.

JFK JR., CHAMPION UNDERDOG'S FRIEND?

The Washington Post, March 13, 1999

by

Lloyd Grove

Back during the campaign of 1960—with Martin Luther King Jr. locked up in the Birmingham jail for opposing segregation—Democratic standard-bearer John F. Kennedy made a sympathetic phone call to the civil rights leader's wife. Thus the future president sent a clear and powerful message of support for racial equality.

Four decades later, history repeated itself. Well, not really—except in an end-of-millennium kind of way. On Thursday night, John F. Kennedy Jr., the slain president's son and the editor in chief of *George* magazine, paid a visit to Mike Tyson, the famously troubled boxer currently serving a year for assault in Montgomery County jail.

The younger Kennedy's message? Powerful, certainly—favoring Tyson with a rare public relations bonanza. But it was also a little bit hazy.

Yesterday, the day after Kennedy's late-night pilgrimage to the Rockville detention center and subsequent press availability before a gaggle of cameras, the air was rife with speculation. Never mind that he forthrightly declared himself "a friend" of the former heavyweight champion, and expressed his conviction that Tyson is "a much different man . . . than his public image would suggest," and said that his year-long sentence, arising out of a fender bender and altercation last year, should be reconsidered.

Kennedy described Tyson—who is on probation for a rape conviction in Indiana, and still trying save his career from the consequences of biting off part of Evander Holyfield's right ear in June 1997—as "a man who really was putting his life back together and has an opportunity to do so in the future." Before climbing into a chauffeured Mercedes, Kennedy added: "I hope perhaps coming here and telling folks that, people might start to believe it, because he's had a difficult life."

But when two of the world's biggest celebrities are involved, surely nothing could be that simple. Was Kennedy laying the ground work for attracting African American Tyson fans for some as-yet-undisclosed candidacy? Was he trying to obtain publicity—or perhaps an interview—for his slick political magazine? Or was he, as he insisted Thursday night, merely standing by a friend?

Kennedy didn't return phone calls, but a couple of his friends offered knowledgeable interpretations.

"John is very sensitive to the idea that the public impression of a celebrity can be really at odds with the real man," said a Kennedy friend who asked not to be named. "From his own experience, he believes that 80 percent of what people know about celebrities is bull. I don't know that this happened, but if somebody called him up and said, 'All this stuff about Tyson is wrong, that woman set him up in that hotel room, in that traffic thing the local police were looking for publicity' or whatever, he'd be real interested. It would sound at least plausible to him. And it certainly would get his attention."

Another friend, who described himself as being "familiar with Kennedy's thinking" on Tyson, said the two met a little over a year ago, when Kennedy assigned author John Edgar Wideman to write a story about Tyson's boxing comeback struggle, and Tyson visited Kennedy at *George*'s Manhattan offices. The article was never published, but a friendship between the boxer and editor blossomed, with Kennedy getting to know Tyson's physician-wife, Monica, and their children.

"I think John has learned to empathize with a figure like Mike Tyson, who is known only in the most superficial way by the press, and made out to be something publicly, when in fact he's quite another thing privately," said this friend. "He's gotten to know Tyson in a different light. He went down there to show support for that person. John has a great amount of empathy for the underdog."

The friend added that Kennedy's support for Tyson is all of a piece with his natural affinity for others beset by bad PR—among them, his father's secretary of defense, Robert McNamara, still widely criticized for his role in the Vietnam War. "At that big (75th anniversary) dinner for *Time* magazine, John got up to toast McNamara. He had gotten to know McNamara in a way not seen by the majority. This was not inconsistent with the way John approaches his relationships or friendships with people with whom he chooses to identify."

Freelance Democratic media consultant Brian Weaver—who said he talked to Kennedy about the Tyson visit—said Kennedy, a former lawyer in the Manhattan district attorney's office, has been disturbed by the severity of Tyson's sentence, which was imposed Feb. 5 after he pleaded no contest to misdemeanor assault.

"As a former prosecutor, John honestly felt that he was put away not because of the crime, but because he was Mike Tyson," Weaver said. "Because he was Mike Tyson, there were preconceived barriers set up so nobody was going to be his advocate."

Other than Tyson's team of well-paid attorneys, of course.

THE FATHER'S KISS

Esquire, June 1999

by

Tom Junod

There are no baby pictures of Mike Tyson. Nobody cared enough either to keep them or to take them in the first place, and so there are no pictures of Mike Tyson smiling without teeth, or sleeping in a crib, or being held aloft in the arms of his father against some white stain of sunlight; no pictures of Mike Tyson's first step, or his first day at school; no way of knowing whether Mike Tyson was a cute infant, a cute toddler, or even a cute little boy. He is around twelve years old by the time of his first extant photograph, and because no pictures of him exist before that one, it's almost as though he didn't, either, until the first click of the shutter nudged him into being, and he was born, on film, fully formed, already *finished*: already stocky, already strong, already brave, already scared, already heartbroken, already truant, already violent, already in trouble, and already captured, thirty-eight times between the ages of ten and thirteen, and delivered into the hands of the law.

His children are, thankfully, another story, an ongoing story, extensively documented. There are lots of baby pictures of Mike Tyson's children. They exist in snapshots, in videos, in studio portraits, in frames on the wall and on top of dressers and counters and shelves, in so many albums and so many camcorder canisters that Tyson's wife, Dr. Monica Turner Tyson, keeps them in stacks, unsorted. His children have a record, and in that record everything is where it should be: birth at the beginning, to applause and tears of joy, and then party hats, pony rides, and the continual performance of children who have been given no reason not to preen. Candles, cake, confetti, clowns: The photographs go from one determined, incantatory celebration to the next, featuring Mikey and Gena and then Rayna and Amir and then Tyson himself, peering in from the edge of the frame. He figures in many of the many photographs of his children, and if, in most of them, he seems as happy as he could ever be, he also seems slightly puzzled, as though figuring something out—as though the glimpse these pictures afford him, of both his kids and of himself, is the closest he will ever come to a glimpse of what he was, and might have been, before the first flash.

Monica comes first, wearing black, holding the sleeping child in her arms. The bodyguard is second, a huge man named Cornelius. Tyson is third, and he comes along so quietly—so obediently—that his presence in the room, when it finally registers, seems sudden and almost sneaky. He is reverent around his boy, his high voice scraped down to a craggy whisper, and the sound in the room dampens around him, until, for a moment, the only things within earshot are those things that are never out of earshot in a place like this: the wads of keys that never stop jingling off the belts of the uniformed men who stand outside in the hallway, and the heavy doors that never stop opening and closing, driven by machines, so that the hallways hum with patient, determined thunder, punctuated by the clang of metal banging against metal.

The room is small. It is smaller than a boxing ring and oblong instead of square, but the way Tyson occupies it is reminiscent of the way he has always occupied the ring before a fight. He has always had a deep fatalism as a prizefighter. He has always seemed funneled into the ring on his way to it, and, once inside the ropes, he has always seemed to accept his presence there not as a choice but as an inevitability—as though for him, and now for his opponent, there was never any real possibility of escape. He is a ritualistic man, formidable in his observances, and even now, in this room, there is something almost sacramental about him, a buzzing stillness at once agitated and extremely deliberate. He looks old; not old in the way other aging athletes look old—he is thirty-two—but old in the way, say, snapping turtles look old: regally old, ancient, relict, the embodiment of some force or principle that predates the existence of everyone else in the room and will certainly outlast them. He has almondy, pit-bullish eyes and small, tattered ears, stuffed, in some of the ridges, with cauliflower. His head is enormous, armored in the brow and slightly pointed at the crown. He is wearing clothes that seem inappropriate to his present circumstance—an open chamois shirt, brown Gucci boots, and a pair of pale-yellow jodhpurs, in a windowpane pattern, that accentuate the shortness of his legs and make him look both huge and shrunken. He has an animal awareness of everyone who walks through the door, the way Sinatra once did, and he looks like no other human being on this earth.

Then he sits on a flimsy, unstable conference table and holds out his arms to accept from Monica the gift of his son. Amir has not woken up, and, with his legs hanging over the basket of his father's arms, he looks as peaceful as a fallen warrior. He is one and a half years old, a beautiful boy, his body already developing within the thick template of his father's, his face wide, his eyelashes long and dark, his head full of soft black curls. Tyson holds him stiffly at first, as if he doesn't want to hurt him. He has not held his son—or any of his children—since he came here nearly two months ago. Then he brings his arms up and dips his head down and extends his lips to kiss Amir on the scalp. He kisses his son as though to taste him or to smell him—as though to make sure that he keeps on smelling and tasting him after he leaves. Tyson is not living with his son right now, or with his daughter, or with Monica, and the place where he is living does not smell like Amir or like children at all. It smells like men. It smells like sweat and socks, like the sour, pukey smell of cheap paint relentlessly applied, like fried food, like meat. Tyson kisses his son again and again, until the boy's curls dampen as if with sweat. The door of the room is still open to the hallway, and a man in a dark-green jumpsuit, shuffling forward with the perversely proud, shit-in-the-pants walk of manacled men, stops to look inside, when someone in a blue uniform prods him to keep moving. Tyson doesn't look at them; his eyes are closed, as if in answer to his son's. The door shuts, and the photographer begins shooting, his lens whirring, his flashes sneezing billows of light. "Is he getting heavy?" he asks Tyson after a while. "He weighs a ton," Tyson says with an almost apologetic smile, and holds the boy closer. His presence is so alien and so removed, so creatural and extreme, that it might seem as if he had to travel some great distance to get here, to the simple human gesture of kissing his son. But what makes the gesture so heart-stopping—so worthy of hope and dread and awe—is the fact that he has not traveled an inch. The heart that made Tyson the most openly sadistic of any of our great fighters is the very same heart that throbs encompassingly against Amir's; the mouth that once tore Evander Holyfield's ear is the very same mouth that applies itself to Amir's soft scalp, the very same mouth that—as Tyson shifts his weight on the table and lifts the little boy as though offering him for consecration—opens to show the glint of two gold teeth and to say these two words:

"My son."

LIKE MIKE

The Washington Post, February 26, 1999

by

William Raspberry

I can't think of Mike Tyson without thinking of the thousands of kids—streetwise, impulsive, tough and undereducated—who, like the former heavyweight boxing champion, are bound for perennial trouble.

Tyson is in the news because, while in jail for an assault after an auto accident, he hurled a TV set across the room in a fit of rage. Tyson said it was because a jail guard hung up the telephone while the fighter was in the middle of a conversation. And oh, yeah, they had taken him off the medication prescribed to calm him down.

(Tyson says his last three violent episodes came after he missed taking his medicine.)

What does that have to do with the kids? Well, if you can forget Tyson the millionaire athlete for a second, you might consider Tyson the kid who grew up poor, abandoned, exploited and, I dare say, unloved. There are lots of such kids out there, though few with Tyson's physical gifts, whose out-of-control behavior will land them behind bars if it hasn't already.

If you're wondering why I am making excuses for violent thugs, you've gone to the heart of the point I'm trying to make: that it's extremely hard to work up any sympathy for people who frighten us. Tyson frightens us. A certain type of young black male frightens us. We want them controlled for as long and by whatever means it takes to make us feel safe. And, of course, we never do.

As psychologist Kenneth Dodge of Duke University put it the other day, "people like Tyson have developed their impulsivity problems across childhood—in their problem-ridden neighborhoods, in inadequate parenting, in insufficient resources, in discrimination, in early academic failure, in peer experiences, in poor social and emotional relations.

"And when they get in trouble, we act as though their behavior is the simple result of free will and moral choice. We would never deprive a child of schooling and then, at age 18, throw him in jail for illiteracy. But isn't that what we're doing with kids who grow up unsocialized in middle-class values and then act out?"

Precisely that—and worse. For not only do we pretend they are otherwise normal young people who choose to misbehave, we also kid ourselves that we can punish them into upright conduct. We take away Tyson's boxing license, give him jail time for that traffic dust-up that a lot of people thought warranted no more than a few days behind bars, then threaten to take away his earned "good time" for the in-jail infraction.

As for the kids whose futures concern me, we respond to their violence and impulsivity by ordering longer prison terms in harsher prisons. And when the awful behavior shows up in younger and younger children, we elect to try adolescents as adults. Surely if we escalate the punishment enough, they'll get the message and go straight.

They don't go straight, of course. They become more violent, as anyone who's ever kept a dog chained up would expect. Indeed, I remember when people would chain dogs in the yard for the precise purpose of making them mean.

I am not suggesting that violent behavior—in Tyson or in those rough and dangerous kids in the nation's ghettos and barrios—should go unpunished. I am suggesting, though, that punishment cannot be our only line of attack.

Dodge, director of Duke's new Child Policy Center, is in the middle of a 10-year experiment on preventing violence in children predisposed to it. That's worth talking about another time. For now, I make only his secondary point: that ratcheted-up punishment doesn't work very well, frequently making violent people worse, and that escalating the punishment takes resources that might have been used for prevention. California, once touted as the national model for public education, now spends more on prisons than on schools, sacrificing education without improving public safety.

To repeat, I am not advocating that violent offenders be let go. They frighten me as much as they frighten you, and until we learn how to control their violence, prison may be the only realistic alternative.

But if we are to avoid making things worse and worse—in fiscal as well as in criminal terms—we had better start paying some attention to identifying causes and possible cures, and then acting on that knowledge.

It's obviously too late to change Mike Tyson's childhood. But can't we at least give him back his medication?

ME AND MIKE TYSON

The Guardian, January 22, 2000

by

Donald McRae

They went back to the old house in Catskill last Saturday afternoon. It was the same rambling white house with the grey roof and the low porch where they had lived so many years before. But, even though they were going home to see the woman who had been a mother to both of them, no one could have mistaken Mike Tyson and Jay Bright for brothers.

When they began their journey upstate by climbing into the fighter's limousine in New York, they provided a study in contrast. It was not just that one was black and the other white, or that Tyson was the infamous boxer and Bright his obscure trainer. Tyson's squat figure was still edged with the menace which once made him the "baddest man on the planet." Bright cut a cuddlier picture with his camp arch of an eyebrow, a silvery beard and his chubby girth.

But they were bound together by the house and, especially, by the couple who had lived there: the late Cus D'Amato and Camille Ewald, the now 94-year-old woman waiting for them in Catskill. The legendary boxing trainer and his partner had rescued both boys as broken 13-year-olds.

Bright still lives at home with Camille, and he and Tyson continue to look after her. As they left the city for Catskill last weekend, that strange link between them glinted again.

"We talked all the way there and back," Bright remembers. "We spoke about boxing and flying to London the following day. We were excited. But we also talked about Camille and Cus, those incredible people who had taken us in.

"We had a great meal with Camille. She'll be 95 in March but she was so happy to see us get our chance in Europe. Mike and me then went out to Cus's grave. Mike said a prayer over the gravestone. It was a wonderful day, a very beautiful day.

"So I find it unfair that everyone expects Mike to be throwing furniture out of his hotel window or chewing the legs off chairs. If Mike was truly the Hannibal Lecter everyone makes him out to be, he wouldn't visit his surrogate mother or pray in private over Cus's grave. Mike Tyson as the raging monster is a colourful metaphor which sells newspapers. It has little to do with the Mike I know."

In March, it will be exactly 20 years since Tyson was first taken to the Catskill house. Abandoned by his father and estranged from his mother, he was already in a kind of jail. But in 1980, as an inmate of the Tryon juvenile detention centre, he had discovered hope in boxing.

When D'Amato saw the massive teenager spar a few rounds he was convinced. He had seen the future heavyweight champion of the world. D'Amato had already won the title with Floyd Patterson—but Patterson had been crushed later by Sonny Liston and humiliated by Muhammad Ali. Tyson was far more imposing. At 13 he had the raw tools of a dark trade. Cus took him inside.

"This is the one I've been waiting for all my life," he told Camille. But she was compelled by a different image. Mike ran up the long drive which stretched from the bottom of their rolling green garden. His face was full of shy delight when he asked if he could pick some flowers to take back to Tryon. He had never seen roses before.

Three months later on June 30 1980, the day he turned 14, Tyson was released into D'Amato's custody. In the Catskill house he was the only black kid alongside seven white boys. Bright was the oldest, having lived there for almost seven years.

When D'Amato first met him the 12-year-old Bright weighed some 385 lb (27 stone). "I had a 56-inch waist," Bright recalls, "but I loved boxing. I used to go up to the Catskill house on my vacations. After a year in Cus's gym I got down to 175 lb (12 stone)."

Bright's mother had died when he was 11. A year later he lost his father and then, less than a year after that, his brother. Three deaths in two years were too much for a 13-year-old boy to take. He asked Cus and Camille if he could stay in Catskill—and he's never really left since.

"It was hard for Mike in the beginning," Bright says. "He was very suspicious. I understood. He came from a neighbourhood where it was eat or be eaten. It takes a long while for those layers of street callousness to dissipate. But slowly he began to open his heart and trust people.

"I sense a similar process in London. After all the cynicism in America it's been so refreshing to be here. Mike's responding to the way British people have embraced him. We should have done this years ago."

Bright's return to Tyson's corner, working alongside Tommy Brooks as co-trainer, is one of the least publicised features of rusty Mike's latest comeback. Within boxing, Bright has always been ridiculed. Teddy Atlas and Kevin Rooney, both former D'Amato disciples, have been particularly scathing since his debut as a Tyson cornerman in 1989.

"Jay Bright has no boxing knowledge," Rooney jeered, "unless you count quiche-making as a useful quality." Atlas sneered of the Bright-Tyson partnership that "it's like wearing plastic thongs under an Armani suit. It's ridiculous."

"Anyone who reinforces the style Cus ingrained in Mike is doing a good job," Bright insists. "I'm just trying to apply Cus's methods."

Bright is a walking talking D'Amato doll. Even if he is unlikely to rekindle in a 34-year-old fighter the dazzling lateral movement and fast combinations which remain the tenets of the Cus creed, his devotion is obvious.

"Cus always said Tyson is at his best when he's calm and cool. When he has that dead calm he sees the openings and, boom, he throws devastating combinations. It's now politically correct to dismiss Mike. But all his problems in the ring have been down to enforced inactivity. He still has the knowledge and technique; even Evander Holyfield said Tyson knocks out Lennox Lewis. The book is not yet closed."

If Bright's boxing dreams appear more romantic than realistic, his personal perceptions of Tyson are no less sentimental.

"Mike is a great guy. With all my heart I don't believe he raped

Desiree Washington. Neither does Camille. She's a tough, smart Ukrainian woman and she never wavered."

Yet the bleak saga of Tyson—both the terrible distress he has caused and the pain he has suffered—is essentially a story of violently broken trust. In 1997 he said: "I've been abused, I've been humiliated, I've been dehumanised. I've been betrayed. I have no friends. When I came out of prison I realised that you can give people all the money in the world and it can't make them loyal to you in their hearts."

Bright was one of those he cast out. He was blamed for Tyson's first defeat by Holyfield and fired. So he was not in the corner when Tyson's parody of *Jaws* ended up with him biting chunks out of Holyfield's ears in the rematch.

"Don King and the rest were whispering to Mike," Bright says. "But I still wished Mike well. I watched the second Holyfield fight on TV and it broke my heart to see what he did. But a few weeks later we spoke again and everything was fine. You see, I was never a hired gun or a mercenary, I was always a friend before anything."

For those of us who have followed Tyson's mazy path for years, it is difficult to believe that he has found serenity. But in Jay Bright he has a staunch believer.

"Mike's very deep. The other day he was having his hands wrapped and we started talking about Alexander the Great. He was articulate and thoughtful. Ask Mike about philosophy and you're in for a treat. Ask him about Nietzsche; that's his man! He knows all that stuff. Is that an uneducated person?"

Bright and Tyson are boxing's definitive odd couple. But it's a sweeter image to think of them discussing philosophical theories of eternal reoccurrence in the gym than to see Tyson repeating the same forlorn pattern of mistakes.

"What you have to do when trouble follows you," Bright says, "is adopt a mature attitude and avoid it. Mike has matured. He is strong and emotionally balanced now. He's focusing on the things that are most important in his life: his boxing and his family."

"And his friends?" I wonder.

"Well," Bright says slowly as he looks away. "Mike knows I'm his friend. He knows I'm loyal. I think he genuinely trusts and respects me. He doesn't feel that about everyone . . ."

WEALTHY IN ALL THINGS, BUT LOVE!

October 25, 2000

by

Mumia Abu-Jamal

Unlove's the heavenless hell and homeless home . . .
lovers alone wear sunlight. —e.e. cummings

This is a tale of two remarkable, relatively young, people— Mike Tyson and Lil' Kim (Kimberly Jones). In an age of media-fueled celebrity, these two send paparazzi and gossip columnists into drooling fits of ecstasy, as they search for the latest morsel to toss to the masses. Two recent tidbits caught this writer's attention, because of the similarity between these very different people.

What could be similar between an intense, bipolar, knockout artist who did prison time, and a tough-talking, blond-wig wearing, rap artist, whose stage presence owes much to the old strip tease?

These are two young black people who used their considerable talents to rise in a rough world, and in rough fields of endeavor, to achieve fame, fortune and relentless media attention.

Mike won his first heavyweight championship belt in 1986 (WBA), one of the youngest to do so in history. His career has netted him millions. Lil' Kim has used rough lyrics and raunchy sexuality on stage to launch a rap career that sends teenage boys into testosterone orbit. By any measure these two figures could be deemed successful in their chosen fields, with Mike earning tens of millions for nonchampi-

WEALTHY IN ALL THINGS, BUT LOVE!

onship fights, and Lil' Kim selling tens (if not hundreds) of thousands of her records (or is it CDs these days?). They have everything, but . . .

In the days leading up to his bout with the formidable Andrew Golota, Tyson exploded at the media, and told some terrible, heart-wrenching truths: "I'm an angry guy, I'm bitter, I'm mean because people I trusted all my life, they (screwed) me . . . (Boxing) brought me money and fame, but it never brought me no happiness." (*USA Today*, 10/18/2000, 2c; 10/20/2000.) "I go to Scotland and England and white people love me; I come back home and black people hate me." (*USA Today*, 10/17/2000, 7c).

Brilliant black feminist scholar Bell Hooks, at a recent NYC promotion for her book, "All About Love: New Visions" (2000), told about an interview that she conducted several years ago with Lil' Kim (before her "blonde ambition" phase) when she asked the diminutive singer about love. "Love? What's that?" she reportedly replied. "I don't know nothin' 'bout that. I ain't never had that," Lil' Kim reportedly exclaimed. The writer described her shock at hearing such a young woman saying such a thing and wondered at the world that would plant such coldness in the heart. She thought of how young blacks could grow into adulthood, feeling unloved, either by intimates, family or the nation of their birth.

Mike with Camille

Nor is this, strictly speaking, a black, or a Brooklyn thing. Years ago, the oil industrialist, John Getty, then perhaps the richest man on earth, remarked to an interviewer, that he would gladly give all of his billions away if only he could find someone who truly loved him, for himself, as opposed to his wealth.

Fame acts as a barrier to love, not a magnet. And it is possible, in a world drunk on its material pursuits, for people to be wealthy beyond dreams, yet because of the lack of love, to be poor indeed.

EMBARRASSMENT TO JUST ABOUT EVERYONE

San Francisco Chronicle, January 30, 2002

by

David Steele

That was painful to watch. A 35-year-old man being judged, peered upon by the entire country (at least the segment that watches ESPNews or MSNBC), hearing his every mistake and misstep recounted and dissected in excruciating length and detail, until the volume became staggering. Then pleading his case, alternately defying his accusers and begging them for another chance.

All while never straying far from pitiful.

That's how Mike Tyson looked yesterday. Not sympathetic, mind you; he cashed in his sympathy card long ago. Tyson, once the Baddest Man on the Planet, sat in front of the Nevada State Athletic Commission and got scolded as though he were a naughty boy. With his expressions and mannerisms, it was as though his mother was standing before him, wagging a finger, wondering when he was going to shape up, praying for the strength to get through that hard head of his one day.

Forget the actual decision; Tyson will fight Lennox Lewis somewhere, for a lot of money and before a large, voyeuristic audience. But can you imagine reaching that age and still being subjected to what Tyson was yesterday? And knowing that you've got no one to blame but yourself?

EMBARRASSMENT TO JUST ABOUT EVERYONE

Yet, Tyson very well might not know that. Dr. Tony Alamo, one of the five commissioners—and one of the four who voted to deny him his license to fight in the state—spoke of what Tyson had done in the first 35½ years of his life, and expressed concern for the next 35½ years. Those first 35½ do not bode well for the rest. They constitute what might be the biggest waste of talent and opportunity in boxing history, if not all of sports.

After the events of the past week, during which I wrestled over exactly how I felt—or if I felt anything—about Tyson, that's all I can get out of it. It's been a big waste. A dozen years since winning the title and what does he have? Not dignity, that's for sure. No belts. Not nearly enough money. Nothing close to his old skills. No glowing stature in the public's eyes. Not much more than the starring role in a nationally televised freak show.

All things considered, in and out of the ring, Tyson might end up as one of the worst heavyweight champions ever. That's the legacy he has carved for himself.

This was going to be an angry column. Before Tyson sat before the commission yesterday, this was written, and Tyson was going to be written off.

As a disgrace to the sport, which routinely sets new standards for disgrace. As a disgrace to human decency, because the way he acts in public and the justifications he offers are inexcusable, regardless of what he has encountered in his life. As a disgrace to his own family— his wife, who constantly must deal with evidence that her husband treats women with something beneath disrespect, and his children, who someday will wonder why he decided to, among other things, grab his crotch and spew vile language across a room of reporters from around the world.

Worse, and most personally, a disgrace to black people everywhere. Particularly to black men, who spend their lives being followed by department-store security guards, pulled over by police on DWB charges (Driving While Black), shrunk away from in elevators, and hearing "compliments" about how "articulate" and "well-mannered" we are.

Largely because, for too many people, Tyson is the prototypical black male, the one they're most familiar with, the one they see on TV acting up all the time. We all have to live him down, every day; we can't exult in, say, Colin Powell without having to address Mike Tyson.

It didn't help that I finally saw the movie "Ali" last weekend and got a chance to see what a heavyweight champion ultimately can be. Talk about polar opposites. It might be asking a lot of boxers, or anyone with that kind of visibility, to emulate Muhammad Ali. It's not asking much to do better than Tyson. The more I thought of what can be attained and what Tyson chose instead, it made me sick.

But how can anger like that last, in light of that wretched scene in Las Vegas yesterday? Actually, it endures pretty well.

Early in the proceedings, commissioner Amy Ayoub grilled Tyson at length about his indiscretions—limiting herself, fairly, to what happened in and surrounding his bouts. Still, she drew a few testy rebuttals from Tyson, as well as his claim that he was "violated" during last week's news conference incident, and was a "victim."

Ayoub's response was that Tyson had earned opportunities and extra chances and money that few from his background could ever hope to get.

"Mr. Tyson," she concluded, "I know you're a human being, but I deeply feel that you're not a victim anymore."

I second that.

LET TYSON FIGHT

salon.com, February 1, 2002

by

King Kaufman

There has been general applause for the Nevada State Athletic Commission's 4-1 decision to deny Mike Tyson a license to box. Finally, the chorus has gone, boxing officials have turned their backs on all that money to be made and done the right thing.

I think I'm the only guy who thinks maybe they didn't do the right thing.

I don't think what the commission did was horribly wrong—as a sports fan, I don't care if Mike Tyson never fights again—but their decision still troubles me. I don't think that just because Tyson is an ass he should be denied the right to make a living. And I don't see what good the commission's suddenly moral stance does anybody, including the ailing Las Vegas tourist industry that's missing out on the dollars a heavyweight championship fight would bring in, dollars that the typing classes are sniffing at these days as somehow tainted because Tyson's the one bringing them in.

To which I say: Tell it to that laid-off waitress over there.

In case you missed it: Tyson was denied a license in the wake of a brawl that he appeared to instigate last week at a New York press conference announcing his April 6 bout in Las Vegas with heavyweight champ Lennox Lewis. This, of course, was only the latest embarrassing incident in the life and troubled times of the 35-year-old former champion, a list that includes spending three years in prison on a rape conviction and three months in jail on a road-rage conviction, biting part of Evander Holyfield's ear off in the ring, punching a referee, testing positive for marijuana after a fight and various out-of-the-ring shenanigans, such as last month's attack on some photographers in Cuba. Remember when he said he wanted to eat Lewis' children? (He said later that he was just fooling around—ha ha!—he knows Lewis doesn't have any children.)

The Nevada commission's decision means the Tyson-Lewis fight won't happen in Vegas, and is essentially a ban on Tyson fighting in the United States, since it's unlikely any state will grant him a license after a leading boxing state has denied him one, though the Los Angeles Times reported Thursday that Tyson will try California. Tyson is free to fight in any country that will let him do so, and it's a big world, so some country will welcome him. They're already forming two lines. Not here, says Denmark. You know how to whistle, dontcha Mike? says South Africa.

I feel that I should say this again: This is not a defense of Tyson. I'm not a fan of his (though I once was), and it affects me not one bit if he never fights again. He is one of history's great screw-ups. Thanks to a winning ticket in the genetic lottery and, yes, years of his own hard work, he found himself in possession of a tool, his body, that was a license to print money and enjoy the good life. All he had to do was stay in shape, fight two or three times a year for a decade or so and not ruin his life and the lives of those around him with stupidity and poor impulse control. A soft assignment, I don't care how hardscrabble your background is, and he failed spectacularly, repeatedly. He makes Elvis Presley look like a sober, steady overachiever.

And worst of all, he's not an interesting fighter. Hasn't been for more than a decade, really. Anyone paying to watch him fight—to watch him try to knock out his usually third-rate opponent with one wild punch, then settle into increasingly bizarre fouling tactics if that strategy fails—is a sucker. But when did the Nevada State Athletic Commission get into the business of legislating morality, and why?

Why do you have to be a good citizen to box? You don't have to be a good citizen to be a pipe fitter or a gardener or a writer for an Internet magazine. Stay out of prison, show up and do your job, and your boss can't ax you just because you got into an off-hours punch-up at Uncle Bubba's Bar. Tyson has been convicted of no crime, accused of none. (At least not yet. Las Vegas police said Wednesday that they're recommending that prosecutors charge Tyson in another rape case, and yet another is being investigated. But all of that is beside the point for this argument—and the commission said it didn't consider the potential charges.) Why this sudden good-behavior clause? Because boxing has standards of sportsmanship and fair play to uphold? As the Englishman Lewis might say: Pull the other one!

If the commission had seen fit to deny Tyson a license for, say, biting Holyfield, or for any of his other between-the-ropes fouls, I'd be all for it. That's what the commission should be for. It should ensure that boxers are medically fit before they're licensed (this job alone is big enough that no state commission has ever fully succeeded at it) and that they follow the rules of the sport after they're licensed. No biting, for instance, one of the old 8th Marquess of Queensbury's basic ones, but also things like no losing on purpose.

How fighters conduct themselves elsewhere, on roadsides or in barrooms or at press conferences, for example, should be the concern only of the promoters and the fans, who can decide not to work with bad people or not to pay to watch them, respectively. Boxing does not need a commission to act like a bar association or medical licensing board. There is no public interest in forcing boxers to be moral, ethical people.

The Nevada commissioners did suspend Tyson's license after the Holyfield fight, but later reinstated him. Though the ear incident and the litany of other Tyson meltdowns has been cited endlessly in the coverage of the commission's decision, it's pretty clear that the press conference brawl is what moved the board to act.

I guess the commissioners are trying to clean up boxing's image. That's a noble pursuit, but the fact is that boxing has far bigger problems than Mike Tyson's behavior. The fact that Tyson, in spite of everything, is still the most famous and popular boxer on the planet speaks volumes about the sport's weaknesses. Public interest is at an all-time

LET TYSON FIGHT

low, thanks in part to a poor product, especially at the crucial heavy-weight level—Lennox Lewis, who has dominated the division for the last half-decade, would have been an also-ran if he'd come along any time before the 1980s—and in part to boxing's well-deserved image as a den of thieves.

Boxing needs better safety standards and some way out of its current system of being run by promoters with no interest other than their own wallets, a system that has left the sport with too many champions who won't fight each other, too many fans turned off by high prices for bad fights with questionable judging, too many lawsuits and not enough good, solid competition.

What can be done? Don't ask me, pal. Smarter people than I have thrown up their hands at the state of the sweet science of bruising. But the Nevada commissioners aren't getting anywhere by denying Tyson a license, and the rest of us aren't accomplishing anything by rushing to pat them on the back for punching out the one guy nobody's going to rise to defend.

NO HAPPY ENDING

Interview March 21, 2002

by

Rudy Gonzalez

Throughout all my years with Mike his most favorite movie, no matter where we traveled, I don't care what port we were in the world, what city we were in, one of his most favorite movies, besides all his cartoon collection, was *Raging Bull*. I don't know if you know it, there's a part in *Raging Bull* where he's losing the fight and Joe Pesci tells DeNiro to bite the opponent in order to stop the fight. Tyson took a chapter out of that movie and he used it to break his contracts with Don King—not that he was crazy, not that he hated Holyfield,

Q—Not that he was afraid of losing the fight?

I think he was frustrated, like any fighter—it wasn't going the way he planned—but Mike would have been able to regroup. Even losing would have been ok for him.

Q—He bit Holyfield deliberately to get out of his contract?

My first question when I embraced him in 2000 in Miami Beach when we met secretly and I asked him I said "Everybody thinks you're crazy for biting Holyfield" and he looked at me and he goes "You know me better than that." He goes "That's the only way I could of got out of the contracts." And it made sense to me then. He suspended himself from the fight; he threw himself out of the sport, in order to void his existing lifetime contracts with King.

Q—I don't understand the legalities. How does being suspended from the sport allow him to break his contract?

Well once he was suspended, then he didn't have a license. You can't have a contract with a licensed boxer who just lost his license. It's sort of as if I was your chauffeur, and I lose my license. I lost my driver's license, so how can you hold me to that agreement? Three months later he filed a lawsuit against Don King, Don King Productions, John Horne, John Horne Entertainment, Rory Holloway, and Rory Holloway records. Basically he filed all the lawsuits against all the principals involved, and it was a total of 600 million dollars that he felt that he was basically screwed out of and I gotta tell you that throughout all the years, the money—I mean Mike Tyson lived an extraordinary life, like many of my celebrity clients do—but nobody, nobody can go through the money the way these guys did. And they were just basically, they were hand-feeding Tyson his money, but in reality he never controlled the bulk of his empire.

Q—Even on a day-to-day level?

Even on a day-to-day level there's only so much you can buy. We had 250 cars; we had a private jet; we had three mansions.

Q—He was living in a golden cage.

Well, he was being fed a golden egg that was really not gold. But he realized that he never had the proper education to understand what was going on in his life. To this day, for example, the Lennox Lewis press conference: if you look at the press conference, and you shut down the noise and you see what it was, it started out as a hype for a fight, then turned into a brawl, only because Tyson is not getting the proper, he doesn't understand what's going on because the hands that are controlling him really are telling him one thing. He walked out on that stage thinking that Lennox Lewis and him were supposed to have this fight. In reality Lennox Lewis knew nothing about this. We met with him last night. And you know I, the last time I saw him was on television, trying to tackle Lennox Lewis. He was told to act like this; it was going to be good for the fight; But once he stepped across that platform, he realized that no one else knew what was going on except him. What does he do now? Does he back up? Well, no. He can't because he's supposed to be the baddest fighter in the world. So he continues his reign and his rage. The press takes that opportunity to write about him: He's like that. And it's a circle that's been repeated. It's a violent circle that keeps repeating. There's no one to stop the circle.

Q—How can King profit from Tyson now?

In order for King to profit from Tyson now is basically he needs Tyson in dilemmas because basically if Tyson's head was straight right now, firstly he wouldn't be boxing. Tyson shouldn't be boxing at this point of his life. At this point of his life he'd be getting ready for a major trial. A federal court trial here in New York City, in federal Supreme Court basically to expose the undertow of what's been going on in his life. But they're not doing that. Let's keep Mike, first of all, let's keep him off balance, let's keep the media hating him— and King is now using that propaganda to throw his hands up and go "the boy's crazy, he's out of control."

Mike should have been stopped at the press conference. He should have never have got into an altercation with a guy from the press. But if you notice they sat there and just like threw their hands up and let Mike go all out. Mike is venting anger. He feels the world hates him. And He feels the worlds hates him because he's painted this picture, you know, it goes back to what's happening with a lot of dogs nowadays, with these pit bulls, that you see these dogs in the streets and they're supposed to be pets but behind the scenes they're being trained to kill and destroy. Now we let this dog out on society: what does the dog do? He does what he's been trained to do. Mike Tyson behind closed doors, in a world that no one sees, is agitated. He's told that everybody hates him. He's charged up to believe that when you go into this press conference the media hates you, man, they all talking about you. And they do this systematically. They do this with my relationship and me with him. As a friend, as a guy who's been in his life for the past 15 years. I'm a threat to these guys. So what do they do? "Oh he's up to no good. He's looking to, he's working for the media." So Mike is skeptical about "well, what does this guy truly want?" But this is why my relationship with Tyson is one way. He calls me. I don't call you for anything. The moment I pick up the phone and call him for something then I open the door for them to use propaganda—"Ah he's looking to do a book on you, he wants this, he's working with so-and-so." But in reality when he feels the need to pick up the phone and call me then that propaganda can't work. And that's why we meet in secret locations and we have dinner together quietly and I try to involve him in my life as much as I can. Because I see the guy that nobody really sees. Everybody thinks they know Mike Tyson but no one's ever taken the time or had the pleasure to really get behind the scene and see the man that I saw, that I respected and that I grew up loving. A guy who's not perfect, he's not perfect but he's not a deranged animal, he's not a menace to society. He's just a guy who has the wrong kind of handlers in his life, the wrong kind of trainers. And he believes the only way he can get respect is to be angry.

He's been manipulated. He doesn't know what's up and what's wrong. He doesn't understand. But the same guy that can go out there and attack the media and attack Lennox Lewis—a month later he's having a private dinner with Christina Aguilera and her entourage, including myself, and he acted like a perfect gentleman. And he was embraced and at that point he earned another fan because someone who didn't like this man, because she was feared of him, got to see this real nice, nice guy that's inside and, fell in love with him. But if I never got Christina to meet with Tyson privately, then all she would have is what the media portray Mike to be. And this has been the misconsumption of this man's life, both inside the ring and outside the ring. And you know he has no friends, and it's a lonely world, even with all the money. At one time I worked for one of the richest men in the world and we would exchange Christmas gifts. What can I buy Mike Tyson? I would think of the most stupidest things to get him. The last gift that I gave him before he went to prison was a train set. He always said that he loved trains. So we went out and bought him a train set. He was like a kid in his room for a month; he did not come out of his room playing with his train set. And he hugged me and said, "Nobody ever gave me anything." It's not about mansions, it's not about cars, it's not about private jets, it was basically the thought that "I love you man." No one ever gave this to him. One thing that I've learned is, sometimes the most dangerous person in the world is the person closest to you. That has happened to Tyson, all the way around. First it was Rory Holloway, and then it was Robin Givens, and then it was Don King, then it was all his guys around him, and then there's all these wannabe white haters, and Muslims that are truly not Muslims—because the Muslim religion doesn't teach hate. It's jailhouse rhetoric that Mike is being taught. They need him angry. Because as long as he's angry, he's out of control, and as long as he's out of control he's predictable. And this works, in boxing.

Q—Does he still want to fight in the ring?

I don't think he wants to fight. I don't think he knows how to fight anymore. I don't think he's had a moment of peace in his life since Cus D'Amato died. Mike Tyson is a modern day Frankenstein who a lot of people had a hand in his creation. Like Frankenstein they all left him alone and he wanders the world by himself. He's a monster that no one really,

really educated. No one spent time in healing his pain. Recently his stepmother died, Camille, which is another layer of pain and the truth is now he doesn't even have her. Here's a woman who could put him in a room and tell him to go upstairs and go to bed. Every safety mechanism in his life is gone.

Q—What about Jay Bright?

Jay Bright to me is a disappointment to the Cus D'Amato days.

Q—He's loyal to Mike.

He's not loyal to Mike because if he was loyal to Mike he would be helping Mike. He's a Yes man. Mike Tyson doesn't need yes men in his life. Mike Tyson needs help. He doesn't need yes men; he needs No men. And Jay Bright isn't loyal, he's a puppy. Mike does not need a puppy. Mike needs people to go in there and tell him the truth. As I did from 1985 to 1992 when we looked at him and told him he was being ripped off by Don King and John Horne and Rory Holloway, and he refused to believe it. If Jay Bright really cared about Mike Tyson, if he really cared about Cus D'Amato, then you know what, then do the right thing, get him out of the ring. Why is it about Mike Tyson fighting? What happened to Mike Tyson the human being? These guys don't care. Because they earn their money through him. Tyson hasn't got time to reflect because he snaps his finger . . . you know Jay Bright is probably the biggest disappointment because he has the power to say, "Hey, Mike, you know what, let's leave this shit alone. Let's go on vacation for two years. Let's find peace in our lives. Let's do something else besides, the fight, the fight, the fight, the fight, the fight." For what? Every time he fights he's broker than when he started. So why would he fight?

Mike is a man who changed my life. A man who gave me . . . you know it's sad but, through his life, I've been able to help other people in his situation. One of the biggest problems with celebrity is trust and who they trust. Who do they trust? And how do they trust? Because of the things I saw happen to Mike Tyson I've taken very strong steps to bring safety mechanisms for my clients. And sometimes it's hard. Sometimes it's hard to have a stranger come into your life and tell you, "Hey, your brother's stealing from you. Hey, your manager's not doing the right thing." But I believe my clients need to know. I believe that because of the pain and suffering that I saw Mike Tyson go through, and not everybody understands that he does go through pain, that this man cries at night; that he feels alone, that he's been betrayed by everyone around him.

Don King took took took took took, but you know what? Why didn't you educate him? Why didn't you send him to college? Why wasn't there a tutor with us on tour? Why not have a professor study with this man? Well Don King's idea of educating Mike Tyson was to tell him that he needed to go to jail. Every great black leader went to jail. King actually compared himself to Malcolm X and Martin Luther King, and he actually believes that the only way you can become something is to go to jail. He believed it. If you notice the pictures of Mike Tyson when he went to jail, he's playing with the handcuffs, and he's smiling at the world because he thought he was doing something good. These guys were actually telling him that every great man, every great black leader has to go to jail. Tyson has been mishandled for a long time. The abuse in his life has never stopped. It just has changed hands.

Q—How could there be a happy ending?

The only way for a happy ending for Mike Tyson, is Mike Tyson has to be banned from the sport of boxing. Mike Tyson needs time to reflect on his life. Mike Tyson needs to embrace the world as the world embraced him. He needs to disengage from the clowns and the characters that control his life. Otherwise, his last destiny is not going to be a happy one. He's being orchestrated, to self-destruct. I never want to see him put on those gloves again, It's not what it's supposed to be.

It's not what Cus wanted. It's not what Jim Jacobs wanted. It's not what Bill Cayton stays alive for. It's not for Steve Lott who still loves him and still thinks there's a chance and a hope for him. He needs to retire. I say that loving him and respecting him more than any one in the world. That will be his salvation.

The next book about Mike Tyson will be about what used to be. There really is no more story to tell, but really where he's headed. I don't think he'll fight in June and I think if he does it will be a disaster. I think King is going to influence everything that goes on and I think Lennox Lewis doesn't really need the fight. . . . He's a boxer. Tyson is enraged. I saw it in his eyes. If you look at any picture of Mike Tyson when he was young, his eyes were clear . . . You look at them now—they're just angry. And he judges everything by color, and race and creed. In 1991, when Mike Tyson should have been sitting in a room with his attorneys discussing his rape charge, King brought him a companion. King hooked him up with Iceberg Slim, a pimp. This pimp stayed with Mike for three months, living in the house, teaching Mike how to whip women and how to bitch smack'em, because he was too weak with them. The next thing you know he's wearing a pink hat, he's walking around with a cane, and he wants to be called "Sugar Daddy." If you look at his entourage now they all look like wannabe gangsters. Well, no one is training; no one is getting him up at 4:00 in the morning like Kevin Rooney. Rooney would kick the door down—and you ran. There's no discipline. Boxing is discipline. It's dedication. I told him something last night, and I hope it went with him. I asked him to take one moment of every day and just think of Cus D'amato. Think of what your doing to Cus's name. Cus died turning you into a champion. Why should you die turning him into a chump?

Q—What was his answer?
He said that he hasn't thought of Cus in a long time. He said, "I don't even think of Cus no more."

• • •

My job with Tyson always had a bottom line to it. I was there to create a safe passage for him. But after fifteen years of seeing his struggles, his betrayals, and the deceit among his people I am saddened to feel that there will never be a happy ending for Mike Tyson.

God Save the King

TALE OF THE TAPE

Undisputed world heavyweight champion: 1987-90
WBC heavyweight champion: 1986-90, 1996
WBA heavyweight champion: 1996
Ring Magazine Fighter of the Year: 1986; 1988
Amateur record: 24-3
Pro record: 49-3-0-1 (43 KOs)
53 Fights: 49 Wins, 3 Losses, 1 No Contest, 43 Knockouts
Weight: 222
Height: 5'11"
Reach: 71"
Chest (Normal): 43"
Chest (Expanded): 45"
Biceps: 16"
Forearm: 14"
Waist: 34"
Thigh: 27"
Calf: 18"
Neck: 19"
Wrist: 8"
Fist: 13"
Ankle: 11"

RING RECORD

1985

Mar. 6—Hector Mercedes, Albany, N.Y., TKO 1

Apr. 10—Trent Singleton, Albany, N.Y., TKO 1

May 23—Don Halpern, Albany, N.Y., KO 4

June 20—Rick Spain, Atlantic City, N.J., KO 1

July 11—John Alderson, Atlantic City, N.J., TKO 2

July 19—Larry Sims, Poughkeepsie, N.Y., KO 3

Aug. 15—Lorenzo Canady, Atlantic City, N.J., TKO 1

Sept. 5—Michael Johnson, Atlantic City, N.J., KO 1

Oct. 9—Donnie Long, Atlantic City, N.J., KO 1

Oct. 25—Robert Colay, Atlantic City, N.J., KO 1

Nov. 1—Sterling Benjamin, Latham, N.Y., TKO 1

Nov. 13—Eddie Richardson, Houston, KO 1

Nov. 22—Conroy Nelson, Latham, N.Y., KO 2

Dec. 6—Sammy Scaff, New York, KO 1

Dec. 27—Mark Young, Latham, N.Y., KO 1

1986

Jan. 10—Dave Jaco, Albany, N.Y., TKO 1

Jan. 24—Mike Jamison, Atlantic City, N.J., TKO 5

Feb. 16—Jesse Ferguson, Troy, N.Y., TKO 6

Mar. 10—Steve Zouski, Uniondale, N.Y., KO 3

May 3—James Tillis, Glen Falls, N.Y., W 10

May 20—Mitch Green, New York, W 10

June 28—William Hosea, Troy, N.Y., KO 1

July 11—Lorenzo Boyd, Swan Lake, N.Y., KO 2

July 26—Marvis Frazier, Glen Falls, N.Y., KO 1

Aug. 17—Jose Ribalta, Atlantic City, N.J., TKO 10

Sept. 6—Alfonzo Ratliff, Las Vegas, KO 2

Nov. 22—Trevor Berbick, Las Vegas, TKO 2

(Won WBC Heavyweight Title)

1987

Mar. 7—James Smith, Las Vegas, W 12

(Won WBA Heavyweight Title/Retained WBC Heavyweight Title)

May 30—Pinklon Thomas, Las Vegas, TKO 6
(Retained WBA/WBC Heavyweight Titles)
Aug. 1—Tony Tucker, Las Vegas, W 12
(Won IBF Heavyweight Title/Retained WBA/WBC Heavyweight Titles/Became Undisputed World Heavyweight Champion)
Oct. 16—Tyrell Biggs, Atlantic City, N.J., TKO 7
(Retained Undisputed World Heavyweight Title)

1988
Jan. 22—Larry Holmes, Atlantic City, N.J., TKO 4
(Retained Undisputed World Heavyweight Title)
Mar. 21—Tony Tubbs, Tokyo, Japan, KO 2
(Retained Undisputed World Heavyweight Title)
June 27—Michael Spinks, Atlantic City, N.J., KO 1
(Retained Undisputed World Heavyweight Title)

1989
Feb. 25—Frank Bruno, Las Vegas, TKO 5
(Retained Undisputed World Heavyweight Title)
July 21—Carl Williams, Atlantic City, N.J., TKO 1
(Retained Undisputed World Heavyweight Title)

1990
Feb. 11—James Douglas, Tokyo, Japan, KO by 10
(Lost World Heavyweight Title)
June 16—Henry Tillman, Las Vegas, KO 1
Dec. 8—Alex Stewart, Atlantic City, N.J., TKO 1

1991
Mar. 18—Donovan Ruddock, Las Vegas, TKO 7
June 28—Donovan Ruddock, Las Vegas, W 10
1995
Aug. 19—Peter McNeeley, Las Vegas, WDSQ 1
Dec. 16—Buster Mathis, Jr., Philadelphia, KO 3

1996
Mar. 16—Frank Bruno, Las Vegas, TKO 3

(Won WBC Heavyweight Title)
Sept. 7—Bruce Seldon, Las Vegas, TKO 1
(Won WBA Heavyweight Title)
Nov. 9—Evander Holyfield, Las Vegas, TKO by 11
(Lost WBA Heavyweight Title)

1997
June 28—Evander Holyfield, Las Vegas, L DQ 3
(For WBA Heavyweight Title)

1999
Jan. 16—Francois Botha, Las Vegas, KO 5
Oct. 23—Orlin Norris, Las Vegas, NC 1

2000
Jan. 29—Julins Francis, Manchester, Englad, TKO 2
June 24—Lou Savarese, Glasgow, Scotland, TKO 1
Oct. 20—Andrew Golota, Detroit, TKO 3

2001
Oct. 13—Brian Nielsen, TKO 7

CONTRIBUTORS

Mumia Abu-Jamal is the author of *Live from Death Row, Death Blossoms,* and *All Things Censored.*

Dave Anderson is a Pulitzer Prize winner (1981), and a 1994 winner of the Associated Press Sports Editors Red Smith Award for distinguished sports column writing. He was inducted into the National Sports Writers and Sportscasters Hall of Fame in 1990. He has been a sports columnist at *The New York Times* since November 1971 and is the author of 21 books and more than 350 magazine articles.

Phil Berger's many books include *Blood Season: Mike Tyson and the World of Boxing, Punch Lines: Berger On Boxing,* and, with Joe Frazier, *Smokin' Joe.* He died in 2001.

Harry Crews is the author of more than twenty books, including *The Gospel Singer, Naked in Garden Hills, This Thing Don't Lead to Heaven, Karate Is a Thing of the Spirit, Car, The Hawk Is Dying, The Gypsy's Curse, A Feast of Snakes, A Childhood: The Biography of a Place, Blood and Grits, The Enthusiast, All We Need of Hell, The Knockout Artist, Body, Scar Lover, The Mulching of America, Celebration,* and *Florida Frenzy.*

Pete Dexter is the author of the novels *The Paperboy, Brotherly Love, Deadwood, God's Pocket,* and *Paris Trout,* which won the National Book Award, and several screenplays including *Paris Trout, Mulholland Falls,* and *Rush.*

Katherine Dunn is the author of the novels *Truck, Attic,* and *Geek Love* and a frequent reporter on boxing (see cyberboxingzone.com.) Her profile of Lucia Rijker appeared in *The New York Times Magazine,* February 27, 2000.

Gerald Early is the editor of several volumes, including *The Sammy Davis, Jr., Reader, The Muhammad Ali Reader,* and *Lure and Loathing: Essays on Race, Identity, and the Ambivalence of Assimilation.* He is the author of *The Culture of Bruising: Essays on Prizefighting, Literature, and*

Modern American Culture (1994 National Book Critics Circle Award), *One Nation Under a Groove: Motown and American Culture, Daughters: On Family and Fatherhood*, and *Tuxedo Junction*.

Martin A. Feigenbaum is an attorney in private practice in Miami. He is the author, with Rudy Gonzalez, of *The Inner Ring*. His essay, "The Preservation of Individual Liberty Through the Separation of Powers and Federalism" was awarded a prize by the Commission on the Bicentennial of the United States Constitution and has been published in the Supreme Court Reporter, one of the few essays to ever receive that honor.

Rudy Gonzalez worked for Mike Tyson for more than five years. He is the author, with Martin A. Feigenbaum, of *The Inner Ring*.

Lloyd Grove has been a staff writer for the *Washington Post* for more than twenty years.

Pete Hamill has been editor-in-chief of both the *New York Post* and the *New York Daily News*. He is the author of *Snow in August, Why Sinatra Matters, Diego Rivera, A Drinking Life*, a memoir, and many other books. He is on the staff of *The New Yorker*.

Peter Heller is the author of *In This Corner!: Forty-Two World Champions Tell Their Stories* and *Bad Intentions: The Mike Tyson Story*.

Evander Holyfield is the first heavyweight to win the title four times and one of only two men to have defeated Mike Tyson in the ring.

June Jordan is Professor of African American Studies at UC-Berkeley. Her books of poetry include *Haruko/Love Poems* and *Naming Our Destiny: New and Selected Poems*. She is also the author of five children's books, a novel, three plays, and five volumes of political essays, the most recent of which is *Affirmative Acts*.

Tom Junod is a staff writer for *Esquire*.

Michael Katz's writing on boxing can be found at maxboxing.com.

King Kaufman is Senior Writer for *salon.com*

Robert Lipsyte is the author of *The Contender, The Brave,* and *In the Country of Illness.* He is the co-author of *The David Kopay Story* and, with Dick Gregory, *Nigger.* He writes for the *New York Times.*

John Lombardi is the manging editor of the *Miami New Times.* He is a former writer and editor for *New York* magazine, *Esquire,* and *The New York Times Magazine.*

Hugh McIlvanney is the chief sports writer at *The Sunday Times* (London). He has been winner of the Sports Writer of the Year on seven occasions and is the only sports journalist to have been voted Journalist of the Year. He is the author of several books, including the collections *The Hardest Game: McIlvanney on Boxing, McIlvanney on Football,* and *McIlvanney on Horseracing.*

Donald McRae is the author of *Dark Trade: Lost in Boxing,* a William Hill Sports Book of the Year, *Winter Colours: Changing Seasons in World Rugby,* and *Nothing Personal: The Business of Sex.*

Barry Meier is an investigative reporter at *The New York Times* specializing in Business and Health related stories.

Jack Newfield is the author of *Only in America: The Life and Crimes of Don King, City for Sale* (with Wayne Barrett), and *Somebody's Gotta Tell It: The Upbeat Memoir of a Working Class Journalist.*

Joyce Carol Oates is a recipient of the National Book Award and the PEN/Malamud Award for Excellence in Short Fiction. She is the author of *On Boxing, We Were the Mulvaneys, Blonde, Beasts,* and many other books. She is the Roger S. Berlind Distinguished Professor of Humanities at Princeton University and has been a member since 1978 of the American Academy of Arts and Letters.

George Plimpton is the founder and editor of *The Paris Review.* His books include *Shadow Box, Edie: American Girl, Paper Lion, Out of My*

League, *The Bogey Man*, *Open Net*, and *Truman Capote: In Which Various Friends, Enemies, Acquaintences and Detractors Recall His Turbulent Career*. He lives in New York City.

William Plummer is the author of *Buttercups and Strong Boys: A Sojourn at the Golden Gloves* and *Wishing My Father Well: A Memoir of Fathers, Sons*, and *Fly-Fishing*. He died in 2001.

William Raspberry is a syndicated columnist writing for the *Washington Post*. He is the author of *Looking Backward at Us*.

Tony Sewell is Senior Lecturer in Education at Kingston University, England and was appointed to Britain's Commission for Racial Equality. He is a regular columnist for *The Voice* (UK), and the author of *Black Masculinities and Schooling: How Black Boys Survive Modern Schooling*.

Tim Smith writes a regular column on boxing for the *New York Daily News*.

David Steele is a staff writer for the *San Francisco Chronicle*.

José Torres is the former world light heavyweight champion and chairman of the New York State Athletic Commission. He is the author of *Fire & Fear: The Inside Story of Mike Tyson* and *Sting Like a Bee: The Muhammad Ali Story*.

Robert Wright is a visiting scholar at the University of Pennsylvania and author of *The Moral Animal and Nonzero: The Logic of Human Destiny*. Wright's first book, *Three Scientists and Their Gods: Looking for Meaning in an Age of Information*, was nominated for a National Book Critics Circle Award. Wright is a contributing editor at *The New Republic*, *Time* magazine, and *Slate*. He previously worked at *The Sciences* magazine, where his column "The Information Age" won the National Magazine Award for Essay and Criticism.

PERMISSIONS

"Cus D'Amato" by William Plummer. Copyright © 1985 by Time, Inc. Originally appeared in *People*, July 15, 1985. ◆ "Dr. K.O." by Jack Newfield. Copyright © 1985 by Jack Newfield. First appeared in the *Village Voice*, December 10, 1985. Reprinted by kind permission of the author. ◆ Excerpt from *Fire & Fear* by José Torres. Copyright © 1989 by José Torres. Reprinted by permission of Warner Books, a division of Time, Inc. ◆ "Mike Tyson" by Joyce Carol Oates. Copyright © 1987 Joyce Carol Oates. Originally appeared in *Life*, March 1987. Reprinted by kind permission of the author and John Hawkins Associates. ◆ "Happy Birthday Ingrate" by Michael Katz. Copyright © 1988 by Michael Katz. Originally appeared in *New York Daily News*, June 30, 1988. Reprinted by kind permission of the author. ◆ "At Ringside with Madonna and Sean" by Harry Crews. Copyright © 1989 by Harry Crews. Reprinted by kind permission of the author and John Hawkins Associates. ◆ Excerpt from *Bad Intentions* by Peter Heller. Copyright © 1989 by Peter Heller. Reprinted by permission of Signet, a division of Penguin Putnam. ◆ "When an Ogre Looks Forlorn" from McIlvanney on *Boxing by Hugh McIlvanney*. Copyright © 1996 by Hugh McIlvanney. Reprinted by permission of Mainstream Publishing. ◆ Excerpt from "The Inner Ring" by Rudy Gonzalez with Martin A. Feigenbaum. Copyright © 1995 by Rudy Gonzalez and Martin A. Feigenbaum. Reprinted by kind permission of the authors. ◆ "The Manly Art of Self-Delusion" by Robert Lipsyte. Copyright © 1991 by the *New York Times*. Originally appeared in the *New York Times*, August 4, 1991. Reprinted by permission of The New York Times Agency. ◆ "Mike Tyson: Tales from the Dark Side" by Phil Berger. Copyright © 1992 by Phil Berger. Originally appeared in *M* Magazine, January 1992. Reprinted by permission of Sundays at Eight. ◆ "Rape and the Boxing Ring" by Joyce Carol Oates. Copyright © 1992 by Joyce Carol Oates. Originally appeared in *Newsweek*, February 24, 1992. Reprinted by kind permission of the author and John Hawkins Associates. ◆ "Requiem for the Champ" by June Jordan. Copyright © 1992 by June Jordan. Originally appeared in *The Progressive*, April 1992. Reprinted by kind permission of the author. ◆ "Unlike Kennedy Kin, Tyson Didn't Pretend" by Pete Dexter. Copyright © 1993 by the *Sacramento Bee*. Originally appeared in the *Sacramento Bee*, March 21, 1993. Reprinted by permission of the *Sacramento Bee*. ◆ Excerpt from *Piecework* by Pete Hamill. Copyright © 1997 by Pete Hamill. Originally appeared in *Esquire*, March 1994. Reprinted by permission of Warner Books. ◆ "Tyson vs. Simpson" by Robert Wright. Copyright © 1995 by *The New Republic*, Inc. Reprinted by permission of *The New Republic*, Inc. ◆ "Tyson Tests His Drawing Power" by Hugh McIlvanney.

PHOTOGRAPHS